FOR REASONS
OF POVERTY

FOR REASONS OF POVERTY

*A Critical Analysis
of the Public Child Welfare
System in the United States*

LEROY H. PELTON

PRAEGER

New York
Westport, Connecticut
London

AIT 8253 - 2/2

Copyright Acknowledgments

Excerpts from the following articles are reprinted with permission from the journals:

Pelton, L. H. (1987). Not for poverty alone: Foster care population trends in the twentieth century. *Journal of Sociology and Social Welfare*, *14*(2), 37-62.

Pelton, L. H. (1987). The institution of adoption: Its sources and perpetuation. *Journal of Social Work and Human Sexuality*, *6*(1), 87-117.

Pelton, L. H., and Rosenthal, M. G. (1988). Whose neglect? The role of poverty-related factors in child neglect cases and court decisions in the United States. *International Journal of Law and the Family*, *2*, 167-82. Excerpts written by the first author.

Library of Congress Cataloging-in-Publication Data

Pelton, Leroy H.
    For reasons of poverty : a critical analysis of the public child
welfare system in the United States / Leroy H. Pelton.
        p. cm.
    Bibliography: p.
    Includes indexes.
    ISBN 0-275-93073-4 (alk. paper)
    1. Child welfare—United States.   2. Social work with children—
United States.   3. Foster home care—United States.   I. Title.
HV741.P445   1989
362.7'0973—dc20   89-33968

Library of Congress Catalog Card Number: 89-33968
ISBN: 0-275-93073-4

First published in 1989

Praeger Publishers, One Madison Avenue, New York, NY 10010
A division of Greenwood Press, Inc.

Printed in the United States of America

♾

The paper used in this book complies with the
Permanent Paper Standard issued by the National
Information Standards Organization (Z39.48-1984).

10 9 8 7 6 5 4 3 2 1

To Matthew, Michael, and Daniel

Contents

Introduction

The thesis of this book is that the modern public child welfare system and its forerunners have failed to serve professed child welfare policies that have been enunciated since the beginning of this century up until the present time.

One of the central issues to be discussed is the separation of children from their parents by child welfare agencies, through no fault of the children. Such children have frequently come from a category of children traditionally referred to as "dependent and neglected" and, more recently, as "abused and neglected."

It will be shown that, throughout this century, child removal has survived as a major tactic in regard to child welfare problems despite a long-standing policy of family preservation. This much is supported by the facts in this book; indeed the presentation of those facts is a major aim of the book. The possible reasons for this persisting discrepancy between policy and reality despite the best intentions of child welfare professionals and advocates is another matter: On this issue our answers can be speculative at best. We can only explore the possible forces, motives, functions, and effects that the tactic of child removal may be propelled by and serve, and the obstacles that have blocked the fulfillment of stated policy.

It will be argued here, making my thesis more specific, that at least since the beginning of the twentieth century up until the mid-1970s, whenever child welfare agencies expanded and staff size increased, then the foster care population increased. It is later hypothesized that this relationship between increased resources, on the one hand, and increased child rescue rather than family preservation outcomes, on the other, is due to the dysfunction of the dual role of the child welfare agency, which is obstructive to child welfare policy. From the early 1960s, the child abuse crusade and the acceptance of the medical model of child abuse and neglect, fueled by greatly expanded resources and the already operational dual role, drove the foster care population to unprecedented heights. In the late 1970s, in response to criticisms of the foster care system, a formal permanency planning movement was launched. Due to conscious efforts, this movement served to decrease the foster care population considerably, although not below levels (in proportion to the total child population in this country) that existed near the beginning of the century. Permanency planning achieved this decline by dramatically decreasing the length of continuous time that children remain in foster care. However, due to the continued dominance of the child abuse crusade and medical model—coupled with the ongoing dual role structure of child welfare agencies and lack of prevention efforts—there has been no decline, and possibly an increase, in the number of children who enter foster care each year. They just do not stay as long anymore; yet in increasing numbers and at increasing rates, they reenter the system after being returned to their parents and after their adoptions are disrupted. In the 1980s, the foster care system has become a huge "revolving door." The permanency planning movement has exchanged the higher one-day-count foster care population of the 1970s for a foster care system in which high numbers of children enter and leave each year. It is argued that the dual role structure continues, as it has since the beginning, to obstruct the implementation of family preservation policy and to impede the development of preventive efforts.

The domain of this book, then, is that of modern public child welfare agencies: their interventions into the lives of dependent and allegedly neglected and abused children and their families, and their operations of protective and preventive services, foster care, and adoption. We will examine these operations, and the policies, laws, and mandates that govern them, in the course of developing the book's thesis.

Child removal was a major strategy for dealing with dependent and neglected children during the nineteenth century, and children were placed in institutions. In the latter half of the century, a preference slowly began to develop for placing children in foster family homes rather than in institutions [even institutions began to develop "cottage" settings (Ashby 1984, p. 30)]. However, it was only by the 1950s that foster family homes came to predominate over institutions as the most frequently used placement setting for dependent, neglected, and abused children (Lerman 1982). It can be argued that the shift in foster care patterns from institutions to foster homes has been the only true major reform that has occurred in child welfare practice in modern times, if we are to measure reform by results rather than by intentions or new administrative structures. For example, it can be argued, as Platt (1977) has done, that the advent of juvenile courts did not signal any less harsh treatment of children brought before them than they would have received before: that is, children were still frequently sent to institutions in the days before the rise of foster family placement. This book supports the position that, despite continuing rhetoric of reform, no other true reform has come about right up until the present time.

There have been many changes, but this study may show that the history of child welfare practice supports the adage that the more things change, the more they remain the same. In some respects, it can even be said that this book is a study in linguistics: Changed philosophies, theories, "treatments," laws, labels, and names have been changes in words only, and not in methods or results. A dependent child is now called a neglected child. Negative moralistic attributions to "offending" parents have been replaced by negative psychological labels, and so on.

Administratively, by the turn of the twentieth century, child rescue work in regard to dependent, neglected, and abused children was being carried out by private agencies, primarily the Societies for the Prevention of Cruelty to Children. By the 1910s, the juvenile courts had become the primary child welfare agencies. It was not until 1929 that most states had county boards of child welfare. State public child welfare agencies as we know them today did not begin to appreciably grow and expand until the 1950s.

In spite of these changes in administrative structure for child welfare services, the functional structure remained constant: The agency would both investigate the family and try to help it. This dual role of social welfare agencies is embodied by the paid agent (who did the investigative work) and the friendly visitor (who offered moral advice) of the Charity Organization Societies begun in the 1870s, and goes back even farther than that. This dual role structure, whether vested in one and the same worker, as it was in the probation officer of the juvenile courts, or in different workers within the same agency, characterizes public child welfare agencies at the present time. I will later argue that the incompatibility of the investigative/coercive and helping/supportive roles is a major reason for the failure of the child welfare system in this country to serve stated child welfare policies.

The policies we speak of began to take form in the 1890s and were formalized by the famous 1909 White House Conference on the Care of Dependent Children. They were shaped by the value placed on family life. On the one hand, this value led to a preference for foster family care over institutional care. The primary policy, however, was a preference for preserving the original family over removing children from the family. It is this policy that is the focal point of the present study. Over the years, many programs have been launched in attempts to fulfill this policy. Yet, ironically, child removal is as frequent today as it was at the time of the 1909 White House Conference.

Why the gap between policy and reality? Between what is intended and what is achieved? Why after so many "reforms" does the system continue in the same direction? The policies tug in one direction, and the day-to-day tactics in individual cases go in another. The dual role structure creates a conflict between family preservation and child rescue.

It is as though a long arm of the past has stretched out of the nineteenth century to determine the operations of public child welfare agencies in the late twentieth century. In one sense, this is true. The child removal strategy of the 1800s—especially as seen in the humane societies of the late 1800s (since these were the direct forerunners of the present public child welfare agencies)—has persisted by tradition into the current child welfare scene. Although the humane societies eventually lined up behind the new family preservation policies of the turn of the century in their public pronouncements and perhaps intentions, they could not escape their history of removing the child from the family. The juvenile courts, certainly guided by the rhetoric of family preservation, nonetheless removed large numbers of dependent and neglected children, taking over much of the function from the humane societies. In addition, the public child welfare agencies—when they arose and traditionally up until the present day— have been child-placing or foster care agencies and little else. This will be shown in the figures presented later on foster care population trends throughout this century, but it is also seen in the operating budgets up until the present time. In the 1950s, 72 percent of the budgets of child welfare agencies was devoted to foster care services, and it is still true today that the greatest proportion of their budgets is allocated to foster care. Thus the persistence of child removal strategies may possibly be attributed to bureaucratic inertia. It is therefore necessary to identify the obstacles that have blocked agencies from shifting their budgets to family preservation strategies, despite the continuing rhetoric of family preservation in statements of child welfare policy and in the mission statements of these agencies.

On the other hand, it can be argued that the past does not determine the present, but rather that the rationale and tactics of child removal are re-created in each successive generation. The inclination to "blame the victim" may be so pervasive that child removal survives as a punitive tactic against parents despite the best intentions of child welfare advocates, both within and outside of child welfare agencies, to enforce family preservation policies. Support for this argument comes from three sources: (1) the fact that child welfare agencies tend to re-create the reasons for removing children from their parents; (2) the fact that, through all these re-creations, the children being removed have largely been from the same population (namely, poor families); and (3) the fact that the possible functions that child removal might serve for society in general are just as much present today as they were in the nineteenth century.

In the nineteenth century, dependency and neglect were viewed as one and the same. The rationale for removing dependent children from their parents was to prevent the children from being contaminated by their parents' moral defects, which presumably had "caused" the parents' poverty in the first place. By the turn of the century, when the social and structural causes of poverty began to be examined, it was still maintained that many poor parents neglected their children, and separate "evidence" for neglect was found to establish wrongdoing apart from poverty. It was of course, the same dependent children who continued to be removed. Neglect continued to be interpreted in terms of the supposed moral shortcomings of the parents, and cruelty to their children was added to the arsenal of blame. By the 1920s, with the popularization of psychodynamic theorizing within the helping professions, the same need to blame poor parents manifested itself in psychologizing rather than moralizing about them; the parents began to be seen as psychologically rather than morally defective. Beginning in the 1960s, with the "discovery" of child abuse, a crusade was launched on the premise that this social problem was "epidemic" in proportion, psychological in nature, and crossed class lines, "afflicting" families of every race, creed, color, and economic status, as a "disease" knowing no bounds. Child abuse reporting laws were passed mandating citizens to report any suspicions of child abuse and neglect, according to their own lights, and a dramatic expansion of child welfare personnel provided an army to investigate these complaints. A logical response to these fears of child abuse was to remove children from their homes in great numbers. It turns out that these children again proved to be the same "dependent and neglected" children of long ago; they were "rescued," and continue to this day to be "rescued," from the poorest families in our society.

In any event, whether driven by historical determinism or by a human inclination to "blame the victim," the great persistence of the child rescue phenomenon moves us to speculate about the possible functions it might serve for society in general. The possibilities, although none are proven, are not difficult to imagine. On the psychological level, allegedly abusive parents can provide targets for "downward comparison" (Wills 1981): We all like to think that we are good parents, and we can enhance our feelings of well-being if we compare ourselves with parents who are so bad that they do not even deserve to have their children.

Child removal can save children from the still-supposed "bad" influences of impoverished parents, and can supposedly protect society from children who would otherwise grow up to plague society. In the old days, dependency, neglect, and juvenile delinquency were lumped together in law and in treatment (especially by the juvenile courts), so intertwined was the relationship thought to be (Ashby 1984, pp. 14–15). Currently, empirical studies of the relationship between child abuse and delinquency have evoked interest among child welfare professionals.

Child removal can serve the function of enforcing supposedly middle-class morality among poor people and of punishing parents who do not conform to such norms. Removal of some parents' children can serve as an example to other parents and thereby promote social conformity among poor parents. In these senses, the child welfare system can serve the function of regulating poor families by removing children from them. Child removal can serve as a warning to other poor people to manage their Aid to Families with Dependent

Children (AFDC) grants better, to get married, to not have too many children, etc.

Likewise, occasional changes in child welfare programs, while maintaining the major thrust of child removal, can be seen as largely adjusted responses to serve changes in the needs and self-interest of society in general. For example, the permanency planning movement of recent years, although largely fueled by criticism and alarm that our foster care system had gotten out of hand, can be seen as serving the function of replacing the diminished supply of white healthy infants for adoption with other types of children. It also can be viewed as serving the function of fulfilling the desires of a growing population of older single adults (particularly women) to become parents.

Most importantly, the focus on investigation, blame, and subsequent child removal might serve the functions of diverting attention from the continuing problem of poverty in this country and its effects on children, and of deflating pressures toward fundamental changes in our social, economic, and public welfare systems.

Although the reader might find evidence tending to support the hypothesis of one or another of these functions in the course of this book, the existence of these functions remains speculative, cannot be proven, and is not the focus of this study. If they do indeed exist, they raise a question as to how realistic any recommendations for change, such as the ones advocated in this book, may be. If the functions served are very important for our society and if they are indeed rooted in a pervasive and deep-seated need to blame the victim, then change might be difficult indeed.

Yet even if it were true that our child welfare system has primarily served the function of regulating poor families by removing children from some of them, and that this function is supported by a deeply rooted need to blame the victim, the fact remains that child welfare policies have been stated otherwise. These policies, in rhetoric at least, have had a different thrust, namely, toward family preservation. If the current child welfare system serves certain functions and needs for society in general, a changed system—more in line with professed policy—might also serve certain functions and needs, whether altruistic or of a social control nature, or both. The current system does not have a monopoly on serving functions and needs, and the conflict that exists between the policy of family preservation and the reality of child rescue tactics itself demonstrates a cognitive dissonance in our collective thinking that could become a force for change.

The child rescue response to child welfare problems has indeed been a sturdy survivor. It has survived many "reforms," such as the already-mentioned establishment of the juvenile courts, which came to deal with dependent and neglected children as well as delinquents, and failed to reduce the frequency of child removal. It survived the rise in the perceived value of children for their own sake rather than for their labor, beginning in the early twentieth century (Katz, 1986, pp. 115–117). This, coupled with the increased emphasis placed on "children's rights" current today, may have led to a concern for removing children from institutions, but did not lead to any lessening of child removal efforts. Indeed, in modern times, the rhetoric of children's rights has been used more to oppose family rights and has rationalized removal of children in alleged child abuse and neglect cases. The child rescue response has survived policies to preserve families. For example, the 1909 White House Conference participants concluded that children should not be removed from their parents "for reasons of poverty," but only for reasons of "inefficiency or immorality." This position was later strengthened by policies that advocated "treating" child abuse and neglect, rather than removing children. It has even survived tangible programs aimed at upholding those policies, such as the mother's pension laws passed in most states in the two decades following the 1909 White House Conference, the Aid to Dependent Children (ADC) program of the Social Security Act of 1935, other programs and aids to the poor (such as food stamps, developed in ensuing years and largely in the 1960s), and finally, the most significant recent "reform" directly concerning child welfare, the federal Adoption Assistance and Child Welfare Act of 1980, with its reiteration of family preservation policies and its support of preventive and "permanency planning" programs.

The current study attempts to document the ascendancy of the child rescue response and to describe the *internal* dynamics of the child welfare system that allow it to persist. It will be shown that the theoretical conflict of family preservation versus child rescue is mirrored in the dual role structure of the child welfare system itself, manifesting itself in the helping/supportive versus investigative/coercive dual role of the public child welfare agency, and often of the individual caseworker. The conclusion will be reached that this fundamental structure is dysfunctional from the point of view of preserving families and protecting children.

There are indeed many harms occurring to the children seen by our public child welfare agencies. It can be questioned, however, whether the investigation of approximately two million child abuse and neglect complaints per year by public child welfare agencies (American Humane Association 1988) is the most effective way to serve these children and their families. In retrospect, it can be argued that our current system has failed them. Thus, this study concludes with recommendations for a fundamental restructuring of our public child welfare system. The recommendations are radical only within the context of the child welfare system itself, and I have limited the book to this context. The restructuring recommended here can be realistically accomplished within the ongoing larger economic and social welfare context, which has proved resistant to change since the Social Security Act. For example, proposals for such measures as a guaranteed minimal income, while supported by the author, are not foreseeable in the near future. The contention here is that the lesser social welfare system of child welfare has room to get its own house in order. Further, while clients of the child welfare system would benefit from more sweeping measures such as those just alluded to, so too would they significantly benefit from a restructuring of the child welfare system in lieu of such measures.

It remains to be seen whether even this more modest proposal (restructuring the child welfare system) is doomed to failure because of all the resistance and reasons for resistance to change cataloged above. In addition, while the restructuring recommended here may look good on paper, it remains to be seen whether its implementation would make a real difference in finally reorienting agencies to act consistently with the prevailing policy of family preservation. After all, other administrative restructurings were enacted in the past without accomplishing this goal, although they were intended to do so.

A more basic and limited purpose of this book is to stimulate our thinking about the current child welfare system. Current scholarly critical analysis, for the most part, is beset by a complacency that allows for criticism of external forces impinging upon the child welfare system, such as funding problems, but not of the internal workings of that system. By gathering facts and developing arguments that challenge current knowledgeable beliefs about the subject, I hope to promote productive controversy about the basic dynamics, philosophical underpinnings, operational structure, and direction of the child welfare system itself.

1

Child Welfare Through the Twentieth Century: Policy and Reality

One can hardly imagine a more profound intrusion of government or society into the lives of families than the separation of children from their parents. When such separation is effected through no fault of the children, the question arises as to what conditions of the family or faults of the parents might be defined by society as rightful or necessary cause for such extreme action.

Institutions were a favored mode of out-of-home placement for dependent, neglected, and orphaned children in the United States during the first half of the nineteenth century, and even through the second half in much of the country. Yet a long and gradual deinstitutionalization process, taking well into the twentieth century, did eventuate in a significant shift in the type of placement of such children from institutions to foster family homes (Lerman, 1982). That shift, however, which represents a significant reform in the history of child welfare in this country, is not the focus of this book. Here we are concerned with the crucial nexus of separation of child from parent, no matter where that child is placed. (In this book, the term "foster care" is defined as including both institutional placement and foster family care.)

At least since the early 1900s, a strongly stated commitment and policy toward maintaining children in their own families, whenever possible, has emerged in the United States. The 1909 White House Conference on the Care of Dependent Children issued the following famous conclusions:

Home life is the highest and finest product of civilization. . . . Children should not be deprived of it except for urgent and compelling reasons. Children of parents of worthy character, suffering from temporary misfortune, and children of reasonably efficient and deserving mothers who are without support of the normal breadwinner, should as a rule be kept with their parents, such aid being given as may be necessary to maintain suitable homes for the rearing of the children. . . . Except in unusual circumstances, the home should not be broken up for reasons of poverty, but only for considerations of inefficiency or immorality. (in Bremner, 1971, p. 365)

This was seemingly the dawn of a new era in child welfare, in which the emphasis—in policy at least—was clearly shifting toward maintaining children in their own homes. The praise of home life represented a growing consensus that children should be raised in families, preferably their own, and not in institutions. The expressed concern that children should not be removed from their parents for reasons of poverty seemed to contrast sharply with the philosophy that predominated through the nineteenth century, which emphasized the "rescuing" of children from pauper families (Leiby, 1978, p. 144).

THE MEANING OF DEPENDENCY AND NEGLECT

In the abstract, at least, it does not appear difficult to define dependency and neglect, nor to distinguish between the two. Dependent children are those who are dependent upon society for financial support, either because their families are destitute or because they were orphaned. Neglected children are those whose parents fail to provide supervision, adequate care, or a "proper" home, or who are "unfit" parents or "immoral." Abandonment and cruelty, or abuse, were often subsumed under neglect, although currently neglect is often subsumed under abuse as a kind of shorthand for abuse and neglect.

It is the vagueness of the terms used to define neglect, and the consequent leeway for subjective judgment, as well as the relationship between poverty and neglect in the real world, that has caused confusion and debate. Implicit in the various actions that have been prescribed to remedy the deprivation of children have been varying interpretations of the causes of such deprivation.

As late as 1899, the first law to establish a juvenile court, in Illinois, lumped dependency and neglect together:

[T] he words dependent child and neglected child shall mean any child who for any reason is destitute or homeless or abandoned; or dependent upon the public for support; or has not proper parental care or guardianship; or who habitually begs or receives alms; or who is found living in any house of ill fame or with any vicious or disreputable person; or whose home, by reason of neglect, cruelty or depravity on the part of its parents . . . is an unfit place for such a child. (in Bremner, 1971, pp. 506-7)

This law, considered a reform because it removed child welfare matters from the criminal court, went on to state that when any child was found to be dependent or neglected, the court may order the commitment of such a child to an institution or foster home. Thus, dependent and neglected children were to be dealt with in like manner.

The Massachusetts "Act relating to indigent and neglected children" of 1882 stated: "Whenever it . . . (appears) . . . any child under 14 years of age, by reason of orphanage, or of the neglect, crime, drunkeness or other vice of his parents, is growing up without education or salutory control, and in circumstances exposing him to lead an idle and dissolute life, or is dependent upon public charity . . . (the) court or magistrate shall . . . commit such child . . ." to what amounted to placement in an institution or foster family (in Bremner, 1971, p. 207). Here we can say that there is some distinction made between dependency and neglect, but in practice the result was again the same, namely placement.

Such approaches to dependency and neglect in the late nineteenth century were the vestiges of long-standing theoretical beliefs that the causes of poverty resided within the poor themselves. It is but a short step from this view to the notion that poor people are not "fit" to raise children, that their pauper characteristics are synonymous with neglect where children are involved, and that children should be rescued from their pauper influence, if not for their own sake, then at least for the sake of society, which will have to live with such children when they become adults. Theoretically, there may never have been much opposition to the idea that poverty alone should not be grounds for breaking up families, or to the premise that parents of "worthy character" who are "efficient and deserving" should keep their children. It was just that poverty was thought to coincide with faulty parenthood and unworthiness of character.

There were some departures from this stance. As early as 1887, the Massachusetts Society for the Prevention of Cruelty to Children stated in its Seventh Annual Report that "we never take neglected children by law from their parents, where the neglect arises from honest poverty alone" (in Bremner, 1971, p. 208). Leaving aside the issue of whether a child is removed "by law" or through other means, the questions raised are how much and whose poverty has been seen as "honest" and "alone," how much and whose behavior has been judged neglectful, and whether changing views of poverty and neglect and their relationship to each other have affected the issue of separation.

There can be no doubt that, in modern times, the verbal banner under which the organized forces of child welfare ride is "protect the child and preserve the family," "prevent" child neglect and abuse as well as foster care placement itself, and foster care only as a "last resort." The byword is prevention. The mere thought, moreover, of placing children for reasons of poverty would seem outrageous to many.

The New Jersey Division of Youth and Family Services (1984), for example, proclaims that its mission is to "protect vulnerable children . . . support family preservation . . . prevent family violence and disruption." The federal Adoption Assistance and Child Welfare Act of 1980 (P.L. 96–272) provides that "reasonable efforts will be made . . . to prevent or eliminate the need for removal of the child from his home, and . . . to make it possible for the child to return to his home. . . ." Although this act has been hailed as a reform, the modern rhetoric of prevention goes back at least as far as 1951, when the American Humane Association's standards for child protective work proclaimed that "protective service . . . is directed not so much at rescuing the child from the home, as preserving, where possible, the home for the child" (in Bremner, 1974, p. 853).

If there has been any change at all in stated policies toward the separation of dependent and neglected children from their parents, from the 1909 White House Conference to the present, it is this: There has been an increasing emphasis on the prevention of child neglect and abuse and, beyond not wishing to separate children for reasons of poverty, on keeping families together even when child maltreatment has occurred, by rehabilitating the parents. The undeniable policy thrust, however, over the course of more than three-quarters of a century, has been to keep families together. This stated policy has, if anything, grown stronger and more unequivocal in its expressed intent of doing whatever may be necessary to prevent the separation of children from their parents.

In fact, however, from long before the turn of the century until the present time, there has always been a considerable number of children in the United States living in foster care. These children had been put there—in foster family homes, institutions, group homes, or other living arrangements—through no fault or handicap of their own, by child welfare agencies. While the rationales and motives for separating children from parents have changed over time, a predominant characteristic of displaced children in this country has not changed: By and large they have continued to be poor children from impoverished families.

My purpose here is to examine trends in the national foster care population through the twentieth century, to explore the possible causes of these trends, and to compare policy to reality.

THE FOSTER CARE POPULATION, 1910–1985

Estimates of the nation's foster care population at various points in time between 1910 and 1985 are presented in Table 1 and plotted in Figure 1. They all refer to one-day counts.

The figures for 1910, 1923, and 1933 are based on U.S. Census statistics.[1] The estimates presented for 1961, 1963, and 1965 are derived from a new state reporting system instituted by the U.S. Children's Bureau in 1960.[2] It is known that the foster care population declined after the mid-1930s, and it is believed that the foster care population did not reach its 1933 numerical level again until 1961–62 (Low, 1966; Boehm, 1970, p. 255). However, the turning point is in doubt, and the upward trend might have begun as early as 1957, and even as early as the late 1940s (as depicted hypothetically by the dashed curve in Figure 1).[3] The estimates for 1975, 1977, 1979, and 1980, and the first estimate listed for 1982 are based on studies, employing varying methodologies, by the Children's Defense Fund; Westat, Inc.; the U.S. Office of Civil Rights; the Child Welfare League of America; and Maximus, Inc., respectively. Finally, the 1981 estimate, the second and third estimates listed for 1982, and the 1983, 1984, and 1985 estimates are derived from surveys by the American Public Welfare Association.[4]

Table 1
Child Population in the United States, Child Population Below the Poverty Level, Foster Care Population, Orphan Population, Child Poverty Rate, Child Placement Rate, and Poverty Placement Rate During the Twentieth Century

Year	U.S. Population under Age 18	Population of Related Children under Age 18 below Poverty Level	Foster Care Population**	Orphan Population	Poverty Rate for Related Children under Age 18 (per 100)	Placement Rate (per 1,000)	Poverty Placement Rate (per 100)
1910	35,061,000		151,441			4.3	
1920	41,486,000			750,000		5.3	
1923			218,523				
1930				450,000			
1933	42,186,000		242,929			5.8.	
1954				60,000			
1960		17,288,000			26.5		
1961	65,791,000	16,708,000*	244,500			3.7	1.5
1963	68,420,000	15,548,000*	259,600			3.8	1.7
1965	69,731,000	14,388,000	283,300		20.7	4.1	2.0
1970		10,235,000			14.9		
1975	67,165,000	10,882,000	448,354		16.8	6.7	4.1
1977	65,772,000*	10,028,000	503,000		16.0	7.6	5.0
1979	64,379,000*	9,993,000	302,000		16.0	4.7	3.0
1980	63,682,000	11,114,000	274,000		17.9	4.3	2.5
1981	63,208,000	12,068,000	273,000		19.5	4.3	2.3
1982	62,811,000	13,139,000	243,000		21.3	3.9	1.8
–			262,000			4.2	2.0
–			263,000			4.2	2.0
1983	62,374,000		269,000			4.3	
1984			270,000				
1985			276,000				

*Interpolated
**The reader is cautioned that methodological and definitional differences in the derivation of these estimates hinder precise comparison, and that the estimates are presented here (and utilized in Figures 1 and 2) to indicate general trends only. (See text and Notes 1–6).

Figure 1
Foster Care Population and Orphan Population During the Twentieth Century

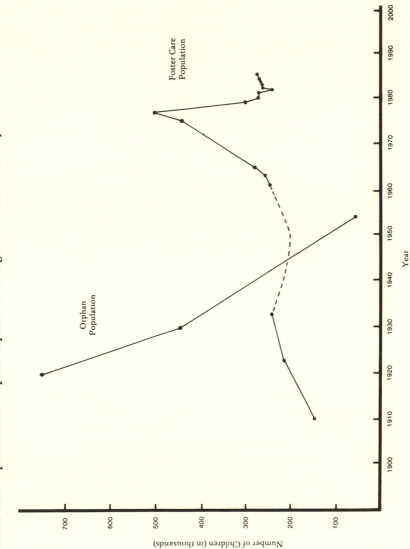

It would be an understatement to say that the various estimates presented here are not strictly comparable. Not only are they derived from several different methodologies, but definitional differences (concerning the types of placement arrangements to be included) plague most comparisons.[5] Moreover, certain implausible fluctuations, such as an apparent decline by 200,000 children in two years (from 1977 to 1979), further diminish our confidence in the precision and consistency of these figures.[6]

Nonetheless, if we were to suspend belief in the various estimates as precise point figures and regard each estimate as merely representing a *range* and having a margin of error of thousands or even tens of thousands, we have reason to be confident in the *trends* that emerge. Thus, for example, we have reason to believe that the high point of the foster care population in this century occurred during 1975–77, based as it is on two independent estimates, although we have little confidence in precisely what the population size was at that time. Indeed, in Figure 1, we observe that a small number of clear trends do emerge, and that at least from 1961 on, the beginning and end of each trend is backed up by estimates at no less than two points in time.

The trends we see are these: The foster care population increased from 1910 until 1933, declined until sometime before 1961, increased until its high point during 1975–77, and declined until 1982. There are indications, based on five estimates derived from consistent studies using the same methodology and procedures (the American Public Welfare Association surveys), that by 1983 the foster care population was on the rise again, and that by 1985, the latest year for which statistics are available, it was still rising.

Since the child population of the United States did not remain static over the course of this century, it is necessary to adjust our figures by calculating child placement rates. The U.S. Census statistics for the population of individuals under 18 years of age are presented in Table 1 (U.S. Bureau of the Census, 1975, Series A29–42, p. 10, and 1984, p. 29, no. 31). The child placement rates, also presented in Table 1 and plotted in Figure 2 (through 1983), indicate the number of children in foster care per 1,000 children living in the United States at the time. We see that these estimated child placement rates indicate the same trends as the absolute foster care population estimates. We can conservatively conclude that the rate of child placement has been no less in recent years than in the early part of this

Figure 2
Child Poverty Rate (per 100 children), Child Placement Rate (per 1,000 children),
and Poverty Placement Rate (per 100 children) During the Twentieth Century

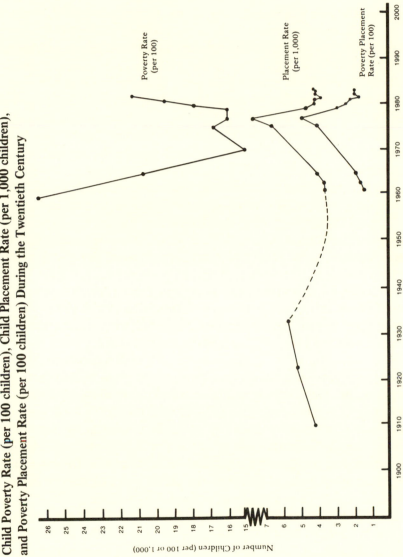

century. (Other numbers and curves in Table 1 and Figures 1 and 2 will be referred to later in this chapter and in later chapters.)

INTERPRETING THE TRENDS

The 1909 White House Conference, through its stand against breaking up families for reasons of poverty alone—and despite its leaders' distaste for public as opposed to private charity—paved the way, together with the emerging recognition in the early 1900s of the social origins of poverty, for mother's pension legislation (Lubove, 1968, pp. 98–99). The first statewide mother's pension law was enacted in Illinois in 1911, and 40 states passed similar legislation by 1920 (Abbott & Breckinridge, 1921, p. 5).

The express intent of the mother's pension movement was to avert the breakup of families for reasons of poverty alone, by giving financial aid to "deserving" mothers at least, to allow them to keep their children (Thompson, 1919, p. 11). Juvenile court judges had been distressed over what they had been forced to do. Reflecting the new understanding of the social origins of poverty, Kansas City juvenile court judge E. E. Porterfield, in arguing for a mother's pension act before the Missouri state legislature, proclaimed: "If the poverty of the mother forces her to neglect her child the poverty should be removed and not the child" (Lubove, 1968, p. 100).

However, competing undercurrents and reservations undermined this intent. The misgivings that private charities had about public pensions, the enduring individualistic view that character deficiencies caused poverty and, beyond that, the fear that aid would promote a "spirit of dependency" and thereby undercut initiative and striving toward economic independence on the part of the mothers, no doubt contributed to the fact that the funds allocated for mothers' pensions were extremely meager and that the individual benefits failed to address the concrete needs created by poverty (Leiby, 1978, p. 151; Lubove, 1968, pp. 101–10; Thompson, 1919, p. 19).

Yet the inadequacy of funding under the mother's pension laws cannot explain, by itself at least, why the child placement rate actually *increased* between 1910 and 1933. This increase is made more remarkable by the fact that the orphan population in our country, once quite large, declined enormously during that time (see Table 1 and Figure 1) (Shudde & Epstein, 1955). There is evidence to suggest that such "full" orphans, when they existed in large numbers, contributed substantially to the foster care population.[7]

To understand the reasons for the increase, we must go back to the origins of twentieth century child rescue efforts, which as the figures indicate, seem to have survived the 1909 White House Conference pronouncements on family preservation.

These origins can be found in the formation of Societies for the Prevention of Cruelty to Children (SPCCs), the first of which was established in New York City in 1874, as an outgrowth of the New York Society for the Prevention of Cruelty to Animals (Tiffin, 1982, p. 40). By 1900, there were 161 humane societies either exclusively for children or combined with animal protection (Giovannoni & Becerra, 1979, p. 47). In 1922, there were 57 SPCCs, and 307 other humane societies combining child and animal work (Shultz, 1924, p. 162). These societies handled a total of 234,577 children in that year (Shultz, 1924, p. 25).

These societies served case-finding and investigatory functions, under the cover of the law, and tended to focus on child removal and "on punishment of the parents as a deterrent to others" (Giovannoni & Becerra, 1979, pp. 47, 59, 66). The Massachusetts SPCC believed child removal to be a warning to other parents, that would instill fear in them (Gordon, 1988, pp. 51–52). Not until the 1920s did most of these societies begin to shift, in policy at least, from child rescue to family preservation (Billingsley & Giovannoni, 1972, pp. 37–38). In 1910, for example, Roswell McCrea, noting that "(i)t is a practical experience . . . that the line between destitute and neglected children is a very shadowy one," praised the Massachusetts SPCC for being a preventive agency, emphasizing prevention of "cruelty" rather than child removal. However, he noted that the New York Society emphasized separating children from their families and that, in fact, of the more than 200 societies in the United States at that time, the large majority were more similar in approach to the New York rather than the Massachusetts SPCC (in Bremner, 1971, pp. 214–216). Yet even the Massachusetts SPCC, at that time, had not really shifted toward prevention in actual practice (Gordon, 1988, p. 72). Societies for the Prevention of Cruelty to Children were the forerunners of today's public child welfare agencies (Rubin, 1979, pp. 35–36).

Paralleling the development of SPCCs, the first statewide children's home society began in Illinois in 1883, and such societies were established in 36 states by 1916 (Thurston, 1930, pp. 140–41, 150).

Children's aid societies, based on the one founded in New York City in 1853 by Charles Loring Brace, also proliferated. By 1923, there were 339 placing agencies of various types (Tiffin, 1982, p. 104). Their functions included case-finding as well as placement (e.g., Thurston, 1930, pp. 134, 148–50; Ashby, 1984, pp. 47–49, 60).

And even though, as already mentioned, there was a decline in the proportion of children in the foster care population who were in institutions as opposed to foster family care during the twentieth century, this shift was ever so gradual, especially between the years 1910 and 1933 (Rubin, 1979, p. 219). At least 13 new institutions were built each year during the first 10 years of this century (Ashby, 1984, p. 13).

In addition, the first juvenile court was established in Illinois in 1899. By 1909, ten states and the District of Columbia had authorized localities to establish juvenile courts, and another 12 states did so within the next three years. By 1925, only two states, Maine and Wyoming, had not established juvenile courts (Tiffin, 1982, pp. 218-19).

It is not clear how many of the children in foster care during those times had been placed there through "voluntary" surrenders by their parents, with their cases never having gone into a court (Thurston, 1930, pp. 134–35). Certainly, before the establishment of juvenile courts, children's home and aid societies usually circumvented courts (Tiffin, 1982, p. 104). Impoverished parents would "turn over" their children to such societies "out of affection, hoping that the youngsters would elsewhere receive opportunities unavailable in their own natural families" (Ashby, 1984, p. 49). Orphan asylums received children in the same manner. The SPCCs, on the other hand, in the matter of separating children from parents, chiefly prosecuted such cases through the courts (Shultz, 1924, pp. 162 ff.).

With the advent of juvenile courts, those cases that were brought to court and previously would have been dealt with through a multitude of adult courts, were now heard before juvenile courts (Tiffin, 1982, p. 284). Cases were initiated through complaints filed by social agencies, parents, relatives, and other individuals to have children declared dependent or neglected (Tiffin, 1982, p. 222). Private relief-giving agencies played a role in case-finding for the juvenile courts, and SPCCs—acting as an arm of the juvenile courts—performed both case-finding and investigative functions. Police and probation officers assigned to the juvenile courts also performed the investigative work (Giovannoni & Becerra, 1979, pp. 59, 66).

Although the primary function of the juvenile courts was to handle cases of juvenile delinquency, dependency and neglect cases did in fact comprise a significant proportion of their caseloads. For example, from a log book for the years 1914 through 1916, 19 percent of the cases settled out of court in the Milwaukee Juvenile Court appear to have involved parental neglect (Schlossman, 1977, p. 147). During a five-year period from 1915 through 1919, 10,631 cases, or 28 percent of those heard by the Chicago Juvenile Court were dependency (and neglect) cases; another 25 percent were mother's aid cases (see below); and 40 percent were delinquency cases (Jeter, 1922, pp. 17–18).

The ascendancy of the juvenile courts to the role of the premier child welfare agencies for dependent and neglected children during the 1910s and 1920s, and the growth of their probation officer staffs during that time, were principal factors responsible for the rise in the foster care population. Ironically, this is so despite the fact that it was in this same time period that all types of agencies involved in case-finding—private relief agencies, children's home and aid societies, and SPCCs—as well as the juvenile courts themselves to which many of the cases were brought and which would investigate and make decisions on the cases, gradually came to embrace—in rhetoric at least—the family preservation philosophy enunciated at the 1909 White House Conference.

Referring to the Milwaukee Juvenile Court that he studied, Schlossman (1977, p. 154) suggests that ". . . the caseload tended to grow with the court: enlargement and improvement of machinery for enforcing the court's original mandate generated 'business.'"

Indeed, until 1905, this court was staffed by volunteers. But after, the caseload grew: ". . . a full-time probation officer had more time and interest in ferreting out juvenile misconduct and in following up local gossip on neglectful parents and abettors of crime than did volunteers" (Schlossman, 1977, p. 154). The probation staff increased from one in 1905, to seven by 1909, to 14 by 1920 (Schlossman, 1977, p. 154). Children appearing in court increased from 594 in 1905 to 2,326 in 1909 (Schlossman, 1977, p. 201). Although even the increased staff is small for a city the size of Milwaukee when compared with today's staffing patterns of public child welfare agencies, we are informed that in 1919, 11 probation officers paid over 8,000 visits to individual homes and received more than 21,000 visits by probationers at their offices (Schlossman, 1977, p. 155).

In the Chicago Juvenile Court, the number of probation officers paid by the county increased from 37 in 1911 to 102 in 1921. In that year, the Probation Department also included 26 police probation officers paid by the City of Chicago (Jeter, 1922, pp. 6, 29). Over a span of 21 years, from the court's inception until the middle of 1920, 79,000 cases were brought into court, but 37,881 cases, or roughly half of this total, were heard by the court in the five-year period of 1915 through 1919 alone, indicating a rapid growth of the caseload (Jeter, 1922, pp. 17–18).

Of the 10,631 dependency cases heard by the court in this five-year period, 4,330 (40.7%) resulted in commitment to institutions, and 491 (4.6%) in commitment to child-placing societies. In another 1,341 cases (12.6%), a guardian was appointed. In these cases, the idea was for the guardian to place the child in a home (in some cases, for adoption). Another 2,805 cases (26.4%) were placed on probation. Of these, 962 (or about a third of the cases of dependent children placed on probation) involved placing the child in a home other than his or her own, usually the home of a friend or a relative, and not one that the court would find (Jeter, 1922, pp. 71–72, 78–79). Thus, not including children placed with friends or relatives, about 58 percent of the cases heard by the court resulted in foster care placement. Although many dependency and neglect complaints were disposed of without court action (Jeter, 1922, pp. 36–39), making the percentages just mentioned subject to interpretation, still a total of 6,162 children were placed in foster care through court action from 1915 through 1919 in Chicago alone, or at a rate of 1,232 children per year.

Such figures bear out contentions that "probation officers and prosecuting attorneys aggressively sought removal of children from their natural parents" (Schlossman, 1977, p. 181) and that juvenile courts had "unprecedented power to intrude into the lives of children and their families" (Katz, 1986, p. 134). Although family preservation had already become a "ritual incantation" (Katz, 1986, p. 115), and the idea was for probation officers to enter the families as helpers and friends, these same probation officers—backed up by court authority—had the power to remove children from their families and "did not hesitate to use this weapon to force parents to conform to the behavioral norms they themselves accepted" (Tiffin, 1982, p. 255).

The dual role of helper and enforcer allowed children to be separated from parents under a facade of friendship, although the parents were not fooled. In dependency cases in the Milwaukee Juvenile Court, the parents, who were almost always impoverished, "were generally called to the court's attention by private and public charity officials who, in the course of processing the parents' claims for financial assistance, decided that in the interests of juvenile welfare, the children should be removed from the home. When brought into court and threatened with loss of their children, most parents responded hostilely, refusing to believe that the court genuinely had the children's best interests at heart" (Schlossman, 1977, p. 160).

The mothers' pensions, along with the juvenile court system, "provided some of the era's most conspicuous examples of government probing into individual life-styles. Some investigators of pension recipients intruded quite deliberately into family lives, searching for evidence of immorality, 'unfitness,' and even inadequate child-rearing techniques" (Ashby, 1984, p. 11).

The mother's pension laws provided for field investigators to judge which mothers were "inefficient" or "immoral," and which were deserving of aid (Lubove, 1968, p. 109; Thompson, 1919). As Lubove (1968, p. 108) states: "An uneasy balance of economic and vague moral criteria complicated the administration of this legislation." Moreover, relief was combined with "social treatment." Again as Lubove (1968, p. 110) points out: "Application for a pension was presumptive evidence of an inadequacy which differentiated the family from the community mainstream and justified intervention in the client's personal life."

As of 1920, the administration of mother's pension laws was placed in the juvenile courts in 21 states, or in more than half of the states that had such laws at that time (Abbott & Breckinridge, 1921, p. 5). Probation officers were often the investigators of relief eligibility (Giovannoni & Beccrra, 1979, p. 63), and although in Chicago, at least, separate officers were attached to a separate division of the court to investigate and supervise mother's pension cases (Jeter, 1922, p. 31), they were under the very same courts that were removing considerable numbers of children from their homes under charges of neglect.

It is possible then, that under the policies of family preservation and not removing children for reasons of poverty alone, and in the absence of appreciable material assistance, increasing numbers of dependent children were being redefined as neglected children, and that the mother's pension laws aided this development by sending out investigators to detect, according to their own lights, deficiencies in the conditions of the home and in the mother's moral character.

In the Chicago Juvenile Court, during the period of August 1, 1913 to March 1, 1915, 532 families with more than 1,400 children had their applications for pensions rejected (Abbott & Breckinridge, 1921, p. 72). Of these families, only 39 (or 7%) were rejected for the reason of "unfitness" of the mother (Abbott & Breckinridge, 1921, p. 73). It appears that in the majority of these cases, steps were taken to "protect" the children, usually by referring the cases to other departments of the court, with the likelihood of placement (Abbott & Breckinridge, 1921, pp. 78-79). Almost all families who received pensions were visited at least once per month (Abbott & Breckinridge, 1921, p. 27), but how many placements might have been initiated through discovery of eventual "unfitness" during supervisory visits has not been reported.

Thus, on the one hand, there is evidence that mother's pension investigations did lead to the placement of some children, but on the other hand, such placements might have accounted for only a small proportion of all placements of dependent and neglected children made through the juvenile courts. Part of the reason for this may be that in the Chicago Juvenile Court, at least, in regard to the 532 families noted above who had their pension applications rejected, only 24 percent had not been known to other social agencies in Chicago (Abbott & Breckinridge, 1921, p. 121). During this same period, only 6 percent of the families whose pensions were approved were not known to such agencies (Abbott & Breckinridge, 1921, p. 121). Thus, most families applying for pensions had already been scrutinized by other agencies.

We may conclude that, given long-standing inclinations to find fault with impoverished parents and to use child removal as a "solution" to their problems, and despite new policies of family preservation, the increase in the foster care population from 1910 on was due primarily to the expansion of the juvenile court system and the growth of probation officer staffs attached to those courts; to a considerable extent to the increase in the number of SPCCs, other humane societies, and children's home and aid societies; and to a minor extent to the provision of field investigators under the mother's pension laws, and the presence of new institutions to accept children.

Finally, it is conceivable that an added spurt was given during the 1920s by the strong influence that psychodynamic theory began to exert on social work practice at that time, leading casework to come to be based upon a psychodynamic model and the casework focus to shift further than in its recent past from the environment to the individual (Woodroofe, 1968, pp. 118–47; Lubove, 1965, pp. 80–117). Children would no longer be removed for reasons of poverty, thus in keeping with the 1909 White House Conference doctrine, but rather for psychological defects of the parents presumably resulting in neglect, and the child placement rate continued to increase.

The subsequent decline in the child placement rate, from the mid-1930s until about the mid-1950s, has been attributed by child welfare experts to the provision of federal funding for Aid to Dependent Children (ADC) under the Social Security Act of 1935 (Low, 1966; Boehm, 1970, pp. 224–25). While the financial benefits under this program were still inadequate, they were to become much better than before. Moreover, they were to cover many more families than did the Mothers' Aid pensions. As late as 1931, only 94,000 families in this country were supported in part by mothers' pensions (Lerman, 1982, pp. 118–19), and widows comprised 82 percent of mothers receiving pensions (Tiffin, 1982, p. 130). Moreover, very few black people ever received mothers' pensions. In Chicago in 1917, for example, only 26 families, or 2.7 percent of the families on the pension roll, were black (Abbott & Breckinridge, 1921, p. 84). By 1940, however, 372,000 families were receiving ADC benefits, compared with 651,000 in 1950 (Lerman, 1982, pp. 118–19).

During the coming decades after the passage of the Social Security Act, many mothers would be denied financial assistance on the grounds of failing to meet locally established "suitable home" criteria (Bell, 1965, pp. 93–110). But since, as previously noted, we cannot pinpoint how long the decline in the child placement rate lasted, it is difficult to determine whether the decline continued despite this phenomenon, or whether this phenomenon contributed to the subsequent upturn.

In any event, it has been suggested that some semblance of material provision, however still inadequate, to address the concrete needs of poverty, had an impact on the rate of child placement by preventing the need for separating children from their parents in many instances. However, the steep decline of the orphan population during that time (see Table 1 and Figure 1) raises an unresolved question of just what proportion, if any, of the decrease in the child placement rate may be attributable to the financial aid itself under the Social Security Act.

In fact, the evidence just reviewed of a link between the expansion of agencies and a growth of personnel available to investigate dependency and neglect cases, and an increase in the foster care placement rate, leads one to suspect that the subsequent decline in that rate may have been due to a possible contraction of agencies and decline in personnel during the 1930s and 1940s. It is conceivable that the Depression and World War II led to a diversion of the public's attention from child welfare issues and decrease in funding for such agencies.

Confirmation of this hypothesis awaits further historical research, of which there has been surprisingly little concerning child welfare issues during this period. But there are indications in the literature that during the Depression years, SPCCs and children's aid societies experienced financial problems that caused agency mergers, attrition, and even the abandonment of protective services (in Bremner, 1974, p. 862). Even before that time, protective service functions had begun shifting from private agencies to state and local governments, and from the juvenile courts to public welfare agencies, but these shifts were accelerated by the Social Security Act of 1935 (Antler & Antler, 1979, p. 200). Yet it was not until the 1950s that public child welfare programs began to expand significantly (Mayo, 1955). Thus, we can surmise that a gap in child welfare services existed during the 1930s and 1940s, which was a transition period. Especially during World War II, personnel shortages developed in the public agencies to which responsibility had shifted (Eliot, 1955). The percentage of vacancies in federally funded child welfare positions in public welfare agencies, for example, increased from 17 percent at the end of 1940 to 39 percent in mid-1943 (U.S. Children's Bureau, 1947). In mid-1946, only 18 percent of all counties in the nation had the services of at least one full-time child welfare worker (U.S. Children's Bureau, 1947).

It should be noted here that public child welfare agencies as we know them today began as public child welfare programs within public welfare agencies. Later, during the 1970s in most states, they became separate agencies under a policy of separation of social services from income maintenance programs. In this book, I will often use the term "public child welfare agencies" to refer to both the earlier programs and the later separate agencies.

We next face the question of why the child placement rate might have risen during the 1950s, and why it soared beginning with the early 1960s.

The rise of the juvenile court's role in handling dependent and neglected children had represented a significant shift in our country to government control of child protection work. But as early as the 1920s, there was a movement afoot to shift some of the court authority over dependent and neglected children to new, more specialized public agencies (Tiffin, 1982, pp. 225-29). The shift toward such agencies, organized on a state or county level, had already begun in such states as Colorado, West Virginia, Minnesota, North Carolina, and Pennsylvania (Shultz, 1924, pp. 223-28).

It was the Social Security Act of 1935, however, that paved the way for separate public child welfare agencies to eventually emerge as the dominant child welfare model, wresting that role from the juvenile courts (Rubin, 1979, p. 217). Title V of this act provided for grants to states to help public welfare agencies to establish, extend, and strengthen child welfare services for the protection of homeless, dependent, and neglected children, "especially in predominantly rural areas." Juvenile courts were operative mainly in urban areas. In 1918, there were 321 courts with separate hearings for juveniles and regular probation services. Of these, only 42 served predominantly rural areas, although about a third were in towns with populations of between 5,000 and 25,000 (Tiffin, 1982, pp. 225-26). It was not until 1947 that federal money was available for foster care, and not until 1958 that amendments to the Social Security Act extended the availability of federal money for "child welfare services" to urban areas (Steiner, 1981, p. 136).

During the 1950s and early 1960s, public spending for child welfare services in this country increased to substantial levels. Such expenditures doubled from $104.9 million in 1950 to $211.5 million in 1960, and the federal share of these expenditures had grown from 4.0 percent to 6.3 percent (Bixby, 1981). Concurrently, the number of employees in public child welfare programs rose considerably (U.S. Children's Bureau, 1953; 1963, Table 21; 1964, Table 21; Low, 1957, Table A).

From the beginning, the emphasis of the new public child welfare services was on child placement, despite rhetoric to the contrary (Rosenthal, 1983, pp. 351-52). The major service of child welfare agencies traditionally has been foster care placement. As Billingsley and Giovannoni (1972, p. 61) state: "The system of child welfare services which had evolved by 1900 in America has undergone modifications in this century. However, the principal modifications have been in the means of providing and administering the services; the services themselves have remained heavily focused on the placement of children away from their parents."

In 1956, for example, 72 percent of total expenditures for child welfare services by state and local agencies went for foster care payments (Low, 1958, Table 1). Thus, increased money available to hire more employees simply meant that more placements *could* be made.

Another factor that may have contributed to the rise in the foster care population from the 1950s on is the extension of child rescue activities to black children. Up until the end of World War I, black children were largely excluded from the child welfare system. In the 1920s and 1930s, the system began to take some notice of them. But it was not until the end of World War II that they began to enter the system in large numbers (Billingsley & Giovannoni, 1972, pp. 34-35, 37-38, 72). When they finally were "allowed" into the system after previous discrimination (it is debatable whether their previous exclusion was not really a blessing in disguise), they constituted an important factor for several reasons. Between 1950 and 1960, the white child population in the United States increased 21 percent, while the nonwhite child population increased 43 percent. Although black children constituted a relatively small proportion of the total dependent child population even at the end of World War II, increasing proportions of poor children have been black children since that time (Billingsley & Giovannoni, 1972, pp. 86, 91, 131). The proportion of the public child welfare caseload consisting of nonwhite children almost doubled between 1945 and 1961, from 14 percent to 27 percent (Billingsley & Giovannoni, 1972, p. 93).

Thus, there has always been a sizable "pool" of impoverished families available from which to rescue children. During the early part of this century, this "pool" was largely stocked by European immigrants, although not out of proportion to native-born impoverished families. The vast majority of poor parents brought into the juvenile courts were immigrants simply because the vast majority of poor people at that time were immigrants (Schlossman, 1977, p. 144; Tiffin, 1983, pp. 41-45). After the Second World War, rescue efforts were extended to black families, at a time when they began to compose increasing proportions of the impoverished population of this country. But rises in the rate of child placement have coincided with increases in the staff available to investigate the families in this "pool" and to do the rescuing.

In the next chapter, I will analyze the events surrounding the unprecedented increase in the foster care placement rate that began in the early 1960s. The decline from 1975–77 until 1982, and the subsequent current rise, will be considered in the discussion of the permanency planning movement in Chapter 4.

NOTES

1. Of the total of 151,441 children in foster care in 1910, 39,927 were outside of institutions (U.S. Bureau of the Census, 1913, p. 28, Table 19). On February 1, 1923, there were 218,523 children in the care of institutions and child-placing societies primarily for the care of dependents (U.S. Bureau of the Census, 1927, p. 18, Table 2). The figure for 1933 indicates the number of children in agencies' institutions and foster homes, representing institutions and agencies caring for dependent and neglected children (U.S. Bureau of the Census, 1935, p. 8, Table 4; p. 1).

2. The figure for 1961 represents children in institutions for the dependent and neglected, in foster family homes, and in group homes (U.S. Children's Bureau, 1962, p. 30, Table 25). The figures for 1963 and 1965 represent the same categories (U.S. Children's Bureau, 1964, p. 9, Table 6; 1966, p. 15, Table 2). The 1960 statistics are not presented here because of an apparent incomplete implementation of the system during its first year of operation (see Jeter, 1962; U.S. Children's Bureau, 1961).

3. See, for example, Jeter and Lajewski (1958). Before 1961, the estimates reported in the Children's Bureau Statistical Series did not include children served only by voluntary child welfare programs. This led to considerable undercounts of children in institutions. For similar reasons, Jeter's (1963) estimate of 177,000 for 1961 is considerably below the Children's Bureau Statistical Series estimate of 244,500 for that year, and the latter figure is used here. The former figure was limited to those children receiving public child welfare services. Considering all available information, our best guess is that it is not likely that the foster care population after 1933 ever dipped below 200,000, nor the child placement rate (see text) below 3.5. In later years (from the 1970s on), almost all children in foster care, even if served by voluntary child welfare agencies, have been served by and known to the public agencies also, and so surveys (see Note 4) could be validly limited to public agencies (see Shyne & Schroeder, 1978, p. 13).

4. The estimate for 1975 is based upon a Children's Defense Fund survey of a random sample of 140 county public child welfare offices (Knitzer et al., 1978, pp. 2, 182, 191). This figure more accurately reflects the report's estimate of the number of children in placement under the aegis of the child welfare system alone, than the higher estimate of 500,000 that I attributed to the report in a

previous publication (Pelton, 1987b). The 1977 estimate, from a Westat study, is based on a sample of almost 10,000 case records from a sample of 315 local public child welfare agencies (Shyne & Schroeder, 1978). The 1979 estimate is based on a survey by the U.S. Office of Civil Rights requesting all of the more than 2,400 public child welfare agencies in the country to provide statistical information (U.S. Office of Civil Rights, 1980). The 1980 estimate was derived from state statistical reports by the Child Welfare League of America (1983). The 243,000 figure for 1982 was due to a study by Maximus, Inc., based on a sampling of case records from a national sample of 167 local public child welfare agencies (Maximus, Inc., 1983). Finally, the American Public Welfare Association estimates for 1981, 1982, 1983, 1984, and 1985 were derived from state statistical reports (see Tatara & Pettiford, 1985, p. 32, Table III; and Tatara et al., 1988, p. 30, Table III). The 1982 figure of 262,000 refers to the last day of fiscal year (FY) 1982; the 1982 figure of 263,000 to the first day of FY 1983, and the 1983 figure of 269,000 to the last day of FY 1983. The 1984 figure of 270,000 refers to the first day of FY 1985, and the 1985 figure of 276,000 to the last day of FY 1985.

5. For example, there has been variation in regard to the inclusion of children in preadoptive homes, emergency care, detention centers, runaway shelters, independent living arrangements, and those living with relatives but whose placements were arranged and/or paid for by public child welfare agencies. According to Dr. Charles Gershenson of the Children's Bureau, 10 different state definitions of foster care are currently in use (Gershenson, personal communication, April 10, 1985). According to Dr. Toshio Tatara, who directs the American Public Welfare Association data collection effort, 34 states define children in preadoptive homes as part of the foster care population, while the remaining states consider such children to have left foster care (Tatara, personal communication, April 16, 1985).

6. According to Dr. Charles Gershenson, it has been determined by Westat and the Children's Bureau that of the apparent decline of 200,000 children from the 1977 Westat estimate to the Office of Civil Rights figure for 1979, 110,000 was due to definitional differences, and therefore was not real.

7. For example, according to a report by the State of New Jersey Pension Survey Commission (1932), there were 3,685 children under state supervision in foster homes and institutions in October 1931. Of these plus another 894 children placed with relatives, 557 were orphans. In 1910, approximately 17 percent of the children in local institutions in New York State were orphans or foundlings (Tiffin, 1982, p. 42).

2

The Crusade Against Child Abuse

In the early 1960s, C. Henry Kempe and his colleagues—a group including radiologists, pediatricians, and psychiatrists—"discovered" or at least "rediscovered" child abuse. Focusing on extremely brutalized young children and infants, this team dramatically called attention to what it labeled the "battered child syndrome," and alluded to psychodynamic causes and "defect in character structure" as underlying this "syndrome" (Kempe et al., 1962). This "discovery" drew an enormous amount of professional and media interest, and child abuse became a national issue (Pfohl, 1977; Antler, 1981; Nelson, 1984). "Although physical abuse . . . was not an unfamiliar problem . . . it was Kempe's formulation that quickly captured the public imagination" (Antler, 1981).

The passage of reporting laws, requiring physicians, social workers, other professionals, and even all citizens, to report cases of suspected child abuse as well as neglect, developed as a major strategy in dealing with child abuse and neglect. By the end of 1963, 13 states had already enacted such laws, and by 1973, every state had passed a mandatory reporting law, an indication of how rapidly and fervently this crusade against child maltreatment took hold (Antler, 1981).

In early 1974, the signing of the federal Child Abuse Prevention and Treatment Act established a National Center on Child Abuse and Neglect (NCCAN) within the Children's Bureau, mandated that this center should compile statistics on the incidence of child abuse and neglect, gave small amounts of money to states for prevention and treatment demonstration projects, provided some funding for individual research, grants, encouraged modifications in state reporting laws, and required that in all court cases a guardian *ad litem* be appointed to represent the child. This act served to draw further attention to the issue of child abuse.

This child abuse movement further encouraged intervention into the lives of families, based on psychodynamic conceptions of the faults of the parents. It will be argued here that this movement was the driving force behind the explosion in the child placement rate that occurred from the early 1960s until the 1975-77 period. However, the movement would not have eventuated in this result if new resources had not become available.

As it happened, Title IV of the Social Security Act was amended in 1961 to make federal monies available to states for court-ordered placement of children from families receiving ADC (later AFDC). It has been claimed that this amendment might have contributed to the rise in the foster care population by inadvertently providing financial disincentives for keeping families together (Rosenthal & Louis, 1981). However, public child welfare agencies continued to circumvent the courts in the majority of their placements (Mnookin, 1973). Thus, if this AFDC-FC program functioned as an incentive to increased placement, it did so to a limited extent.

More importantly, the Public Welfare Amendments (to the Social Security Act) of 1962 provided grants-in-aid to the states for social services. These amendments compelled the federal government to match, by 75 percent, whatever state government spent on "social services," a term that was left ill-defined, with no ceiling placed on the amount that could be spent (Derthick, 1975, pp. 1-14). The amendments of 1967 further expanded the scope of spending. Under these amendments, federal spending for social services rose from $194 million in 1963 to $354 million in 1969, and then soared to $1.7 billion by 1972, after which Congress enacted a $2.5 billion ceiling (Derthick, 1975, pp. 1-14). Federal spending did reach $2.5 billion by 1977 (Bixby, 1981). It is not known exactly how all of this money was spent, but there are indications that a large proportion did go for foster care (Derthick, 1975, p. 2; Mott, 1976, p. 25). Total expenditures (including federal, state, and local) for social services increased from $712.6 million in 1970 to $3.2 billion by 1977 (Bixby, 1981).

In addition, under these same amendments, fixed federal grants to states specifically earmarked for child welfare services rose from $13.4 million in 1960 to $56.5 million by 1977 (Bixby, 1981). These expenditures, however, continued to constitute only a small portion of total expenditures specifically designated as child welfare spending, which rose from $211.5 million in 1960 to $810 million by 1977, indicating that the states themselves contributed heavily to increased child welfare spending (Bixby, 1981).

Public child welfare agencies expanded enormously during this period, allowing these agencies to investigate more and more cases. In New Jersey, for example, the number of employees of the state child welfare agency rose from under 500 in 1965 (when it was the Bureau of Children's Services) to over 2,000 in 1975 (as the Division of Youth and Family Services) (*Governor's Budget Message*, 1966, 1977). The caseload more than doubled from 19,249 children in 1968 to 44,688 children in 1974 (New Jersey Bureau of Children's Services, 1968; New Jersey Division of Youth and Family Services, 1974).

Ironically, although the intent of the amendments was to "strengthen family life," they served to provide the resources for a child abuse crusade whose thrust was to detect psychological defects in impoverished parents rather than to provide concrete services in the home. The crusade provided the reports to be investigated and the rationale for child removal; the amendments provided the resources for more caseworkers to be hired who could investigate more reports and remove more children.

An increase in the number of caseworkers would not necessarily have led to more removals were it not for the fact that foster care was the primary resource that child welfare agencies possessed. The agencies did not have other resources available to deal with identified problems. The fact is that, from a fiscal perspective, these agencies were foster care agencies. That is, their budgetary emphases were on foster care. Having only a hammer, they perceived every problem to need hammering. For example, an analysis of the State Aid portion of the budget of the New Jersey Division of Youth and Family Services in 1981 indicated that less than 5.8 percent of State Aid expenditures went for preventive services, while over 90 percent went for foster-care payments (Pelton, 1981a). If these agencies had used the social services monies to develop concrete supportive services for the home, then the increased number of workers could have provided more of these, rather than more foster care.

But of great significance was the fact that child neglect had been redefined, in a sense, as child abuse (Wolock & Horowitz, 1984). The image created in the public's mind through the media, often through vivid photographs, was of brutally battered children of the type that Kempe had seen in his Denver hospital. The large, often exaggerated numbers, however, cited by proponents of the movement in order to claim that child abuse had reached "epidemic proportions," referred mainly to cases of far milder abuse, and to the many more cases of marginal neglect seen by public agencies (Pelton, 1978a). Aiding this conception of an epidemic was the psychodynamic medical model of child abuse introduced by Kempe and his associates, which the social work profession—long enamored of psychodynamic explanations of behavior—embraced wholeheartedly, and the contention that child abuse and neglect "afflicted" families without regard to socioeconomic standing (Pelton, 1978a).

Hence child neglect, together with abuse, was seen no longer as an aspect or result of poverty, but as a psychological problem, calling for psychological treatment. When the suspect parents did not respond to "treatment," the children were more likely to be shipped off to foster care; this removal was aided by the new and more severe image of what neglect entailed. The fact that the children removed were—as such children have always been—among the poorest children in our society did not deter the removers, who held, and continue to hold, a belief in the myth of classlessness (Pelton, 1978a). Blinded by their own treatment fantasies and demographic myths, professionals involved with child welfare have been led by the psychodynamic medical model to blame the individual results of the conditions of poverty on poor people. By encouraging workers to look for personal defects in poor people, this perspective has made it easier to decide to remove children from their parents rather than to provide concrete services within the home. Under the influence of the new model, even if more money had been wrested from foster care, it more likely would have gone for more counseling and therapy than for concrete services. In any event, the psychodynamic medical model and the myth of classlessness have facilitated child removal by encouraging the already-present inclinations to look for personal deficits in poor people and to overlook the socioeconomic factors involved.

So powerful was the combination of forces being described here that it led to the increase in the child placement rate despite the fact that, at least from the late 1950s on, many studies and reports began to indicate to child welfare professionals that separation and the foster care system were doing considerable harm to children (e.g., Maas & Engler, 1969; see Wald, 1976). Eventually, however, the permanency planning movement developed to address these concerns, as will be discussed in Chapter 4.

THE PSYCHODYNAMIC MEDICAL MODEL

During the 1960s, a psychodynamic orientation toward child abuse and neglect, within the context of a medical model of disease, treatment, and cure, became the dominant viewpoint within the field (Antler, 1981). It was presumed that there are certain personality deficits that distinguish most abusing and neglecting parents from all other people and that explain the phenomena. In the context of this approach, the parent-client is regarded as a patient, whose "illness" involves his or her entire personality and who is an object of treatment. The psychodynamic medical orientation led researchers and agencies to be more concerned with psychological defects thought to characterize such parents than with the situational realities of their daily lives.

The authors of a guide for child welfare workers attributed "infantilism" to neglectful mothers, due to a "stunting of psychological growth" (Polansky et al., 1972). They went on to describe the following personality types of neglectful mothers: the apathetic-futile mother, the impulse-ridden mother, the mentally retarded mother, the mother in a reactive depression, and the psychotic mother. Abusive and neglectful parents had been characterized as hostile, manipulative, and deceitful (Young, 1964). Gelles (1973) gleaned from the literature a partial catalog of the plethora of personality deficits that had been attributed to abusing parents. They were said to have severe emotional problems, defective character structure, poor emotional control, pervasive anger, psychosomatic illnesses, and a perverse fascination with punishment of children. They had also been described by various authors as impulsive, immature, depressed, sadomasochistic, quick to react with poorly controlled aggression, inadequate, self-centered, hypersensitive, dependent, egocentric, narcissistic, demanding, and insecure. They also presumably suffered from "transference psychosis."

Gelles (1973) identified the following problems of the psychopathological approach to child abuse. Most of the discussions were inconsistent and contradictory as to the nature and presence of various personality deficits. There was little agreement as to the attributed personality traits. "Of nineteen traits listed by the authors there was agreement by two or more authors on only four traits." Most studies did not test the assumptions they made: Attributions were made simply on the basis of the abusing behavior and were then offered as explanations. Finally, inadequate sampling procedures were used, coupled with the absence of comparable control groups of non-abusers. Thus we would have no way of knowing whether the proposed attributions could be generalized to all abusers, or whether they differentiate abusers from nonabusers.

Be that as it may, the significant point is that child abuse and neglect, either singularly or together, had been conceptualized as singular entities in themselves that could be "explained" as being "caused" by a particular set of personality characteristics lying within the parents themselves. A dictionary definition of a syndrome, as in "battered child syndrome," is "a group of signs and symptoms that occur together and characterize a particular abnormality." In the case of child abuse and neglect, the signs and symptoms had been attributed to the parents themselves, despite occasional lip service to environmental factors, and it was implied that child abuse and neglect were a singular entity replete with its own diagnosis and cure, a phenomenon that could be "explained" by a unitary theory that awaited discovery by researchers.

As late as 1977, a public relations manual published by the National Center on Child Abuse and Neglect (1977) promoted the medical model mythology by including such statements as "(Abusing and neglecting) parents are sick" and "Child abuse is contagious. If you caught it from your parents, you may give it to your kids." In fact, no greater incidence of psychoses is found among "abusing" parents than in the general population (Pelton, 1977a), and there is no evidence of a cause-effect relationship between having been abused as a child and becoming an abuser as a parent (Kaufman & Zigler, 1987). But again, the significant point here is that the conceptualization of child abuse and neglect as a "disease" was continuing to be promoted.

Due to the cover of medical metaphors, and the fact that, as we will see, many dangers and serious harms do beset children in our society—especially those living in impoverished families—for which the parents can be held partially responsible, a more sophisticated version of "blaming the victim" (Ryan, 1971) arose than heretofore imagined. Indeed, the very terms "abuse and neglect," which predate the medical model, are packed with meaning: They refer not only to harm and risk of harm to children, but also carry the judgmental inference that the parent is responsible for that harm or risk. Moreover, they are accusatory terms that *focus* on the responsibility of the parent and imply that the parent is *solely* responsible.

As we will see later, in many cases labeled as "abuse and neglect," it can be argued that there are multiple sources of responsibility and patterns of multiple causation. Moreover, a great diversity of situations and behaviors have been labeled as "abuse and neglect" cases. There is no reason in nature why, just because we have decided to lump them together into a construed singular "social problem," they should succumb to a singular theory or explanation, and certainly not one that locates the "problem" in the personalities of the parents. Yet the construction of child abuse and neglect as a unitary entity fostered the illusion that its prevalence could be counted, and the attribution of fault to the parents fueled the fervor to encourage the reporting of parents to child protection agencies. Indeed, evidence that could be seized upon to show that abuse and neglect was occurring in "epidemic" proportions would complete the medical metaphor.

THE NUMBERS ILLUSION

"More than a million American children suffer physical abuse or neglect each year, and at least one in five of the young victims die from their mistreatment, the Government announced today." Printed in the *New York Times* (November 30, 1975), this UPI report went on to cite the "epidemic" proportions of the abuse and neglect problem, and reiterated that the yearly death toll is 200,000 children. This death figure continued to gain nationwide publicity through the news media for several weeks. In fact, it was repeated by at least one state's commissioner of human services, in a news release, and by Cornell's famed expert on human development and the family, Urie Bronfenbrenner, in a magazine article reprinted in the *Washington Post*.

Douglas Besharov, then director of the government's National Center on Child Abuse and Neglect, on whose interview the report was based, claims that he had said 2,000. Even this figure was just a guess, being well beyond officially confirmed deaths due to abuse or neglect, and might well have been a gross overestimate. However, the significant matter here is not that a human error was made somewhere along the line, but that such a preposterous figure as 200,000 could be so carelessly repeated even by government officials and experts. We can only conclude that the number did not *mean* a specific quantity to those who echoed it, but rather merely signified the concept "huge, enormous." In this light, one large figure means the same as another. Yet paradoxically, there has been a vigorous pursuit of numbers. Numbers possess an aura of authority, of precise scientific fact. As such, they have been used politically, often by individuals other than those who have tried to collect them, to dramatize and draw attention to issues, to gain resources, and in this case, to fuel a crusade against child abuse based on the psychodynamic medical model.

Previously, the propensity for exaggeration of the death rates was clear, for example, at the 1973 Senate Hearings on the Child Abuse Prevention and Treatment Act, where Congressman Mario Biaggi (1973) referred to abuse and neglect as the "number one killer of children in America today." In fact birth complications, congenital anomalies, motor vehicle accidents, and other accidents have been the leading causes of child death, *each* of which have accounted for far more deaths than can be attributed with any certainty to child abuse and neglect (National Center for Health Statistics, 1988).

The first attempt to gain an estimate of the overall incidence of child maltreatment in the United States was made by David Gil (1970), in a survey designed to obtain an "indirect estimate" of the extent of child abuse alone. Defining child abuse as the physical injury of a child by a caretaker deliberately or in anger, the survey was conducted in 1965 on a nationally representative sample of 1,520 adults.

Only six of the respondents, or .4 percent of the sample, answered affirmatively to the question: "Did you ever actually lose control of yourself and injure a child?" But when the respondents were asked whether they personally knew families involved in incidents of child abuse during the past year, 45 people, or 3 percent, said that they did, although hardly any reported knowledge of more than one incident. From this statistic, Gil extrapolated to the entire population of American adults, and arrived at the conclusion that between 2.5 and 4.1 million adults in the United States knew personally of families involved in child abuse incidents during a one-year period.

There are obvious difficulties with such a procedure, many of which were pointed out by Gil himself. Most importantly, each person was asked to report knowledge of an incident that he or she probably did not actually witness, and that could have been at the level of mere rumor, leaving the investigator with only hearsay to report to us. Yet numbers speak louder than stipulations. The estimate came to be frequently repeated, and there was little inclination to heed Gil's (1973) statement to former Senator Walter Mondale at the Senate Hearings on the Child Abuse Prevention and Treatment Act: "Sir, there is no connection whatsoever between the statistics and reality on this particular issue. . . . The statistics are meaningless. I say this as a person who has tried to collect them for several years."

The tenuousness of Gil's data did not prevent Harvard's Richard Light (1973) from reevaluating them. Creating a mathematical model, and using an extensive series of assumptions and assigned values (at one point he invites any dissatisfied reader to plug in his or her *own* numerical values), he arrived at the range of 200,000 to 500,000 as the estimated number of physical abuse incidents. A few assumptions and mathematical manipulations later, he found that if we include the categories of sexual abuse and child neglect, we could estimate that between 665,000 and 1.7 million abuse and neglect incidents occur each year.

Against this backdrop, it was not altogether surprising to hear the CBS Evening News, in February of 1977, announce the latest findings that 2 million children in this country between the ages of three and 17 have been beaten up by their parents, "two million have been threatened with a knife or gun," and at least a million children have been shot, shot at, or stabbed by their parents. "The results," Roger Mudd solemnly proclaimed to the nation, "shocked even the researchers."

The news item was based on a report of a survey of couples with a child between three and 17 years old. One parent in each of the families was asked whether or not he or she had directed certain actions, specified by the interviewer, toward that child (Gelles, 1977).

Of the 1,146 parents who were interviewed, 71 percent admitted to ever having slapped or spanked the child, and over 46 percent to ever having pushed, grabbed, or shoved him or her. Twenty percent of the parents acknowledged ever having hit the child with something, and almost 8 percent confessed that they had ever kicked, bit, or hit the child with a fist. While 1.3 percent admitted that they "beat up" the child within the past year, 4.2 percent said that they ever had done so. Finally, one-tenth of one percent of all parents claimed to have threatened the child with a knife or gun, and exactly the same percentage to have *used* a knife or gun, once within the past year. The figures were 2.8 percent and 2.9 percent, respectively, for having ever done so.

Extrapolating from these figures to the total population of 46 million children (between ages three and 17) who lived with both parents in 1975 (the survey year), Gelles estimated that between 3 and 4 million had ever been kicked, bit, or punched. He concluded that about 2 million had ever been "beat up," and that between a half and three-quarters of a million had been "beat up" in 1975. Finally, he estimated that between 1 and 1.4 million children had ever had a gun or knife used on them by their parents, and that 46,000 children had undergone such an event in 1975. The broadcast statement that *2* million children had been *threatened* with a knife or a gun appears to have been the inadvertent fabrication of CBS News.

The methodological difficulties of this survey have been debated elsewhere (Pelton, 1979; Gelles, 1979). Briefly, the most important issues raised concern the extrapolation from very small numbers of affirmative responses to an entire population, and the interpretation of words by individual respondents. For example, in the course of interviewing 1,146 parents, only *one* parent (.1%) was found who answered affirmatively to having "used" a knife or gun on the child within the past year. No meaningful extrapolation can be made to a population of 46 million children on the basis of the response of a solitary parent. Moreover, although Gelles (1978, p. 591) suggested the words "shooting or stabbing" himself, elsewhere in his paper he conceded that "we do not know exactly what is meant by 'using a gun or a knife.'" Indeed, despite the potential for varying interpretations of such words as "beat up" or "used," no instructions were given to the 300 interviewers employed as to how to interpret the words or meaningfully respond to parents' requests for clarification. For example, the rare person who answered affirmatively to the "used a knife or gun" question might have meant that he or she once brandished the knife or gun, hit the child on the rear with a gun, rapped the child's knuckles with a butter knife or indeed, shot at or stabbed the child. In addition, to one parent "beat up" might signify the repeated severe hitting of a child in a manner that leaves injuries, while to another, it might mean spanking the child a few times on the rear.

Perhaps the most accurate conclusion that can be drawn from Gelles' study is that a very large proportion of parents admit to having ever slapped, spanked, pushed, grabbed, or shoved their children, and a substantial minority to having ever hit them with something. Although important in what it says about child-rearing practices in our country, this conclusion is a far cry from the notion, seized upon by the news media, that severe violence by parents, such as the beating up, shooting, and stabbing of their children, is rampant throughout our society.

What I refer to as the "numbers illusion" is the notion that the incidence of child abuse and neglect can be counted, and the impression that comes to be conveyed that these numbers refer largely to brutally battered children. For example, newspapers are attracted to the dramatic and novel, which often manifests itself in extremes. Thus, what makes the news in regard to child abuse and neglect are the deaths and maimings, and the largest numbers. Typical of the abuse and neglect incidents reported in the *New York Times* during 1974 (the *New York Times Index*, 1974, pp. 353–54) were such items as:

—Newark, New Jersey, couple is charged with murder in beating-and-scalding death of three-year-old son.

—New York City fireman finds body of six-month-old baby girl in refrigerator with eyes and mouth covered with tape while fighting one-alarm fire in Brooklyn's Bedford-Stuyvesant section; says mother died with burns over entire body and with 10 stab wounds.

—Man is arrested for allegedly torturing and imprisoning a mother and four children with whom he lived; allegedly shut seven-year-old boy in lighted gas oven.

—Mother charged with murder of 22-month-old son after she admits punching him in chest for slowness in learning to walk; body allegedly marked by other beatings and bites.

This same newspaper, it will be recalled, later reported that 1 million children are abused and neglected each year.

At different moments during the same congressional hearings, sociologists have reported large numbers that refer predominantly to mild and even nonexistent cases, and pediatricians who specialize in child abuse have described and illustrated battered children from their very limited range of case experience—limited only to hospitals where only the worst cases are seen. Thus again, the numbers illusion is generated.

The situation I have just described has been summed up by one pair of commentators (Cohen & Sussman, 1975) thusly:

Estimates of the number of maltreated children in the United States abound in the literature. Authors are fond of presenting alarming figures in order to alert their readers to the breadth of the problem. The data advanced vary among experts; and the suggested figures, often stated in probabilistic terms, are highly unreliable. Additional confusion results from the fact that authors tend to blur distinctions between suspected and confirmed cases of abuse as well as between cases of child battering and all other forms of maltreatment.

Aside from the national survey approach, numbers have also been pursued by adding up the official reports of child abuse and neglect made to mandated authorities in the various states and territories. At a time when central registries were just being established, Gil (1970) compiled the data and counted 9,563 reports for 1967 and almost 11,000 reports for 1968. At the time of the 1973 Senate hearings, Dr. C. Henry Kempe (1973), the "discoverer" of the "battered child syndrome," claimed that 60,000 children are reported each year "as being suspected of being in need of protection by society."

The American Humane Association (AHA), as part of an ongoing national study, compiled data based on official reports made to state and territory authorities in 1975, and announced a total of 294,796 reports of abuse and neglect for that year (AHA, 1977). However, of those reports actually followed up and investigated by the appropriate authorities, only 139,267, or 60 percent, were found to be valid. Moreover, of the children who were physically abused, only about 3,000 were found to have suffered burns, scaldings, or major physical injuries.

It was on the basis of such data from AHA that NCCAN had widely publicized the estimate of 1 million children who suffer abuse and neglect each year. Since it was claimed that some states did not count neglect reports and otherwise had incomplete reporting, a projected estimate of substantiated instances was presumably made from the actual data.

Actually, the AHA data collection is based on reports of *incidents*, and so contains some duplication in terms of children. That is, the same child may be the subject of more than one report, even within the same year. It is the official reports, however—eminently countable in themselves—that are most directly relevant for understanding the rise in the foster care population from the early 1960s through the mid-1970s. For it is the official reports, when "validated," that pave the way for coercive government intervention into families and for the possibility of child removal. However, during these years, when central registries were just getting started, and during the mid-1970s, when the AHA system for gathering data on official reports was just being developed, it is likely that few reports of public child welfare agencies made their way into central registries, and it is known that few reports were being made available to AHA for counting. Yet, from the early 1960s on, it is likely that the child abuse crusade and resultant reporting laws were resulting in increased numbers of reports being made to the public child welfare agencies. From 1975 on, due to both increasing numbers of reports to the agencies, and improved systems of passing on information to AHA, the annual national estimate reported by AHA escalated tremendously, from 669,000 in 1976, to 838,000 in 1977, to 1.2 million by 1980, and to 1.7 million in 1984 (AHA, 1988).

By 1986, AHA (1988) was able to reliably estimate, based on report counts obtained from child protective service agencies in the various states, that over 2 million reports were received within that year, and that approximately 40 percent were "substantiated" by the agencies. Slightly over half of the reports originated from professionals, and slightly under half from nonprofessionals, such as friends, neighbors, and relatives. Less than 3 percent of the reports were said to have involved major physical injury, including burns, scalds, severe cuts, and bone fractures, but more than half indicated "deprivation of necessities," including nourishment, shelter, clothing, health care, and supervision. It is this latter category, "deprivation of necessities," which is indicated in so large a proportion of reports, and that certainly can lead to severe harm to children, that we will focus upon in later chapters as a key to proposing new directions in child welfare.

There is wide agreement among the experts that the escalating numbers of reports over the years have not signified a rise in the actual incidence of abuse and neglect, but rather, reflect heightened public awareness and concern and improved reporting systems. But the crusade against child abuse has been fueled by misleading statements. Thus, Senator Harrison Williams (1973) claimed in a letter published in the 1973 Senate hearings that "recent studies" show that child abuse has been "tragically increasing," and a state government press release in 1975 attributed to New Jersey's human services commissioner the statement that "the incidence of child abuse and neglect is growing at an alarming rate all over the nation" (December 9, 1975). The NCCAN public relations manual noted earlier in this chapter contained the remark: "Child abuse is dramatically increasing in New Jersey. . . ." Actually, only *reports* of child abuse have dramatically increased, in part due to expanded public awareness campaigns and the installment of child abuse telephone "hot lines." Anywhere from 40 to 60 percent of these reports have turned out to be invalid upon investigation, even by child welfare agencies' vague standards of what constitutes child abuse and neglect.

At first glance, it would appear that in counting actual reports that have been "validated," we are at last on firm ground for ascertaining at least the lower limit of the incidence of abuse and neglect in the country. Unfortunately, this is not the case, for exactly *what* is being counted remains unclear. The counts have not been based upon a uniform definition of child abuse and neglect. In fact, each state has its own definition, and these definitions have ranged widely between the states. Moreover, many state child protection (child welfare) agencies have utilized definitions that are extremely vague and broad. As late as 1977, at least, in response to my letter to agencies asking them to supply their guidelines, I found that various child protection agency regulations among the states had defined a neglected child as one who has a "foul odor," does not receive "proper care and attention," or whose parent "is found in a disreputable place or associates with vagrant, vicious, or immoral persons," or does not make sure that the child gets to school regularly (Pelton, 1977b).

The data collected in the AHA study give us a rough proportionate characterization of the nature of the incidents that are being reported as "abuse and neglect" to child protection agencies. However, it is futile to ask what the "true" incidence rate is, since each methodology will yield a different estimate, as will each variation of the definition of abuse and neglect that is employed.

At the 1977 Congressional Hearings on the Child Abuse Prevention and Treatment Act, Department of Health, Education and Welfare (DHEW) Assistant Secretary Arabella Martinez (1977) was asked why, despite numerous studies, we still do not know the actual incidence of abuse and neglect in the United States. She answered, in part, that the previous studies have had certain "deficiencies," such as "widely disparate estimates, ranging from 60,000 to four million cases a year." She went on to reveal that the National Center had by then identified no less than 18 different methodologies that could be used in studying the incidence of child abuse and neglect. What she neglected to add was that we also have many alternative definitions of abuse and neglect, and each could be used in conjunction with any one of the methods. The various possible combinations of each methodology with each definition would yield literally dozens of greatly different estimates. Thus, it is obvious that the question "How many?" has no definitive answer.

THE MYTH OF CLASSLESSNESS

Aiding the portrayal of child abuse and neglect as a personal disease that was running rampant throughout our society was the notion that, like the popular conception of an epidemic disease, it was afflicting families without regard to socioeconomic class. Indeed, attempts to disassociate the problems being labeled as abuse and neglect from poverty were vigorously pursued by many child welfare professionals (Pelton, 1978a).

The politicians, for their part, had just come through a "war on poverty" and an ironic concommitant rise in the AFDC caseloads (see Piven & Cloward, 1971) and were disinclined to deal with any more poverty-related problems. But to pass laws to combat a disease that was blind to class would be more politic. They could appear to be aggressively dealing with the phenomenon of child "battering," which the public already perceived as a "sickness," by promoting public awareness campaigns and reporting law strategies.

Although David Gil (1970) had taken pains to unravel the structural factors underlying child abuse—chief among them poverty—these were brushed aside by politicians, most notably at the 1973 Senate hearings by then-Senator Walter Mondale, who pressed hard in his questioning of Gil (1973) to try to establish that child abuse "is not a poverty problem." What interested Mondale more were the numbers, and the prospect of many unreported cases avoiding public detection occurring in upper- and middle-class families.

The myth of classlessness has allowed the problems of abuse and neglect to be portrayed as broader than they actually are, by implying that they are distributed proportionately across all strata of our society. It has served to uphold the medical model perspective and the view of abuse and neglect as psychodynamic problems rather than predominantly social and poverty-related problems. In so doing, it has diverted funding to deal with the problems from concrete services aimed at the poverty-related aspects of the problems to counseling and "talking cures." Moreover, together with the psychodynamic perspective, it has served to mask the possibility that children being removed from their parents for reasons of child abuse and neglect were actually being placed in foster care for reasons ultimately stemming from poverty.

THE OBSCURED REALITY

There is by now overwhelming evidence of a strong relationship between poverty and child abuse and neglect. The great majority of families to whom child abuse and neglect have been attributed live in poverty or near-poverty circumstances. This finding has been obtained across a range of methodologies and definitions. Moreover, poverty is the single most prevalent characteristic of these families (Pelton, 1977a), who tend to be the *poorest* of the poor (Wolock & Horowitz, 1979).

Every national survey of officially reported child neglect and abuse incidents has indicated that the preponderance of the reports have involved families from the lowest socioeconomic levels. In the earliest of these studies, a nationwide survey of child-abuse reports made to central registries, Gil (1970) found that nearly 60 percent of the families involved in the abuse incidents had been on welfare during or prior to the study year of 1967, and 37.2 percent of the abusive families had been receiving public assistance at the time of the incident.

Data collected by AHA, through its annual national study of official child abuse and neglect reporting, have showed that for the year 1976, for example, 42 percent of the families in validated reports were receiving public assistance (AHA, 1978). The median family income was $5,051 (which is at the 1976 poverty level for a family of four), compared with about $13,900 for all American families in 1976. About two-thirds of the families in validated reports had incomes under $7,000, and only 9 percent of the families had incomes of $13,000 or more. For reports of neglect only, the median income was slightly lower ($4,250) than for abuse only ($6,882).

These same trends have continued year after year in a rather stable fashion. The AHA data for the year 1977 indicated that 47.1 percent of the involved families in substantiated reports had incomes of less than $5,000 per year, while only 5.9 percent had incomes of at least $16,000, which was the median family income for all U.S. families in 1977 (AHA, 1979). Moreover, 43.7 percent of the families were receiving public assistance. The AHA data for the year 1981 showed 43 percent of the reported families were receiving public assistance, compared with 11 percent of all U.S. families (AHA, 1983). In 1986, 48.9 percent of the reported families were receiving public assistance, compared with 12 percent of all U.S. families (AHA, 1988).

This poverty relationship is not just a recent phenomenon, of course. In a study of cases known to the Massachusetts SPCC and other private social service agencies in the Boston area from 1880 to 1960, Gordon (1988, pp. 8, 148–49, 307–8) documented that the most pronounced characteristic of the clients in family violence cases was their poverty.

While it is true, as has often been argued, that poor people are more susceptible to public scrutiny and are thus more likely than others to be *reported* for abuse or neglect, it has been shown that the relationship between poverty and child abuse and neglect is not just an anomaly of reporting systems (Pelton, 1978a). First, while greater public awareness and new reporting laws led to a significant increase in official reporting over the years, the socioeconomic pattern of these reports has not changed appreciably. We might have expected an expanded and more vigilant public watch to produce an increased proportion of reports from above the lower class, but this has not happened.

Second, the "public scrutiny" argument cannot explain the evidence that child abuse and neglect are related to *degrees* of poverty, even *within* that same lower class which is acknowledgedly more open to public scrutiny (Giovannoni & Billingsley, 1970; Wolock & Horowitz, 1979). In the Wolock and Horowitz study, AFDC families involved in child abuse and neglect cases were found to be living in more crowded and dilapidated households, to have been more likely to have gone hungry, and in general, to be existing at a lower material level of living than the other AFDC families studied.

Third, the "public scrutiny" argument cannot explain why the severest injuries have occurred within the poorest families, even among the reported cases (Gil, 1970). Moreover, it cannot explain why child homicide studies have indicated that child abuse and neglect fatalities, which are certainly less easy to hide from public scrutiny than milder abuse and neglect incidents, have predominantly occurred in poor families (Weston, 1974; Kaplun & Reich, 1976; Mayor's Task Force, 1983, 1987).

Finally, evidence of a more direct nature was collected in the Westat National Incidence Study, which was designed to go beyond the officially reported cases of child abuse and neglect known to child protective service agencies (U.S. Department of Health and Human Services, 1981). It did so by additionally gathering information on abuse and neglect incidents directly from other agencies, such as police and public health departments, and from professionals in hospitals, mental health facilities, other social service agencies, and public schools. The study found that the annual income of the families of 43 percent of the victims was under $7,000, compared with an estimated 17 percent of all U.S. children who lived in families with income that low. Fully 82 percent of the victims were from families with incomes below $15,000, in comparison with 45 percent of all U.S. children. Only 6 percent of the victims were from families with incomes of $25,000 or more. The relationship between low income and child maltreatment was less pronounced for abuse than for neglect, but still strong. The study concluded that the strong relationship between poverty and child abuse and neglect is not largely explainable in terms of reporting biases because the relationship "is almost as strong for unreported cases as for those which are reported to Child Protective Services." A follow-up to the National Incidence Study showed that, in the year 1986, the relationship between low income and overall maltreatment continued to be strong. In fact, in only 6 percent of the cases was the family income $30,000 or more (U.S. Department of Health and Human Services, 1988).

In light of these facts, the conclusion that problems of poverty might be partial determinants of child abuse and neglect is inescapable. Indeed, it has been theorized that the problems of poverty may generate stressful experiences that become precipitating factors in child abuse and neglect (Gil, 1970; Pelton, 1978a). Such factors as unemployment, dilapidated and overcrowded housing, and insufficient money, food, recreation, or hope can provide the stressful context for abusive as well as neglectful behavior. Such stresses can provoke the anger that may lead to abuse, as well as the despair that may lead to neglect when, for example, a single parent attempts to raise a large family in cramped and unsafe living quarters with no help and little money.

Certainly, parents are responsible for their own behavior, regardless of whether we interpret it in terms of stress or other factors. Yet in most cases, there is multiple causation of the risk of harm to children, and a sole fixation on the parents themselves, which has indeed been fostered by the framing of child welfare problems in terms of "abuse and neglect" and by the psychodynamic medical model, would be overly simplistic.

Impoverished families tend to live, though not by choice, in neighborhoods with the highest crime rates, in apartments that are not secure, and in homes made dangerous by lack of heating, poor wiring and exposed lead paint, to name only a few of the health and safety hazards associated with poverty. These conditions, which are among the very same ones that may cause indirect danger to children by generating stressful experiences for the parents, also cause direct danger for which it is all too easy to implicate the parents for not preventing. Moreover, in the presence of these conditions, poor people have very little leeway for lapses in responsibility.

In addition, a low-income mother with many children cannot easily obtain or pay for a babysitter every time she wants or needs to leave the house. If she leaves her children alone, she is gambling with their safety; if she stays with them, she may be unable to do her shopping in order to provide food and other necessities. Thus, she may be caught up in a difficult situation that has less to do with her adequacy and responsibility as a parent than with the hard circumstances of her life.

It is true that only a small proportion of poor people are even alleged to abuse or neglect their children (Pelton, 1977a). The most reasonable conclusion that can be drawn from the nature of the relationship between poverty and child abuse and neglect is that poverty is often a contributing factor, a partial determinant that often provides the context for abuse and neglect, and that there must be other *mediating* factors between poverty and these resultants. These mediators might well include parent-centered, personal, and psychological problems and characteristics, although just what characteristics these might be remains unclear. However, the doubts cast upon the validity of the personality characteristics that have been implied in the literature, together with the strong relationship found between poverty and child abuse and neglect, lead one to suspect that if any personal traits are prevalent among parents in abuse and neglect cases, they might be ones that have more to do with the ability or inability to cope with poverty and its stresses than anything else. Indeed, other factors frequently associated with child protection cases include health problems, social isolation, family discord, and alcohol or drug dependence (AHA, 1978, 1981; Pelton, 1981b).

Regardless of how we or society decide to apportion blame or responsibility, one thing is clear: Many of the families in child abuse and neglect cases lack resources and need help. Yet in a large proportion of the cases reported to public child welfare agencies, the result has not been help to the family as a whole, but child removal.

Indeed, the proponents of the myth of classlessness, by invoking the public scrutiny argument in attempting to deny the relationship of child abuse and neglect and poverty, were obscuring the significance of the fact of the strong relationship between *reported* alleged abuse and neglect and poverty. The significance is that the families being reported to child protection agencies in the 1970s were, just as they had always been throughout this century and before, predominantly from among the poorest families in our society, and that therefore the children being removed into foster care were the same ones as they had always been in this respect. The only difference was that in the 1960s and 1970s (and, as we will see, up to the present time), due to a child abuse crusade backed by unprecedented funding, more poor families than ever before were being reported to and investigated by child protection agencies, and more such children than ever before were being removed.

The crusade against sexual abuse did not get started until the late 1970s, as reflected in the vastly increased reporting rates since that time (Finkelhor, 1984, pp. 1, 3). As a proportion of all child abuse and neglect reports, sexual abuse reports have increased from 3.2 percent in 1976 (AHA, 1987), to 5.8 percent in 1977 (AHA, 1979), 9 percent in 1983, and 16 percent in 1986 (AHA, 1988).

However, the majority of sexual abuse reports does not fit within the generally accepted definitions of all other forms of child abuse and neglect, in that such definitions designate the parents or other primary caretakers as the perpetrators. Whereas the alleged perpetrator is a parent (including stepparent) in 81 percent of all child abuse and neglect reports, the alleged perpetrator is a nonparent relative or unrelated to the child in 58 percent of sexual abuse reports (AHA, 1988). While not to minimize the seriousness of particular incidents, it can be said that the inclusion of sexual abuse reports involving non-parent relatives, acquaintances, and strangers, in a reporting system in which all other forms of maltreatment primarily involve parents, does create the illusion that most sexual abuse is being perpetrated by parents.

Furthermore, studies reporting high rates of sexual abuse have defined the term very broadly, combining quite disparate types of incidents. Such studies have lumped together intercourse and oral-genital contact with encounters with "flashers" or instances in which someone exhibited his or her genital organs (Finkelhor, 1984, pp. 24, 74, 83). Also included have been instances of a child being fondled through clothing, in addition to sexual requests and other noncontact experiences (Finkelhor, 1984, pp. 74, 83). Thus, a numbers illusion has been generated in regard to sexual abuse no less than in regard to other forms of child maltreatment.

In addition, definitions of sexual abuse accepted by professionals usually involve a motivational component; that is, the adult perpetrator touches the child's genital areas, for example, with the intent of gaining sexual gratification from this act (Biller & Solomon, 1986, p. 55). However, all other forms of child abuse and neglect, at least when taken together, are defined in terms of a failure in responsibility, whether due to omission or commission, and whether intentional or not, and thus the question of motivation is not strictly relevant to the definition. Since motivation is not directly observable but must be inferred, the door is left open to greater possibilities of misinterpretation in regard to sexual abuse than in other forms of abuse. Indeed, it has been claimed by professionals who deal with such cases that increasing numbers of fathers involved in divorce proceedings and custody disputes are being accused of child sexual abuse, and that increasing proportions of such allegations are false (Dullca, 1987). In such cases, the mother might charge the father with having touched a two-year-old child's genital organs. Although the father might have done so in the course of bathing the child, the mother may allege that sexual intent was involved. There is some preliminary evidence suggesting that the rate of unsubstantiated sexual abuse reports may be much higher for reports emanating from parents in custody disputes than for reports from other sources (Dillon, 1987).

Nothing I have said here about sexual abuse is meant to deny the seriousness of the concept. But we must clarify, in our laws, policies, and programs, what types of incidents we consider serious enough to call sexual abuse, and we must develop better methods of determining the validity of sexual abuse charges while not violating the procedural rights of the accused nor (further) traumatizing the child. Otherwise, we might do more harm than good.

Whereas the dominance of the psychodynamic medical model has diminished somewhat in the scholarly literature during the past decade or so in regard to our understanding of child maltreatment in general, the model's grip in the area of sexual abuse has remained as strong as ever, with only beginning signs of a possible shift away from a psychopathological focus (Finkelhor, 1984, pp. 35, 53 ff.; Biller & Solomon, 1986, p. 60). This intransigence is present despite the fact that poverty is just as much associated with sexual abuse as with other forms of child maltreatment. The first Westat National Incidence Study, mentioned above, found the relationship between low income and sexual abuse to be just as strong as that between low income and overall child abuse and neglect, in that 80 percent of the families of sexual abuse victims had annual incomes under $15,000, and only 2 percent had incomes of $25,000 or more (U.S. Department of Health and Human Services, 1981). The follow-up National Incidence Study, also mentioned above, showed that in 1986, the low-income relationship continued to be strong for sexual abuse (U.S. Department of Health and Human Services, 1988). The incidence of sexual abuse was four to five times higher among children from families whose income was less than $15,000 than those from families whose income was $15,000 or more.

These studies included incidents not involving genital contact in their definitions of sexual abuse, but only when there was evidence that such noncontact experiences might have caused at least some physical or emotional trauma to the child. Other studies, employing broader definitions and a variety of methodologies, have not always found this low-income relationship (Finkelhor, 1984, pp. 24, 78, 86; see Finkelhor, 1986, pp. 67–69). Since the preponderance of the incidents counted in the National Incidence studies did involve genital contact, it is clear that the low-income relationship holds for these more severe forms of sexual abuse, and it is likely that the relationship between low income and sexual abuse has been "washed out" in some studies through the inclusion of higher proportions of incidents involving noncontact and questionable forms of sexual abuse. Any adequate perspectives on sexual abuse will have to take the socioeconomic facts into account.

To sum up, the factors responsible for the explosion in the foster care placement rates during the 1960s and 1970s were: (1) the psychodynamic medical model, which encouraged us to blame the individual results of the conditions of poverty on poor people and to look for personal defects in them; (2) the myth of classlessness, which encouraged the inclination to label impoverished parents as psychologically defective and to ignore the socioeconomic factors involved; (3) the numbers illusion, which encouraged the public's apparent inclination to blame parents and to believe that there were many cruel parents out there deliberately battering their children; (4) the public awareness campaigns and reporting laws, which were both cause and effect of the child abuse crusade; and (5) the social service funding that was misguidedly funneled into investigation and foster care rather than into the provision of concrete services.

3

Whose Neglect? The State Intervenes

As already indicated, the primary responsibility for the investigation and handling of child protection problems over the past several decades has belonged to the public child welfare agencies. Under a philosophy of family preservation, these agencies are charged with the task of investigating for the purpose of helping, and have the dual goal to protect the child and preserve the family.

In this chapter we will examine how the public child welfare agencies responded to the child abuse crusade and have intervened, and continue to intervene, in child protection cases. We will also examine the consequences of these decisions, particularly in regard to the foster care system. As we have seen, the child abuse crusade generated an increasing number of reports to public child welfare agencies, and a major outcome of this crusade was a greatly expanding foster care population, at least during the 1960s and up until past the mid-1970s.

The removal of a child from his or her natural parents is one of the gravest actions that can be taken by a democratic society that highly values both individual and family rights. Child removal is the ultimate intrusion into the privacy and sanctity of family life. Yet few people would deny that a humane society has the responsibility to protect the welfare of its citizens, especially those who cannot protect themselves, and in the course of so doing may, on occasion, have to remove a child from his or her natural home.

One might imagine, then, that such decisions would be made by courts of law operating under precise guidelines. In fact, this has not usually been the case, in part due to a long history of confusion in child welfare matters as to whether state intervention is a police-type action to protect the child or a benevolent service to help the family, and whether child removal is a voluntary treatment or a coercive punishment and indeed, whether the client is the child, the parent, or the family.

Courts have been involved in such decisions, and perhaps increasingly so in recent years, and so their role will be discussed in this chapter. However, most cases of state-sponsored child placement—whether they are court-ordered or, on the other hand, involve procedures that are formally called voluntary (in which case the child welfare agencies have implicitly decided to deliver child placement rather than other services, and have urged the parents to sign placement agreements)—are initiated by the public child welfare agencies in their decisions to *seek* removals. The key decision-making power, if sometimes limited to the decision to seek removal, rests with the public child welfare agencies, for even in court, the bulk of the testimony that judges have relied upon to make their own decisions have been provided by the child welfare agencies.

THE PROCESS OF CHILD REMOVAL

In fact, it has been estimated that in the 1960s and 1970s at least, perhaps more than 50 percent of foster care placements were arranged by state social welfare departments without any court involvement (Mnookin, 1973). In a study of child abuse and neglect cases active in 1975 in Mercer County, New Jersey, I found that only 32 percent of the children who had been placed had ever experienced court-ordered placement, and 78 percent had experienced noncourt-ordered placement at some time (Pelton, 1977a).

Thus, many parents had been asked to sign voluntary placement agreements. But as Mnookin (1973, p. 601) pointed out:

A substantial degree of state coercion may be involved in many so-called voluntary placements, making the distinction between voluntary and coercive placement illusory. Many social welfare departments routinely ask parents to agree to give up their children before initiating neglect proceedings in court. Some parents who would have been willing to keep their children may consent to placement to avoid a court proceeding against them. If one were to use the legal standards of voluntariness and informed consent applied in the criminal law to confessions and to the waiver of important legal rights, many cases of relinquishment after state intervention may not be considered voluntary.

There were parents interviewed in the Mercer County study who told me that they had not wanted their children removed but had signed "voluntary" placement agreements because of threats by case-workers that unrelated prior convictions would be brought up in court and that they would lose the case; that if they did not consent to the removal of one of the children, in court the judge would order the removal of all of the children; and that if the parents did not sign, the children would be removed permanently rather than temporarily (Pelton, 1977a).

As one commentator noted:

Parents who enter into such agreements are frequently uneducated and without legal advice except for that offered by the social worker encouraging the placement. . . . Parents may sign a voluntary agreement although foster care is not truly necessary; they may believe that the law requires them to surrender their child, or that the child cannot be provided with necessities unless they sign. Once the child is in voluntary placement, parents may find that they are unable to rescind the agreements and retake custody of their children . . . (Musewicz, 1981, p. 639)

There are indications that a high proportion of "voluntary" placements has continued into the 1980s. For example, it has been esti-mated that a majority of the children in foster care in New Jersey in 1988 had entered foster care through "voluntary" agreements (Wick-ley, 1989). In Massachusetts, it was estimated that a majority of all children in placement on June 30, 1984 might have entered place-ment through "voluntary" agreements, even though the status of some of these placements was changed to court-ordered some time after entry (Herskowitz & Smith, 1985).

As noted in Chapter 2, many state child welfare agencies have had criteria for defining child abuse and neglect that are extremely vague and broad. Moreover, many such agencies have not had written cri-teria or guidelines for seeking child removal (Pelton, 1977b).

However, even the statutes governing court interventions have been extremely vague and broad. As Mnookin (1973, p. 604) has stated:

They are vague and open-ended, they require highly subjective determinations, and they permit intervention not only when the child has been demonstrably harmed or is physically endangered but also when parental habits or attitudes are adverse to the inculcation of proper moral values. Typical statutory provisions allow court intrusion to protect a child who is not receiving "proper parental care," "proper attention," "whose home is an unfit place for him by reason of neglect, cruelty, depravity, or physical abuse," or whose parents neglect to provide the "care necessary for his health, morals or well-being."

Given this looseness of definition, it is not surprising, then, that courts have removed children in the past because the mother "frequented taverns," adhered to "extreme" religious practices, lived in a communal setting, had "illegitimate" children, or was a lesbian (Wald, 1975, p. 1033). There was no evidence of harm to the child in any of these cases. Courts have also removed children from "dirty" homes without requiring any evidence that the physical conditions of the home had harmed the children. As Mnookin (1973, p. 621) put it: "Some 'dirty homes' may seriously endanger a child's growth and well-being, but most merely offend middle-class sensibilities."

The vagueness and broadness of standards pertaining to child removal have enhanced the possibility of extreme variability in judgments among decision makers. Indeed, one study revealed that three highly experienced practitioners, when asked to examine a number of cases and render a decision as to whether the child should be placed, did not agree in the majority of cases (Phillips et al., 1971). It was also found that among the factors these practitioners listed as having affected their decisions were the mother's degree of hostility toward the agency and worker, the mother's "cooperation" with the worker, whether or not the mother "appears" emotionally disturbed, the mother's "ability to verbalize," whether or not the mother is "withdrawn or depressed," and the "suspiciousness" of the mother.

When factors so remotely and debatably related to the reasonable goal of protecting children from harm are allowed to influence child placement decisions, there is no wonder that there is little consensus on such decisions.

Irrespective of the issue of court-ordered versus noncourt-ordered placements, it can be said that there have been two types of unnecessary placements that no doubt have contributed to the large size of the foster care population in this country. The first type, alluded to above, has involved the removal of children from their parents arbitrarily, through determinations influenced by moralistic prejudices and middle-class biases in reference to others' life-styles and child-rearing practices. Such arbitrary removal has been contributed to by vague standards for intervention, which continue to exist (Besharov, 1985). We have no way of knowing what proportion of the total foster care population this type of unnecessary placement had accounted for during the 1960s and 1970s, nor what proportion of foster care placements it accounts for today. But such cases have been documented with enough frequency to indicate that they have not been rare occurrences.

In the type of unnecessary placement just discussed, the placements would have been unnecessary to protect the children *even if no services at all had been provided* to the children and their families. The second type of unnecessary placement has occurred when public agencies have failed to provide reasonable resources and services that might have protected the child in the home and thereby prevented the need for placement. It is this type of unnecessary placement that was addressed by the federal Adoption Assistance and Child Welfare Act of 1980, in its provision that, in order for a state to be eligible for certain federal child welfare monies, the state must have a plan to provide that "reasonable efforts will be made (a) prior to the placement of the child in foster care, to prevent or eliminate the need for removal of the child from his home and (b) to make it possible for the child to return to his home . . ." [P.L. 96–272, Section 471 (a) (15)].

As already discussed, there is considerable evidence that the great majority of families in child abuse and neglect cases live in poverty or near-poverty circumstances. Later in this chapter, we will review the evidence that the children who enter foster care are predominantly from poor families. In light of these facts, the conclusion that problems of poverty might be partial determinants of child abuse and neglect and foster care placement is inescapable. In many cases, impoverished living conditions may have been mistakenly attributed to neglect, although as we shall see shortly, while child abuse and neglect are among the most common reasons cited for placement, they have not been the only reasons.

Despite the relationship between poverty and child abuse and neglect, and foster care placement, only a small proportion of poor people are alleged to maltreat their children, and not all poor children wind up in foster care. As Jenkins and Norman (1972, p. 19) have stated in regard to foster care: "For most households poverty is a necessary but not a sufficient condition for placement. It is the marginal family, whose characteristics and social circumstances are such that it cannot sustain further stress, which utilizes the placement system as a last resort when its own fragile support systems break down."

Indeed, a study of a sample of almost 700 case records of children who entered foster care in New Jersey during the first three-quarters of 1983 revealed that homelessness was the precipitating reason for placement in 14 percent of the cases, and that altogether, the families of 40 percent of the children had at some time experienced homelessness or severe housing difficulties (Tomaszewicz, 1985). In 1984, inadequate housing was the most prevalent of all reasons for foster care placement in New Jersey, accounting for 15 percent of the children residing in foster care at that time (New Jersey State Child Placement Advisory Council, 1984).

Other reasons for placement frequently identified in studies of foster care, usually based on caseworkers' judgments, include "parent unable to cope," child neglect, abandonment, child abuse, child's behavior problems, parent's drug or alcohol abuse, parent's physical illness, and "hospitalization" (New Jersey State Child Placement Advisory Council, 1984).[1] Parents may often initially be reported to the agency for abuse or neglect, and later, during the course of the case, have their children removed for other reasons. However, if poverty does not constitute a "sufficient condition" for placement, neither do the "reasons" cited in the foster care studies. For example, the mother's illness or hospitalization cannot be sufficient reason, since there are many mothers similarly indisposed whose children are *not* placed. Even alleged child abuse or neglect is not sufficient reason for placement, since many children who have been abused or neglected in the past can be served and protected in their own homes. The strong relationship that has consistently been found between alleged child abuse and neglect and poverty suggests that the problem most often is the parent's lack of ability to cope with poverty and its stresses without help (Pelton, 1978a; 1982b). The more accurate reason for placement is very often that the family, frequently due to poverty, does not have the resources to offset the impact of situational or personal problems, which themselves are often caused by poverty, *and the agencies have failed to provide the needed supports.* Most children in foster care are there because their parents were unable, or did not have the personal resources, to overcome family crises without additional outside assistance, which was not forthcoming.

We should reasonably expect that a child will be removed from his or her home only when it is apparent that the child is in danger of specific severe harms that can be prevented only by removal. We should be convinced that less drastic, reasonable measures, aimed at protecting the child while he or she remains in the home, will not be effective. But such "reasons" for removal as mental or physical illness refer to characteristics and conditions of the parents and not to the protection of the child per se. Even abuse and neglect, as we have seen, have been defined so broadly and vaguely in both state laws and agency regulations that it is evident that caseworkers are not explicitly asked to justify child removal decisions on the basis of protection of the child.

Thus, in terms of practice, it would be far more fruitful to ask what services could have prevented placement rather than what the reasons are for placement. When we look at the classifications of "reasons" for placement listed in the foster care studies, and more surely, at the actual placement cases on a case-by-case basis, we find in many instances that the services most frequently requested by the clients themselves—such as babysitting, homemaking, day care, financial assistance, and housing assistance (Pelton, 1982b)—are also the ones that best and most logically fit the situational deficits, and the personal deficits and problems, that prompted placement. However, such reasonable services public child welfare agencies have frequently failed to provide (Knitzer, et al., 1978; Wald, 1976; Musewicz, 1981).

Although, as already mentioned, it was this problem that the Adoption Assistance and Child Welfare Act of 1980 addressed in its statement that "reasonable efforts" must be made to prevent the need for child removal, the proliferation of class action suits in recent years to force state and local governments to make such "reasonable efforts" indicates that such efforts have been lacking (Pelton & Rosenthal, 1988).

THE FOSTER CARE SYSTEM

Beginning at least as far back as the late 1950s, research studies and reports gradually called attention to serious faults in the foster care system in the United States (see, e.g., Maas & Engler, 1959;

Maas, 1969; Wald, 1976; Fanshel & Shinn, 1978; Shyne & Schroeder, 1978; Gruber, 1978). At the same time, as already noted, the number of children in foster care in this country began to grow enormously, reaching its high point of an estimated 500,000 children during 1975–77 (Knitzer et al., 1978; Shyne & Schroeder, 1978; Pelton, 1987b). They had been put there—mainly in foster homes, but also in institutions, group homes, and other living arrangements—by public child welfare agencies, or were there under the responsibility of such agencies. Knitzer et al. (1978) speculated that, in addition to an estimated almost half-million children in foster care in 1975 under the aegis of public child welfare agencies alone, perhaps more than another quarter of a million were there under the aegis of other public agencies responsible for juvenile justice, mental health, mental retardation, and special education. Our concern throughout this book, however, is limited to the child welfare agencies and the children in placement under their auspices. But even these estimates have not reflected the full scope of the child displacement situation in our country, because they refer to one-day counts; that is, they only indicate how many children were in foster care at a particular point in time. They do not reveal how many children living in the United States at that time had ever experienced foster care. While many childrem have remained in foster care for many consecutive years, many others have entered, left, and even reentered, at a fairly rapid rate.

Due to eventual alarm over the large number of children in foster care (under the responsibility of the child welfare agencies) and in response to mounting professional criticism that they stayed too long and moved too much, "permanency planning" became a broad and popular movement within the child welfare field during the mid to late 1970s, and later became a major aspect of the Adoption Assistance and Child Welfare Act of 1980. The main thrust of the permanency planning movement has been aimed at children already in foster care: to either get them returned home or, if this is deemed not possible, freed for adoption. The permanency planning movement and its outcomes will be discussed more fully in the next chapter, although some of its outcomes will be referred to here.

Foster care has been regarded as a "temporary" living arrangement for children during a period in which the parents are presumably helped to "get back on their feet." Yet the fact is that many children have stayed in foster care for many years. In a study of 624 New York City children who entered foster care in 1966 at the age of 12 years or younger and who had remained at least 90 days, it was found that 36 percent were still in foster care five years later (Fanshel & Shinn, 1978). Half of the children who were under two years old when they entered foster care in 1966 were still there after five years, as were almost half (47%) of the black children. In an earlier study of children in foster care at least three months, it was found that 31 percent were still there after ten years (Maas, 1969).

For the more than 40,000 children in foster care in New York State on June 30, 1980, the average length of time in care was 4.4 years. While 43 percent had been there for under two years, 14 percent had been there for 10 years or more (Fanshel & Grundy, 1980).

The national survey cited earlier, which found that there were over a half-million children in foster care at the end of March 1977, also found that 100,000 of these children had been in foster care for at least six years (Shyne & Schroeder, 1978).

In New Jersey, the average length of stay of the 7,363 children who were in boarding foster family home care as of December 3, 1978 was 3.5 years. While 32 percent of these children had been there for under one year, and another 17 percent for under two years, 22 percent had been there for six years or more (Magura, 1979).

It is apparent that once displaced into foster care, many children have spent a large part of their childhoods there. However, by the 1980s, the length of time in care generally had shortened considerably. By fiscal year (FY) 1984, based on data from 27 states, only 10 percent of the children in foster care were found to have been there for six years or more (Tatara et al., 1987, p. 82). Using roughly comparable data from other studies, Tatara and his associates (1987, p. 83, Table 13) determined that the *median* length of time in care (which would tend to be lower than a mean average, which was reported for New York and New Jersey above) declined from 2.4 years in 1977 to 1.5 years in FY 1984. This general shortening of the length of continuous time that children spend in foster care can be viewed as one of the most dramatic outcomes of the permanency planning thrust.

Perhaps one of the greatest inadequacies of the foster care system has been the frequent movement of children from one foster care setting to another. The problem had been noted as far back as the turn of the century, and in 1913, in evaluating its own operations, the Boston Children's Aid Society found an inordinate amount of replacement (Tiffin, 1982, pp. 257, 273). The fact that many displaced children have undergone multiple displacements is well-documented. On the basis of his review of foster care studies, Wald (1976) concluded that at least 50 percent of all foster children experience more than one move, and at least 20 percent experience three or more moves.

The study of 624 New York City children who entered foster care in 1966 showed that, over the five-year study period, 42 percent of these children had experienced just one foster care setting; 30 percent had experienced two foster care settings; and 28 percent had experienced three or more such settings. This study also revealed a direct linear relationship between the length of time a child stays in foster care and the number of moves he or she undergoes while there (Fanshel & Shinn, 1978).

A study of children in foster care in Massachusetts showed that 50 percent of the children had experienced only one placement setting; 25 percent had two displacements, 12 percent had three, and 13 percent experienced four or more displacements (Gruber, 1978). The study of child protection cases in Mercer County, New Jersey, showed that the situation there was not much different. This study found that children who had been displaced had experienced an average of 2.5 foster care settings and that 55 percent had experienced at least two such settings (Pelton, 1977a).

Surprisingly, given that the length of continuous time that children spend in foster care has decreased, the most recent findings, based on data from 23 states, indicate that for only 51 percent of the children in foster care on the last day of FY 1985 was their current placement setting their first one during the preceding three years (Tatara et al., 1988, p. 77). Including the current placement, 26 percent of the children had experienced three or more placements during the preceding three years. These percentages seem remarkably similar to those from previous studies. But how can this be if the length of continuous time in foster care has been considerably shortened since the other studies were done, and if the number of moves a child undergoes while in foster care is related to the length of time that he or she stays in foster care? The probable explanation is that now that children are staying in the foster care system for less continuous time, they are exiting and *reentering* the system at a faster rate. Tatara et al. (1988) included in their counts of foster care settings for each child such settings experienced during previous *periods* spent within the foster care system within the preceding three years. Indeed, they found that 25 percent of the children who entered foster care during FY 1985 (based on data from 25 states) had been in the system before, just within the preceding 12 months alone (Tatara et al., 1988, p. 33). In other words, they were one-year recidivists. The exasperating conclusion must be that children similar to the ones in the 1970s who moved from one foster home to another now, in the 1980s, move from parents to foster home, back to parents, and back into the foster care system again (although the New York City and Mercer County, New Jersey studies had also included foster care settings during previous periods in the foster care system in their counts).

These facts imply an instability of caretaker-child relationships, and frequent changes in friends, schools, neighborhoods, and authority figures for many children. They also imply the frequent loss of potential love objects, uncertainty about the immediate future, and the lack of opportunity to form appropriate disciplinary expectations. Such upheavals may lead to perceptions of rejection, feelings that no one really cares, confusion over identity, and feelings of low self-worth. Such speculated outcomes, however, have not been conclusively documented by research.

Maas and Engler (1959) did report that from 40 percent to 60 percent of the foster children in their large sample exhibited symptoms of psychological disturbance that were associated "not with the length of time they spent in care, but with the number of different moves they had made in foster care." Eisenberg (1962) found that the rate of admission of foster children to psychiatric care was ten times that of the general population and was associated with both the length and number of foster care placements.

It is not possible to determine whether these emotional impairments originated in preplacement experiences and then precipitated the moves in foster care and the lengthiness of placement, or whether the moves and length of stay caused the impairments. However, there is reason to believe that both processes are operative. There is substantial evidence that separations cause immediate emotional trauma and pain in young children (Rutter, 1972). According to Yarrow (1961, p. 485): "Direct observation of children undergoing the experience of maternal separation shows a variety of immediate disturbances in behavior, permitting the simple conclusion that this is a stressful experience for children." These effects can only be multiplied by repeated moves in foster care, and in and out of foster care.

In one study, adults who had previously been in foster care testified to distress experienced in childhood by repeated removals and replacements in foster care (Meier, 1962). Interviews with 160 former foster children in Holland revealed that most (about 75%) had severed contact with their foster parents and hold strong negative feelings about them (Van der Walls, 1960). In addition, clinical reports do indicate that foster children experience loyalty conflicts, identity confusion, and difficulty in making emotional commitments to their caretakers and friends (Wald, 1976, p. 672).

Moreover, there is evidence of child abuse in placement. In his nationwide study of reported child abuse incidents, Gil (1970) found that 2 percent of all abuse reports concerned children in placement. The Mercer County, New Jersey, study revealed that there was reason to believe that abuse in placement had occurred in 10 percent of the abuse and neglect cases in which children had been placed (Pelton, 1977a).

Based on available evidence, it may be possible to conclude that the immediate negative impacts of foster care, such as separation trauma, are well-established, but that the findings on the long-term effects of foster care are inconclusive. In regard to the immediate impacts, the immediacy with which certain harms follow upon certain conditions makes the cause-effect relationship obvious and not speculative. Studies of the long-term effects of foster care, on the other hand, have been hampered by a number of methodological problems, which have been reviewed elsewhere (Pelton, 1978b; Wald et al., 1988). Even then, the findings of the studies of long-term effects have been inconsistent. For example, some studies have reported high rates of deviancy in adulthood for children who had been in foster care (McCord et al., 1960; Murphy, 1964; Ferguson, 1966). Others have reported that, on the whole, foster care is not detrimental to the development of children, in terms of physical, emotional, and cognitive development, academic performance, and personal satisfaction, and that foster care may even allow improvement in these areas (Fanshel & Shinn, 1978; Festinger, 1983; Wald et al., 1988).

It should not be surprising, after all, to find that few general conclusions can be drawn about the effects of foster care on children. As Rutter (1972) points out, the *quality* of the child care experience is the most important factor. This could vary greatly from one foster home to another. More specifically, it could be added that the most important factor is the quality of the *relationship* between the foster child and foster parents. Many children are already sufficiently disturbed when they enter foster care that the failure of a foster care placement does not necessarily reflect negatively on the quality of care which the foster parents were capable of providing.

Although the vast majority of foster children placed by the child welfare system in our country reside in foster family homes, many are in institutions. The quality of care in these institutions has spanned a wide range. A few have been of exceptional high quality, most could be termed adequate, and a few terrible. Within two years after forming an evaluation team in the mid-1970s to visit institutions in which it had placed children, New Jersey's state child welfare agency saw fit to "close" (i.e., to remove or stop placement of New Jersey children) roughly 10 percent of the 70 to 80 institutions visited.

At one out-of-state institution, the evaluation team found that there had been a number of unexplained injuries to children and, in fact, widespread institutional abuse and neglect (Nicholas, 1976). It found, in part, that:

The number and nature of serious incidents present a clear and present threat to the physical safety and emotional well-being of (New Jersey) children. . . . (New Jersey) children interviewed stated that they are routinely hit by staff members. . . . A review of medical records indicated that some injuries have occurred as a result of staff intervention. . . . A review of [the institution's] logs indicated that degrading and humiliating punishments have been used by staff in response to some situations.

The team found that even the structure and maintenance of the physical environment was dismally poor. Weeds had overgrown the outside playground equipment. The children played in the parking area, and during the team's visit, one child's foot was run over by a car. The dormitories, dining hall, classrooms, and bathrooms were dirty. Insects, both dead and alive, were found in all of the buildings. An open septic tank stood behind one building. No privacy at all was afforded to the residents, and staff supervision was inadequate.

The cost of placement of a child at that institution was $15,000 per year at that time. Today, rates as high as $45,000 are not uncommon in institutions. Institutions often justify such rates on the basis of psychological treatments they purport to offer. But the institution discussed above could not even insure the minimal *physical* welfare and safety of its children, much less attend to their psychological needs.

Although most children are no doubt better off in foster family homes than in institutions, there is probably nothing inherent in institutions that would make poor quality of care inevitable, just as there is nothing inherently poor about foster homes. There are good institutions and good foster homes. However, foster care is a *social system* and as such it has its own inherent characteristics quite apart from the qualities of the people—the staff and foster parents—who operate within that system. There are certain built-in structural deficits of the system that cannot be corrected.

For example, the separation trauma that many children experience when removed from their parents are due to the necessities of the foster care system, which by definition entails separation. Yet this is just the beginning of the problems inherent in the system. Focusing on foster family care, we can say that the child now has two sets of parents. The child may become increasingly attached to the foster parents and, if this particular foster placement is to "work out," they to him or her. Yet, to the degree that the foster parents and child do become attached to each other, the relationship of the natural parents to the child may become more strained. This obviously works against the professed purpose of foster care in most cases, which is to provide a temporary living arrangement after which the child will be returned to the natural parents.

Thus, the foster care system is beset by an inherent paradox. This paradox has led to bizarre and contradictory instructions to foster parents, who have been told not to get too attached to the child, not to love him or her too much, for this is only a temporary arrangement. But if the foster relationship is indeed a good one, this advice represents an emotional and psychological impossibility. If it is not a good one, the advice becomes all too easy to follow, and the child will soon be moved from one foster home to another. Incidentally, one of the primary reasons for the frequent movement of a child from one foster home to another is the foster parents' claim that the child has become too difficult to handle. However, the more moves made, the more difficult the child may become, and thus a vicious circle may be inherent in the system.

The natural parents, on the other hand, have often been prevented or discouraged from visiting the child in foster care, despite the fact that eventual return of the child is the "case plan" in most instances, and that research has shown a strong inverse relationship between the frequency of parental visiting and the length of time that children spend in foster care (Fanshel & Shinn, 1978). In this same research, it was found that almost two-thirds of the children who remained in foster care for five years had essentially lost contact with their parents. Even between one-and-a-half and two years after entry into foster care, almost one-third of the children still in care at that time were not being visited at all by their parents, and another 11 percent had been visited rarely. In the Massachusetts study of children in foster care, it was found that 62 percent of the children had not seen their parents for at least six months (Gruber, 1978).

Agencies have discouraged visitation by having no written policies on it for their caseworkers, by not asking parents to plan for regular visits, by severely restricting the time and place of visits, by insisting that the caseworker be present, and by failing to provide funds for transportation (Knitzer et al., 1978; Musewicz, 1981). In the Mercer County study, I found that some parents had only been allowed to visit with their children for an hour or so at a time, in the agency's district office, a rather cold and inappropriate meeting ground for parent and child (Pelton, 1977a). As a member of a New Jersey child placement citizen review board later, I was disappointed to find that this practice had continued into the 1980s.

A well-intentioned mother, looking out for the best interests of her child, and her own emotional well-being, might decide that no visits at all are preferable to visits such as these. Other mothers, allowed to visit their children in the foster home, might fear upsetting the foster family situation. It is also likely that some mothers avoid visiting because they find the sight of their children living in someone else's home a depressing and humiliating experience. For other impoverished mothers, the geographical distance of the placement, and lack of transportation, has provided the subtle discouragement from visiting.

Having the natural parents and children become strangers to each other will obviously create difficulties of adjustment when the child is eventually returned. Yet the caseworker has often feared that visits will emotionally disrupt the child and strain the fragile foster parent–child relationship. Indeed, the foster parents themselves sometimes exhort the caseworker to prevent the visits. Thus, again we see a paradoxical strain inherent in the foster care system itself.

Despite these barriers to visiting, it has not been uncommon for a child welfare agency to use the fact that the natural parents did not visit as a reason for not returning their children to them. Their failure to visit has been taken as a prime indicant that they do not care all that much about the children and so are not ready to have them returned.

Finally, it should be noted that many children in foster care have been illegally held there against the parents' will. A parent who signs a voluntary agreement to have his or her child placed should be able to get the child returned on demand, unless the case is immediately taken to court by the agency. It is illegal to withhold the child without court order if the parent has made such demand. Yet there are documented cases in which parents who had signed voluntary agreements had their children illegally withheld from them by the state agency after they had demanded return (Pelton, 1977a).

Who are the children in foster care? The most recent statistics, based on data from 29 states, indicate that 60 percent of the children who *entered* care in FY 1985 were 12 years of age or younger, and their median age was 10.2 years old (Tatara et al., 1988, p. 43). However, we must remember that many of these children were not entering care for the first time (we know that one-fourth of them had entered before just in the previous one year). The median age of children at *first* entry into foster care has not been reported, but we can deduce that it is considerably lower than 10.2 years old, and that considerably more than 60 percent first enter at 12 years of age or younger. Roughly 58 percent of the children who entered care in FY 1985 were white, 24 percent were black, 10 percent were Hispanic, and 6 percent were from other racial and ethnic minority groups (Tatara et al., 1988, p. 46).

Statistics based on data from 32 states indicate that 54.5 percent of the children *in* care at the end of FY 1985 were 12 years of age or younger, and their median age was 11.9 years old (Tatara et al., 1988, pp. 63–64). Data from 41 states indicate that roughly 52 percent of the children in care at the end of FY 1985 were white, 33 percent black, 9 percent Hispanic, and 5 percent of other racial and ethnic minority groups (Tatara et al., 1988, p. 65). Slightly more children were male than female (Tatara et al., 1988, p. 67).

However, the characteristics of children in foster family homes, the largest part of the foster care population, tend to be considerably different than those of the far smaller number of children in residential/institutional facilities, when looked at separately. The significance of this distinction is that children tend to be placed in foster family homes for child protection reasons, whereas child-centered reasons tend to predominate in residential/institutional placements. In New Jersey in 1980, for example, while more than three-quarters of the children in residential/institutional care were 13 years of age or older, 70 percent were boys, and a majority were white; the majority of children in foster family homes were black, only 43 percent were 13 years of age and older, and slightly more than half were boys. (These statistics are from computerized runs specially generated by the New Jersey Division of Youth and Family Services from its Child Master Record.)

Who are the children in foster care? Interestingly, there have never been efforts made to gather national statistics on the economic origins of children in foster care. Occasional state and local research studies, however, have left no doubt that they have continued to be predominantly poor children from impoverished families (e.g., Jenkins & Norman, 1972; Claburn & Magura, 1977; Gruber, 1978; Levit, 1979). For example, in a study of children in foster care in New York City, it was found that 52 percent of the families from which the children came had been receiving some form of public assistance at the time of placement (Jenkins & Norman, 1972). The authors observed that just prior to placement, "most of the children in the study lived in impoverished households located in the poorest neighborhoods" of that city (p. 19). In a study of children in foster family care in Massachusetts, it was found that in 1972, 61 percent of the biological families had incomes of less than $5,000 per year, and 37 percent even received less than $3,000. Forty percent of the families were receiving public assistance (Gruber, 1978).

In New Jersey, case record analysis of a sample of children who entered foster care in 1971 revealed that no one in the natural family was employed in 68 percent of the cases (Claburn & Magura, 1977). A study of children placed in foster care in New Jersey during 1977 showed that 60 percent of the natural families had annual incomes of under $5,000, and 56 percent were receiving some form of public assistance (Levit, 1979). This study also indicated that the general economic status of the natural families of children in foster family care is lower than that of the families of children in residential-institutional care (although it was generally low for these families also), when foster care is divided into these two subgroups. Eighty percent of the natural families of children in foster family care had annual incomes of under $5,000, and less than 1 percent had incomes above $10,000 per year. Sixty-eight percent were receiving some form of public assistance.

FOSTER CARE FOR WHOM?

The use of foster care is not subject to a merely empirical question, to be favored or disfavored on the basis of research findings on the impact of foster care on children's development. There are the matters of values and priorities, and the question of where we should place our resources. As one commentator has put it, "better prospective development in foster care is in itself no justification for removing a child from his/her own home" (Magura, in press).

In New Jersey, Gloria Downey, a 17-year-old unmarried mother, placed her infant in foster care through the state's child welfare agency, under a voluntary placement agreement, because she did not have the means to house or care for the child at the time (*Doe* v. *Downey*, 1976). In December 1974, during a visit, Ms. Downey retained physical possession of the child and did not return her to the foster parents with whom the child had been residing for more than a year. In July 1975, the foster parents filed a complaint charging Ms. Downey with neglect, and asked that physical custody of the child be awarded to them. The next month, Ms. Downey's custody was terminated by court order, and the child was placed back with the foster parents. In December 1975, the court issued an order claiming the child to have been abused and neglected, and continuing the physical custody of the child with the foster parents. The mother appealed the court's decision.

It had been claimed that, while living with Ms. Downey, the child was residing in overcrowded, "disorganized and filthy" living conditions, was in poor health, did not have a bed of her own, and was observed playing with cockroaches. A psychiatrist testified that Ms. Downey was "immature, of inadequate personality and poor ego strength" and that the child showed signs of emotional disturbance. The trial judge (the original court) had concluded that the mother, since she was receiving public assistance, was financially able to provide minimal shelter for the child and had failed to do so; therefore, neglect was involved. He alluded to the crowded living conditions, the lack of a crib, and the sharing of a bed with other children. He further concluded that the "education" provided in Ms. Downey's household was not conducive to the child's mental growth and development, and that the continuance of physical custody in the hands of the foster parents was in the child's best interests.

On appeal, the Appellate Division reversed the order and returned the child to Ms. Downey, on several grounds. The judge concluded that:

While [substandard, dirty and inadequate sleeping conditions] may be unfortunate incidents of poverty, they do not establish child neglect or abuse. Adoption of such facts as a basis for a finding of child neglect or abuse might result in mass transfers of children from ghettos and disadvantaged areas into more luxurious living accomodations but with resultant destruction of the natural parental bond. (*Doe* v. *Downey*, 1976)

The appellate court further concluded that whatever emotional harm the child might have suffered was not caused by home conditions, but was due instead to "being shuttled between the two divergent and conflicting environments" and that much of this shuttling had been done by the state child welfare agency. (The agency had arranged weekend visits with the foster parents after the child was back in the care and custody of the mother.) Moreover, the court held that the alleged failure of Ms. Downey to provide her preschool child with education or intellectual stimulation in the home was not relevant under the child abuse and neglect law and that the "best interests of the child," which might imply a preference for a wealthy family over a poor one, is not the standard adopted by this statute as the basis for child removal. The Appellate Division's decision was later affirmed by the New Jersey Supreme Court (*Doe* v. *Downey*, 1977).

Similar wording was used in an earlier case in Missouri, in which a mother was faced with the termination of parental rights to her three children on the grounds that she had "abandoned" them, had "willfully" neglected them, and had "refused" to give them "necessary care and protection." The charges arose from the circumstances that the children had been placed in foster care (in 1968), and while in foster care, as alleged by two caseworkers, the mother did not request to see or visit her children and did not send clothing, cards, or gifts. One of the caseworkers testified that the mother, who was often in the hospital for leg ulcers and varicose veins, was not able (in the worker's opinion) to provide the children with "the stability and the stimulation and incentive they need to perform to capacity," and would be "better off" in an adoptive home. In 1971, the Juvenile Court (the court of original jurisdiction) ordered the termination of parental rights.

On appeal, the higher court ruled that there was no abandonment or willful neglect. The mother in fact was sometimes discouraged by the caseworker from visiting her children, and did express interest in them. This higher court perceived that the real issue was whether or not parental rights may be terminated on the grounds that the children would be "better off" in another home. The court concluded: "In the extreme this could lead to a redistribution of a great mass of the minor population." The court ruled that it does not have the authority under state law to terminate parental rights merely because the children might be "better off" with someone else (*S. K. L.* v. *Smith*).

We have here a sequence of events that occurs in many "neglect" cases. The conditions of poverty first bring the mother to the attention of the state child welfare agency. In the Downey case above, the mother "voluntarily" placed the child because she did not have the means to shelter or care for her. Voluntariness is a relative term that must be evaluated in the context of the range of options available. The state was quite willing to offer and finance foster care for the child, but made no offer of housing assistance, emergency financial assistance, or increases in public assistance benefits. In fact, foster care payments to foster parents in New Jersey, as in other states, are higher than AFDC payments that the natural mother would receive for the same child. If adequate financial or housing assistance had been offered, it is likely that the mother would not have "opted" for foster care.

In other cases, certain conditions of poverty are construed to be indications of "neglect" at the outset, and the state child welfare agency itself, without the mother coming forth, aggressively seeks the "voluntary" placement of the child. In the Downey case, the conditions of poverty were construed as neglect only after the mother had made repeated requests for the return of the child, which the agency did not honor although the mother "was entitled to the return of her child since there was at no time any adjudication that she was an unfit mother," (*Doe* v. *Downey*, 1976) and after she physically took possession of the child from the foster home on a visit.

A large proportion of all placements are "voluntary," and a state child welfare agency's failure to honor a legitimate request for return is not uncommon. Ms. Downey's action in retrieving her child is rare and is what precipitated her court battle. The lower court then interpreted the conditions of her poverty as "neglect," as is done in many cases that ever get to a trial court hearing, and then turned an additional argument upon the mother, which is again not infrequent: It was argued, in effect, that the child has been "better off" in foster care and should remain there. Another rarity in this case was that the mother appealed to a higher court, to which hardly any "neglect" cases ever get. Although that appeal resulted in a reversal, the Downey case has had little measurable impact on "neglect" cases in New Jersey, because many cases never go to court and are "adjudicated" by the state agency through so-called voluntary agreements.

Despite the inherent deficiencies in the foster care system, it is definitely needed for some children. The question is for which children and how many?

There are certainly some children of those endangered by severe harm for whom placement in foster care, despite its known deficiencies and attendant harms, would be the relatively *least* detrimental alternative. But who are these children who cannot be protected in their own homes by less disruptive and relatively harmful means than child removal? It is my belief that not only are there many children in foster care who should *not* have been placed there, but that there are other children who are being wrongfully *left in* their natural homes. In short, children are being removed from their homes in the *wrong* cases and being left at home in the *wrong* cases. Furthermore, it is my belief that if only those children were placed in foster care who would actually need it, we would have very *few* children in foster care.

One of the most anguishing stories to hear about is that of a child who has been murdered or severely injured by his or her parents after the family has already been made known to child welfare authorities. A distressingly large proportion of child homicides fall into this category. A study of child homicides in New York City found that 49 percent of the families had previously been reported to the public child welfare agency, most within a year prior to the death (Mayor's Task Force, 1983). A quarter of the children were even involved in an active child protection case at the time of death.

There are several possible interpretations or implications of this finding. First, since it is impossible to have knowledge about how many children child welfare officials (and judges) *save* from death and severe injury (i.e., how many children would have otherwise been killed or severely injured), it is possible to argue that the overall success-failure rate might be so great, that without evidence to the contrary, no cause is presented for a change in child welfare procedures. Child welfare agencies should just keep on doing what they have been doing. This view ignores the fact that current child welfare procedures in regard to child removal have resulted in the arbitrary removal of many children in cases in which there was no intrinsic reason to believe that the child would have been severely harmed if left in the natural home, and in cases in which a relatively small amount of concrete assistance would have eliminated any danger of severe harm that did exist.

Secondly, it is possible to argue that the fact that many child homicides occur in cases already known to child welfare agencies means that these agencies have not been removing *enough* children from their homes. What is needed is *more* of the same: Agencies should increase the numbers of children they put in foster homes. Indeed, it is probably the pressures of public outrage wrought by dramatic publicity of the relatively rare cases of child battering and child homicide that has contributed to the fact that there has continued to be a high number of children sent into foster care each year. The argument that *more* child removal is called for ignores the very real possibility that, without an improved capacity on the part of child welfare officials and judges to discriminate between cases in which there is danger of severe harm to the child and no alternative means of eliminating that danger, and cases in which no such danger exists, child removal will continue to be arbitrary and counterproductive. That is, even *more* children will be *inappropriately* removed, and there will be hardly any increase in the removal of children actually in danger of death or maiming.

This brings us to the third and final alternative: It is possible to entertain the hypothesis that the application of more appropriate child removal criteria would reduce errors. A definite policy can be formulated that would eliminate child removal for arbitrary reasons, and that would increase the chances of detecting for removal those few children who are in danger of severe harm or death and cannot be protected from such consequences in any other way.

Violence against children is often repetitive. The single best indicant that a child is in serious danger of severe harm may be a pattern of repeated severe violence or—whether or not deliberate acts were involved or can be proved—prior unexplained and suspicious severe injuries, and not the personality characteristics of the parents, which are far more variable in child abuse and neglect cases. In his nationwide survey of child abuse reports made to central registries during the years 1967 and 1968, Gil (1970) determined that at least half of the children, and quite likely over 60 percent, had been previously abused. He also found that "at least 31.6% of mothers and 39.9% of fathers had been perpetrators of abuse in the past." Moreover, in 21.1 percent of the families, siblings of the abused child had been abused in the past. According to Gil (1970, p. 108): "It thus seems that physical abuse of children is more often than not an indication of a prevailing pattern of caretaker-child interaction in a given home rather than of an isolated incident." However, many of the past and current incidents were not serious in terms of injuries, and it remains to be definitively determined whether or not severe violence is adequately forecast by prior repeated severe violence.

A New York City child homicide study revealed that 90 percent of the victims and/or their siblings had been physically abused or neglected before the fatal incidents (Kaplun & Reich, 1976). It also showed that in 79 percent of the cases in which children remained in the home following the homicide, "there was evidence of possible jeopardy, and in 32%, continued neglect or abuse was a matter of record." The authors concluded: "The murder of a child is the final chapter in his history of maltreatment. That history develops against a background of poverty and violence. . . . [The] assault is unpremediated and impulsive, and similar ones directed against siblings or spouses occur before and after the killings." In a Philadelphia homicide study, Weston (1974) found that 64 percent of the fatal victims of child abuse had a history of previous trauma. Again, whether or not such prior and subsequent incidents arc serious are a matter for further research, although a British study revealed that 60 percent of battered children who are returned home are rebattered (Skinner & Castle, 1969).

Severe injury (or injury severe enough to require hospitalization or emergency room treatment) occurs in only a minority of child abuse and neglect incidents. Even in many of those incidents in which such injury has occurred, the problems could be remedied in a far less drastic manner than by placing the child in foster care. However, it may be that in most cases in which the child has been brutally beaten or tortured, the violent acts are impulsive, uncontrollable, repetitive, and often indiscriminate (in many of these cases the offender, at various times, may have assaulted other children, the spouse, other relatives, and even acquaintances and strangers), and there is extremely little or no chance that the perpetrator can be changed within a reasonable period of time by any currently known means.

The findings of the various studies reviewed here raise the possibility that the best indicant that the child will be violently injured in the future is that he or she has been violently injured in the past. Such studies also found other factors frequently present, such as alcoholism, narcotics use, and in some cases (Smith et al., 1975) abnormal electroencephalogram (EEG) patterns. Some of the children's assailants were also judged to be aggressive psychopaths and to exhibit "poor impulse control." But prior violence may be the most solid indicant and there are, after all, many alcoholics, drug addicts, and persons with aggressive personality disorders, poor impulse control, and abnormal EEGs who do *not* physically abuse their children. Moreover, having abnormal EEGs is not a crime; the assault of an individual is.

Psychological predictors are misleading. The injuries and the actual criminal acts may be far more predictive, and in fact constitute legal grounds for restraining a person from doing it again, without the possible violations of civil liberties that acting against the parents on the basis of psychological factors would entail. In many cases, a child who *should* have been removed is left in a home in which he or she has been repeatedly harmed, because the caseworker or psychiatrist had not perceived the parents to possess "abnormal" characteristics.

Just as one cannot be convicted for possessing a characteristic that bears some weak statistical association with a certain form of criminal activity, he or she should not be punished for it (by losing his or her children) by the helping establishment. The trouble with concentrating on a pattern of repetitive violence and severe injury rather than upon "psychological predictors," some will argue, is that we cannot predict, nor therefore take action to protect the child from, the *first* violent act against him or her. This is true, but we cannot adequately predict the first act anyway, and in any event, to incarcerate or punish an individual on the basis that he or she might commit a crime in the future is entirely unjust and smacks of police state tactics. Simply stated, one must commit a crime before he or she is punished for it.

In severe child abuse cases, parents are hardly ever arrested. A British study of 134 battered infants and children under five years of age, most of whom had been admitted to hospitals, revealed that while 19 percent of the children's siblings had been previously battered, only 1 percent of the parents had been charged with cruelty or neglect (Smith et al., 1975).

In reviewing a subset of 60 of the cases in the earlier New York City child homicide study, the authors found that no suspect was arrested in one-third of the cases (Kaplun & Reich, 1976). Of 17 cases in which postarrest information was available and in which the suspects had gone to trial, virtually all were given short sentences on reduced charges in return for guilty pleas. One case was dismissed because the testimony of the ten-year-old sibling who was the sole witness to the killing was deemed inadmissible because of age. There was a conviction for first-degree murder in only one case.

Thus in child homicide cases, conviction of the offender on the charge of first-degree murder is an extremely rare event. Most of those who even go to trial are given short sentences on reduced charges in exchange for guilty pleas. The offenders are soon free to abuse their other children, if no state action is taken to protect them. In most cases, such action is not taken. In fact, in most cases in which a child was killed, the parents had not been charged with abuse to begin with for a previous battering of the victim or his or her siblings.

In a child protection case in New Jersey in 1975, a three-year-old boy had suffered burns over 40 percent of his body that were so severe that he was hospitalized for over three months and required skin grafting. It was suspected that his stepfather had submerged him in a bathtub filled with hot water. Within the next year, numerous complaints of abuse and neglect were received from relatives and neighbors and many suspicious injuries were found on the boy and his siblings, including bruises, welts, and cigarette burns. Also, the boy told at least two professionals that his stepfather had been responsible for the original hot water scalding.

In this case, the state *did* bring child abuse charges against the stepfather, but failed to win the case in court, perhaps because only evidence pertaining to one incident, the hot water scalding, was deemed admissible, and not that pertaining to a *pattern* of injuries.

About one year and three months after the scalding incident, the boy died after ingesting three-quarters of a bottle of rum. The other children were found suffering from malnutrition and other injuries. The stepfather was convicted and given a long prison term.

Previously in this complex and tragic case, psychiatric evaluations of both parents revealed no psychopathology. Actually, parents have been diagnosed as psychotic in only a very small percentage of child abuse and neglect cases. In this case, the injuries were usually "unexplained" or "suspicious." But proving abuse, which implies intention, in court is difficult, and at one point the court even ended the state child welfare agency's supervision. The stepfather was finally convicted when all previous suspicious injuries were allowed to be introduced as evidence into the court proceedings.

Although proving abuse is difficult, a series of suspicious severe injuries of unknown origin should be enough to establish drastically inadequate supervision, or neglect. In cases of suspected severe abuse, it might be less difficult to establish neglect rather than abuse, under the law. A pattern of *repeated severe injuries to the child*, whether or not it can be established that those injuries were the result of deliberate violent acts, may be predictive of future severe injuries, and may be indicative of neglect.

The series of severe injuries that occurred prior to death made this case a far more serious one than scores of cases I have studied in which children had been "voluntarily" placed. However, this case differed from most other cases in significant ways that raise serious questions of class, and perhaps racial discrimination, in the child welfare system. This case had involved a white middle-class family. With the aid of a private lawyer, the parents in this instance were able to terminate the state child welfare agency's supervision of the case because child abuse had not been proven. Now there are countless cases, many involving poor black families, in which agency supervision continues despite the fact that there is less reason for suspicion than in this case, in which the risk of harm is less, and in which past injuries, if any, were less severe. We must face the fact that many families continue under supervision, and under risk of child removal, merely because the parents are ignorant of their legal rights or too poor to retain a private lawyer. The child welfare system ultimately rests upon a foundation of ignorance and poverty, and this is an unjust basis for any system.

Parents have the responsibility to protect the child from severe harm, and not to do so is a crime. If the parents have completely abdicated that responsibility, it is clear that the state must replace the parents, perhaps by placing the child in foster care. In some cases, such abdication is so obvious even before any serious injury has in fact occurred to the child, that preventive action can and should be taken, because the abdication itself is a crime. In other cases, the pattern of previous severe injuries itself is indicative of such extreme neglect. However, the problem has been that children have been removed from homes in which no severe injuries had occurred to them, in which whatever dangers of severe harm existed could have been remedied in far less drastic ways, and in which there had been no firm or obvious basis to believe that the child was in such danger.

As we will discuss later, many severe harms do occur to children in child welfare cases, and many risks of severe harm are present in such cases. Yet few severe harms are due to actual child abuse incidents, and few can be attributed solely to neglect. Most harm and risk of harm is attributable to configurations of multiple causation and is nonintentional. Thus, they are amenable to preventive efforts, aimed at one or several elements of those configurations. There are a few extreme cases, however, in which immediate causation is not multiple, but concentrated within a parent, and the risk of harm that the parent presents is so great and severe, that nothing short of an unlikely drastic change in the parent would protect the child. Rather than to allow the labels "abuse and neglect" to color our vision and guide our handling of increasingly greater portions of the multiple causation spectrum, we should narrow our use of these terms to cases in which the parent's responsibility and culpability is so paramount in causing severe harm or the risk thereof that other elements in the immediate context play little or no role. These cases of obvious culpability might more realistically be handled as police matters.

PROVISION OF SERVICES

Critics of the foster care system have not advocated that it be abolished. They recognize that, despite its detrimental aspects, foster care is necessary at certain times for certain children. But they have argued that foster care has been overused as a supposed "solution" to child welfare problems.

In recognition of the detrimental aspects of removing children from the parents on the children themselves, critics have advised that a child should be removed only in cases in which it has been determined that the child is at risk of suffering severe harm within the home, that this harm is greater than that which he or she is likely to suffer within the foster care system, and that all reasonable services have been provided in an effort to protect the child from severe harm within the home and thereby avert the need of foster care.

Earlier in this chapter, two types of unnecessary placements were discussed. The first is due to vagueness in laws and administrative guidelines that has allowed much arbitrariness to enter into decision-making processes, with placement decisions being based on factors far removed from the factor of risk of harm. The second type has been due to lack of reasonable efforts being made through provision of appropriate services that might address the risk of harm within the home and avert the need for placement.

As already indicated earlier in this chapter, such reasonable efforts continue to be lacking. In New York City, for example, Special Services for Children (SSC), the city agency responsible for child welfare services, revealed in its own annual reports and plans that in federal fiscal year (FY) 1979 and 1980, it provided homemaker service for less than 1 percent of the children reported to it for abuse or neglect. It planned to provide homemaker service to only 355, or 1 percent of such children in FY 1982. Similarly, it provided day care as a protective service for only 160 children in FY 1981 and planned to increase this figure to only 180 in FY 1982 and only 280 in FY 1984. These are just a few of the examples of the meager level of preventive services continuing to be offered. Overall, SSC planned to spend 82 percent of its FY 1982 budget of $354.6 million on foster care, only 5 percent on preventive services and 5 percent on protective services, and 7 percent on adoption. Thus, SSC spends more than eight times more money on foster care than it does on protective and preventive services.

It can be validly argued that our country needs to put far more money into the child welfare system than it currently does, in order to raise the level of services devoted to child welfare cases. However, as already noted in Chapter 1, public child welfare agencies traditionally have been foster care agencies: in 1956, 72 percent of total expenditures for child welfare services by state and local agencies went for foster care payments (Low, 1958, Table 1). As noted in Chapter 2, when federal spending for social services did increase considerably during the 1960s and 1970s, much of it was channeled into foster care. By the end of the 1970s, nearly three-quarters of all child welfare monies in this country were still being channeled into foster care (Burt & Pittman, 1985, p. 31). Thus, what is needed is a shift in the budgetary emphasis in the child welfare system, from foster care to prevention-of-placement services, in regard to the monies already allocated to the system. However, attempts to accomplish that shift within the current system have obviously failed. It will be argued in the last chapter that nothing less than a restructuring of the system will be necessary to reverse this emphasis, and to insure that larger proportions of any future additional monies allocated to child welfare flow to prevention as opposed to placement.

In light of the continuing failure of child welfare agencies to provide the concrete and supportive services that the clients want and need, it is difficult to accept claims that many parents known to the system "want" their children removed, as indicated by their signing of "voluntary" placement agreements. Poor people may have rather low expectations of what government can, or even should, provide to families to help keep them together. There are many cases in which a mother, because of inadequate housing, perhaps compounded by physical illness or emotional strain, is urged by caseworkers to "temporarily" place her children in foster care. In some cases, the mother may look upon such an offer as a favor, since she knows that she is unable at the moment to care for her children without help. Gratefulness for such assistance, however, may occur only in the subjective context of not expecting the agency to offer housing assistance, emergency financial assistance, and in-home supportive services such as baby-sitting. In other words, the mother may perceive a limited range of options for gaining help for her family, and in that context may indeed be grateful for any assistance offered. To be sure, studies have shown that agencies in general have been more interested in offering, aside from foster care itself, psychological and educative services rather than concrete and supportive services, although it is concrete and supportive services that clients have been most interested in receiving (see Sudia, 1981, and Pelton, 1982b, for reviews of this research). Thus, the agencies have shaped and reinforced the parents' limited expectations. The agencies themselves have restricted the range of clients' response options to such questions as whether or not they want their children removed.

NEED FOR STANDARDS AND GUIDELINES

In a child welfare agency, caseworkers and supervisors are constantly called upon to make decisions that significantly affect the lives of many individuals. They are faced with decisions regarding coercive intervention into family life, the selection of services, child removal, child return, termination of parental rights, and case termination. But there has been a lack of standards and guidelines to aid them in making such decisions. This situation has contributed to great variability and arbitrariness in decision making, and to the uncertainty and confusion of parents who must deal with such agencies.

In the absence of clear and specific agency standards and guidelines, each worker is left to his or her own devices. The implicit standards and guidelines that one worker or supervisor may employ in decision making is likely to vary greatly from that of the next worker or supervisor. Moreover, such individualistic conceptions are likely to be vague, and unwittingly subject to social, class, and cultural biases regarding minimally adequate child care.

This vagueness has been reflected in agency case records (Pelton, 1977a). Actual harms that might have befallen the child have sometimes not been recorded or described. Often no clear accounting of services actually offered or received have appeared in the case record. If the child had been placed, the precise reasons for placement, and an explanation of why placement seemed to be the least detrimental alternative in the particular case, have often not appeared in the case record. Moreover, when and under what conditions a child would be returned to his or her parents have often not been specified. The Adoption Assistance and Child Welfare Act of 1980 was designed, in part, to overcome some of these deficiencies in recording and accountability by mandating implementation of statewide information systems, case review systems, and case plans for children in foster care. Despite the implementation of these systems in most states, much vagueness still remains in individual cases.

Greater specificity is still needed in many areas: identifying actual harm to the child; determining what conditions in a particular case place the child at risk of harm; identifying the causes of the harm in the given case; selecting services to be offered that "fit" the conditions and problems identified; determining the need to seek placement and the conditions that have to be satisfied for return; and justifying the need for all significant actions taken.

STAFFING INADEQUACIES

These continuing problems have been due, in part, to the wide-spread and well-documented facts that caseworkers in public child welfare agencies have been overburdened with excessively high case-loads, that they have received inadequate training, and that they have experienced extremely high turnover rates (Knitzer et al., 1978). In recent years, caseworker turnover rates of up to 50 percent per year have been reported in various parts of the country. Under these circumstances, the ability of public child welfare agencies to monitor, assess, plan for, and actually help troubled children and their families may be marginal at best.

In the Mercer County study, I found that most parents held positive attitudes toward the caseworkers themselves and were favorably impressed with their personal conduct (Pelton, 1977a). They tended to perceive the workers as nonaccusatory, polite, respectful, and sincerely interested in helping. The parents told of many acts of personal humaneness on the part of the caseworkers that seemed to go beyond the "call of duty."

Indeed, one cannot help but be impressed, on the whole, with the caseworkers' extraordinary dedication and sincerity, and deep concern for the children and families. However, they must operate within a system that offers built-in dilemmas and "catch-22s," and that provides the caseworkers with few tools to carry out their tasks. They must perform an almost impossible dual role, that of both helper and coercive investigator. They are faced with ambiguous agency policy, few firm guidelines for action, a dearth of appropriate services to offer, and the failure of social science to generate solid knowledge of practical value in meeting the kinds of social problems facing a child welfare agency. Given few resources with which to work and little guidance by those who administer the system, these workers are thrown onto the "front lines" of society's clumsy, feeble, and hesitant attempts to deal with the effects of poverty. They are sent out with few adequate tools with which to repair the ravages of poverty, and are largely left to their own devices. However, their personal humaneness and resourcefulness are not enough to effectively cope with the social problems they are asked to deal with, and ultimately they become accomplices of a system that often does more harm than good.

NOTE

1. CWIS/CCRS Special Report Series, New York City, Series A, Status date 3/31/81, p. 6, Table 13, and pp. 36–37, Table 34.

4

The Permanency Planning Movement

As already noted, from at least as early as the late 1950s, many studies and reports began to call attention to serious faults in the foster care system in the United States (see, e.g., Maas & Engler, 1959; Maas, 1969; Wald, 1976; Fanshel & Shinn, 1978; Shyne & Schroeder, 1978; Gruber, 1978). Despite these concerns, and due to the combination of forces behind the child abuse crusade as described in Chapter 2, the foster care population in this country grew enormously during the 1960s and most of the 1970s, reaching its high point during 1975-77 (Knitzer et al., 1978; Shyne & Schroeder, 1978; Pelton, 1987b; see Table 1 and Figures 1 and 2 in Chapter 1).

However, as also already indicated, due to eventual alarm over the large number of children in foster care and in response to mounting professional criticism that they stayed too long and moved too much, "permanency planning" became a broad and popular movement within the child welfare field during the mid to late 1970s, and later became a major aspect of the federal Adoption Assistance and Child Welfare Act (AACWA) of 1980 (P.L. 96-272). Basically, it was the belief that many children were being harmed by a system in which they stayed indefinitely and drifted from one home to another, without close monitoring of their cases and without plans for more permanent and stable living arrangements, that led to the establishment of permanency planning programs in child welfare agencies, and mechanisms for periodic review of children in foster care guided by a permanency planning philosophy. The permanency planning philosophy has been that every child has a right to a permanent and stable home, and that a plan should be made for every child in foster care for a more permanent living arrangement.

The main thrust of the permanency planning movement has been aimed at children already in foster care: to either get them returned home or, if this is deemed not possible, freed for adoption. Other options include legal guardianship and planned long-term foster care. While some commentators wish to expand our understanding of the concept of permanency planning to include the prevention of foster care placement in the first instance (Stein & Gambrill, 1985), the reality is that the Oregon Permanency Planning Demonstration Project, which has served as a model for the movement, dealt with children already in foster care, and the emphasis was on adoption (Emlen et al., 1978). Moreover, permanency planning units in public child welfare agencies usually have dealt with children already in foster care, and most external review mechanisms (e.g., citizen review boards) developed in the last decade are also so focused, and indeed are often called foster care review boards.

In fact, as far back as 1969 (in New York State) but mainly during the 1970s, states passed laws to provide adoption subsidies to adoptive parents in order to facilitate the adoption of so-called "hard-to-place" children out of foster care. The AACWA of 1980 introduced federal money into adoption subsidies, in order to facilitate permanency planning efforts. Also, within the past decade, many states have "liberalized" their laws concerning termination of parental rights in order to make it easier to free children for adoption.

The decline in the child placement population and rate between 1977 and 1982 (see Table 1 and Figures 1 and 2 in Chapter 1) can be attributed to conscious efforts on the part of public child welfare agencies to decrease the size of the foster care population. However, the child placement population and rate was on the rise again by 1983 (see Table 1 and Figures 1 and 2 in Chapter 1). Indeed, despite the provision of the AACWA of 1980 that "reasonable efforts" should be made to prevent the need for child removal, as well as to make it possible for a child to return home, there are indications that the decline in the foster care population that did take place between 1977 and 1982 may be attributable more to an increase in the number of children who exited from foster care than to a decrease in the number who entered, and that the most recent rise in the foster care population, beginning in 1983, is due to a continuing failure to deal with the "front end" of the foster care system, that is, prevention of foster care placement in the first instance (Pelton, 1987b).

THE FOSTER CARE FLOW

What impact has the permanency planning movement had on child welfare and foster care? As we have already seen in Chapter 3, the median length of continuous time that children spend in foster care has decreased considerably in recent years. This can only mean that children have been *exiting* from foster care at a faster rate. This fact alone can account for the decline in the foster care population that took place between 1977 and 1982.

Although national statistics are not available on the number of *entries* into foster care per year prior to 1982, we do know that in FY 1982, more children *left* foster care than entered, but that in FY 1983 as well as in FY 1984 and FY 1985, slightly more children *entered* than *left* care (Tatara et al., 1988, p. 37). Both the number of entries and exits increased over these years, but the changed ratio accounts for the increase in the foster care population that began in 1983. During FY 1985, there were 190,000 entries into foster care, and 184,000 exits from foster care. Although there were 276,000 children in foster care on one day at the end of FY 1985, 460,000 children had experienced foster care sometime during that year, and this figure was up from 434,000 in FY 1982. Thus in FY 1985, two-fifths of all children who had experienced foster care for at least some part of FY 1985 had entered within that same year. Similarly, about two-fifths of the 276,000 children in foster care on a single day at the end of FY 1985 had entered within the previous year (Tatara et al., 1988, pp. 37, 81).

Thus, we can conclude that our foster care system has become a huge "revolving door," with many children entering and exiting each year. Adding to this revolving-door concept is the fact, already noted in Chapter 3, that 25 percent of the children who entered foster care during FY 1985 were the *same* children who had *exited* from foster care at least once before, within the 12 months prior to the current entry alone. What percentage of all children who entered foster care in FY 1985 had *ever* been in the system previously is not known, but must be considerably higher.

Although national statistics are not available to us on entries and exits prior to FY 1982, we can piece together reasonable inferences as to the patterns that have occurred. We can assume that during the 1960s and up until the mid-1970s, the annual number of entries into foster care grew considerably, the annual number of exits increased slightly, and the annual number of entries heavily predominated over the annual number of exits, thus accounting for the increase in the foster care population to one-day counts of about a half-million during 1975–77. Between 1977 and 1982, the annual number of entries into foster care either continued to increase or stabilized, but the annual number of exits increased enormously, and the annual number of exits heavily predominated over annual number of entries, bringing the foster care population back down to one-day-count levels similar to those at the beginning of the 1960s. By 1983, the annual number of exits began to stabilize, and with the number of entries increasing slightly, the number of entries began to predominate over exits, and the foster care population began to rise again. At this time, the rates of entry and exit had reached such high levels that it is evident that the foster care system has become a revolving door. In this situation, the difference between a one-day count of the foster care population and the count of children who experienced foster care at least sometime during the year must be far greater than it was in 1975–77. We do not know how much greater than a half-million that latter count was for 1975–77, but in 1985 it had reached almost half a million, even though the one-day count was 276,000. In the coming years, we may expect both counts (or at least the placement rates per child population) to stabilize at current levels, with high numbers of children both entering and exiting foster care. The higher one-day foster care population counts in the mid-1970s have been traded for a revolving door in the 1980s.

In any event, it is possible that the recent rise in the one-day count is due to a continuing failure to deal with the "front end" of the foster care system, namely, prevention of foster care placement in the first instance. It can be charged that the permanency planning movement, because it has largely been directed at children already in foster care, has failed to address this issue. It is as though the child welfare establishment wants to have it both ways: The child abuse crusade continues unabated so that children are placed in foster care as readily as before, and attempts are made to keep the foster care population down by getting children out of foster care more quickly. Prevention continues to take a back seat.

Where do the children who leave foster care go? In FY 1985, based on data from 27 states, about 67 percent were returned to parents or relatives (or other caretakers), 10 percent were adopted (or placed for adoption, although most states consider children placed for adoption to still be in foster care), 9 percent were emancipated or reached the age of majority, 3 percent ran away, and 2 percent were discharged to other public agencies (Tatara et al., 1988, pp. 54–56). Others left foster care for a variety of reasons including marriage, death, incarceration, and having legal guardianship established.

If we could apply the previously mentioned 25 percent one-year recidivism rate to the children who *left* foster care in FY 1985, and if we were to further assume that recidivism is confined almost exclusively to those who were returned to parents or relatives, we could speculate that perhaps almost one in three of the children who were returned to their parents or relatives reentered foster care within a year thereafter. We might then conclude either that little in the way of preparation or preventive services are being given to the parents or relatives to whom the children are being returned, or that preventive services currently being utilized are not effective, at least when given to families from whom the child has already been separated at least once before. We will look at recent studies of the efficacy of preventive services later in this chapter. However, while the above statistical speculations might not be too far from the truth, the fact is that increasing numbers of children recently *adopted* out of the foster care system are probably also contributing to the recidivism problem. Because adoption is the second largest destination for children leaving foster care (next to being returned home or to relatives), and because a push toward adoptions of children from foster care has been a key element in the permanency planning movement, we next turn to the issue of adoptions, and then adoption disruptions.

THE INSTITUTION OF ADOPTION

The separation of children from their parents has taken many forms, but none has been more extreme than the modern version of adoption. In adoption, the state has sanctioned the complete severance of all parental rights and responsibilities, as well as of all contact between the parents and child, and the withholding of all knowledge about each other from both the parents and child. While adoption, in this extreme form, might have been practiced at other times and in other places, it is really a very recent phenomenon in the Western world, having been practiced as such, with some gradual loosening of secrecy requirements, for only the past 50 years.

By contrast, in foster care, the prospect exists that the child and parents will be reunited after the factors that have seemingly necessitated the separation have been ameliorated. In theory, if not always in practice, the child and parents have the right to know the physical location of each other, and can visit and be in written and telephone contact with each other. Moreover, the parents must be consulted in regard to medical decisions concerning the child. Other forms of separation of children from living parents, of course, such as giving them to relatives to raise, hospitalization, or sending them to boarding school or summer camp, do not involve relinquishment of legal rights or responsibilities, do permit continued contact and communication between children and parents, and are usually temporary arrangements.

From this perspective, adoption is a peculiar institution. It is quite different from more limited forms of separation that ostensibly serve the most basic and obvious reason for separation at all: to allow the child to be cared for when the parents presumably cannot or will not do so, or to enhance the development of the child.

The institution of adoption would not exist, obviously, if there were not a source of children for it, as well as willing receivers for this ultimate form of child transference. The purpose of this discussion is to explore the changing nature of the source. Where do the children come from?

THE SHIFTING SOURCES OF CHILDREN FOR ADOPTION

Our concern here is with adoptions by nonrelatives. The other type, related adoptions, most often involves the adoption of a child by his or her stepfather, in which separation from the mother does not occur.

The annual number of nonrelated adoptions in the United States rose rather steadily from an estimated 33,800 in 1951 to a peak of 89,200 in 1970, and then, more abruptly, declined to an estimated 47,700 in 1975, the last year for which statistics were collected by

the National Center for Social Statistics. These estimates, as summarized recently by Maza (1984), are presented in Table 2. The best
more recently available estimate, derived from a national survey conducted by the National Committee for Adoption for the year 1982,
indicates that the annual number of adoptions might have reached
another turning point, rising slightly since 1975 to 50,720 (National

Table 2
**Estimates of Total Nonrelated Adoptions and Public Agency Adoptions in the
United States, and Public Agency Adoptions as a Percentage of Total Nonrelated
Adoptions, for 1951–82**

Year	Total Nonrelated Adoptions	Public Agency Adoptions	Public Agency Percentage
1951	33,800	6,100	18
1955	48,400	9,700	20
1957	48,200	10,600	22
1958	50,900	10,200	20
1959	54,100	11,400	21
1960	57,800	13,300	23
1961	61,600	15,400	25
1962	62,900	14,500	23
1963	67,300	17,500	26
1964	71,600	18,600	26
1965	76,700	20,700	27
1966	80,600	23,400	29
1967	83,700	23,100	30
1968	86,300	26,800	31
1969	88,900	28,400	32
1970	89,200	29,500	33
1971	82,800	29,800	36
1972	67,300	25,600	38
1973	59,200	22,500	38
1974	49,700	19,400	39
1975	47,700	18,600	39
1982	50,720	19,428	38

Sources: Maza (1984) for 1951–75, and National Committee for Adoption
(1985) for 1982.

Committee for Adoption, 1985; see Table 2). There is independent corroboration from another source of data that there has been a slight increase since 1975 (Bachrach, 1986). From these statistics, it is apparent that there are currently well over 2 million living Americans who have been adopted by nonrelated parents.

Most commentators agree that the major factors responsible for the overall decline in nonrelated adoptions since 1970 include the decreased social stigmatization of unwed mothers in our society, the increased availability of contraceptives, and the legalization of abortion. (The U.S. Supreme Court struck down anti-abortion laws in 1973.) This decline took place despite the fact that the annual number of illegitimate births had risen dramatically, more than doubling between 1957 and 1974 (Bonham, 1977).

National statistics are also available, for the same years noted above, in regard to the routes through which nonrelated adoptions have been accomplished. In Table 2, we see a rough parallel between the trend for total nonrelated adoptions and that number effected through public agencies; that is, there is a gradual annual increase up until 1970–71, and then a decline through 1975. There is a slight increase between 1975 and 1982 (Maza, 1984; National Committee for Adoption, 1985). As a proportion of all nonrelated adoptions, public agency adoptions rose rather continuously from 18 percent in 1951 to 39 percent in 1975, with only a possible minor decline to 38 percent in 1982 (see Table 2).

However, as opposed to the National Committee for Adoption's (1985) estimate of 19,428 public agency adoptions in 1982, Tatara et al. (1987, p. 88), through their annual surveys, have estimated 22,000 to 24,000 public agency adoptions in FY 1982. They also indicate a decline to 19,000 to 21,000 estimated public agency adoptions in FY 1983, and 18,000 to 20,000 public agency adoptions in FY 1984. Still, this possible decline did not bring recent annual public agency adoption totals below those of 1974 and 1975, and there is little doubt that public agency adoptions continue to constitute a larger share of all nonrelated adoptions than they did before the 1970s.

The remaining proportion of nonrelated adoptions were effected through the routes of private agency and independent adoptions. While there have been fluctuations in the division of nonpublic agency adoptions between private agency and independent, the public agency's proportion has constituted the highest proportion of all three routes since 1974 (Pelton, 1987a).

It would seem that unlike public agencies, the fortunes of private agencies, in regard to adoptions, rose and fell with their ability to deliver healthy white infants to prospective adoptive parents. Prospective parents for such infants then turned to independent means, and the private agencies were left with a decreasing proportion of a decreasing pie. The public agencies, although not having reached the numbers of adoptions they effected during 1970–71, have held their own in terms of the proportion of the total pie due to the permanency planning movement, the effects of which will be discussed shortly.

Currently, we can estimate that the majority of nonrelated adoptions in this country, perhaps 53 percent and rising, are a combination of adoptions of children coming from the public agency foster care system, and foreign adoptions, which are constituting an increasing proportion of nonpublic agency (independent and private agency) adoptions.

While public agency adoptions are holding their own in regard to numbers and proportion of total nonrelated adoptions due to the permanency planning movement, the growth sector of nonrelated adoptions in recent years, in terms of both numbers and proportion, has been foreign adoptions.

Adoptions of children from foreign countries began as a trickle in the post-World War II years. From 314 in 1949 and 189 in 1950, the number reached almost 3,000 in 1959 (Krichefsky, 1961). It averaged less than 2,000 per year through the 1960s, and then climbed until the mid-1970s. While it declined again somewhat over the next few years, it has risen steadily since 1981 (Immigration and Naturalization Service, 1980, Table 12).[1] By 1986, the annual number had reached 9,945, the highest number of annual foreign adoptions in our country's history, representing more than a doubling since 1981 (Immigration and Naturalization Service, 1987).[2] By 1987, it had reached 10,097 (Immigration and Naturalization Service, 1988). In 1982, foreign adoptions represented 11.3 percent of all nonrelated adoptions. If the total number of nonrelated adoptions remained steady since 1982, save for the rise in foreign adoptions, then foreign adoptions would have constituted as much as 17 percent of all nonrelated adoptions in 1985.

In the post-World War II years, almost all foreign adoptions came from European war-torn countries, mostly from Greece, Germany, and Italy (Krichefsky, 1961). Beginning in 1953, Japan and South Korea became significant contributors to this stream of foreign adoptions (Krichefsky, 1961; Adams & Kim, 1971). By about 1958, South Korea had become the largest single contributor to foreign adoptions in the United States (Krichefsky, 1961), and has remained so (Weil, 1984; Immigration and Naturalization Service, 1980, Table 12).[3] By 1976, 59 percent of all foreign adoptions were coming from South Korea and only 3 percent from Europe. Colombia was the second highest contributor with 8.5 percent of the total (Immigration and Naturalization Service, 1980, Table 12).

In 1985, a total of 10 countries accounted for 92 percent of all foreign adoptions: South Korea, Colombia, the Philippines, India, El Salvador, Brazil, Chile, Honduras, Guatemala, and Mexico (see Pelton, 1987a). In that year, South Korea provided more foreign adoptions than any previous year and by itself accounted for 61 percent of all foreign adoptions.[4] In 1987, these same 10 countries continued to account for over 90 percent of all foreign adoptions, and South Korea alone accounted for 65 percent of all foreign adoptions (Immigration and Naturalization Service, 1988).

The trends are clear. A handful of developing countries in Asia and Latin America are providing almost all of the foreign adoptions to the United States. In 1980, Europe was a source of less than 1 percent of such adoptions. In European and other developed countries, too, the influx of foreign adoptions has been mounting, and their sources are also Asia and Latin America (see Pelton, 1987a).

THE THREE STAGES OF THE
PERMANENCY PLANNING MOVEMENT

What impact has the advent of the permanency planning philosophy had on public agency adoption trends? As previously noted, the annual number of adoptions through public agencies rose until its high point in 1970–71 and declined until 1975, with a slight increase shown in 1982 over 1975. Thus, although national estimates are not available for the years 1976–81, the estimates that are available indicate that the permanency planning movement, at the very least, halted the decline in public agency adoptions during those years, although a slight new decline might have begun in 1983.

The permanency planning movement also played a role in the dramatic change that has occurred in the characteristics and indeed the sources of children placed for adoption through the public agencies. In 1971, the median age of children involved in public agency adoptions in the United States (based on data from 36 states) was only four months at the time of adoptive placement (i.e., 50% of the children adopted were under four months old when placed in adoptive homes); 73 percent of the children were under one year, and only 7 percent were six years old or more (National Center for Social Statistics, 1973). In FY 1984 (based on data from 24 states), the median age of children whose adoptions were finalized through public agencies was 5.6 years; only 11 percent were under one year, and 46 percent were six years old or more (Tatara et al., 1987, p. 90).

Most of the children adopted in 1971 obviously could not have spent much time in foster care, since they were placed for adoption as infants. Now, most of the children being placed for adoption through public agencies have been residing in the foster care system for several years. Indeed, in New Jersey, for example, 68 percent of adoptive home placements in 1985 were with foster parents, compared with only 27 percent in 1970.[5]

Other characteristics of the children have also changed. In New Jersey, for example, 31 percent of the public agency adoptive placements in 1970 were of nonwhite children, compared with 68 percent in 1985.[6] In Tennessee, the nonwhite percentage was 10 percent in state fiscal year (SFY) 1970 compared with 25 percent in SFY 1985.[7] As we will see later, an increasing proportion of adoptive placements involve handicapped children, but the statistics showing this are available for only the last few years.

Three distinct stages in this overall transformation are discernible. The first occurred between 1971 and 1974, at a time when total non-related adoptions as well as the number of public agency adoptions were declining, and during a time when the foster care population was increasing considerably. An age increase in public agency adoptions took place that in some states, at least, was due not only to a decline in the availability of white infants for adoption, but also to an apparent informal permanency planning movement that focused on efforts to get older foster children adopted. The median age of children in New Jersey involved in public agency adoptions in 1971 was a mere 5.6 months at the time of adoptive placement (National Center for Social Statistics, 1973). By 1973, it had jumped to 15.4 months, and as early as SFY 1974, children six years of age and older constituted 47 percent of all New Jersey public agency adoptive placements (National Center for Social Statistics, 1975).[8]

This change could not have been due to the decline in availability of white infants alone. Nationwide, only 7 percent of public agency adoptions in 1971 were of children who were six years of age and older at the time of adoptive placement (National Center for Social Statistics, 1973). If we apply this statistic to New Jersey, we can estimate that only 48 children in that age group were placed for adoption through the public agency in 1971.[9] In SFY 1974, however, 188 children in that age group were placed for adoption in New Jersey.[10] Thus an increased number, as well as proportion, of the children were in that age group, indicating that special efforts were being made.

In Tennessee, however, a far more modest change occurred during this period, while its total adoptive placements plummetted. The median age of children involved in adoptive placements rose from 4.0 months in 1971 to 4.4 months in 1974 (National Center for Social Statistics, 1973, 1976). Its adoptive placements of children six years of age and older went from 5 percent or 28 children, in SFY 1970, to 17 percent, or 48 children in SFY 1974.[11]

Nevertheless, the evidence suggests that the permanency planning philosophy began to imbue the child welfare field before the mid-1970s. The permanency planning movement began as a thrust to get children adopted, and it did so, at least in some states, as soon as a downturn started in the number of white infants available for adoption.

For example, as early as November 5, 1970, the Commissioner of the Tennessee Department of Public Welfare advised his staff that "Region I is to be commended for their [sic] efforts in placing many older children for adoption" (Yeatman, 1970). In 1971, his successor noted: "With the decrease in the number of infants available (for adoption), more and more couples are becoming interested in the school-age child" (Friend, 1971). In 1972, the same commissioner advised: "With the decrease in the number of preschool children, staff must devote more time to children in legal custody who can be legally freed for adoption" (Friend, 1972). In 1973, he stated: "More attention must be given those children for whom an adoption subsidy would make it possible for the children to have permanent homes" (Friend, 1973). Earlier in that year, he had been advised: "It has been brought to your attention that we have far more applications for the normal white infant than we have normal white infants" (Hooe, 1973). By 1976, a succeeding commissioner was advised: "With the moratorium (on the acceptance of applications for normal white preschoolers), we have seen an increase in the number of applicants for the hard-to-place child as families have stopped to seriously consider their ability to accept a child with special needs" (Slack, 1976).

The next two stages involve the formal permanency planning movement, the first during the mid to late 1970s, and the second after the passage of the AACWA in 1980. In New Jersey, children six years of age and older consituted 47 percent of public agency adoptive placements in SFY 1974, 57 percent in SFY 1977, 46 percent in 1980, and 56 percent in 1985.[12] In Tennessee, children in this age category constituted 17 percent of such placements in SFY 1974, 30 percent in SFY 1977, 19 percent in SFY 1978, 31 percent in SFY 1980, and 51 percent in SFY 1984.[13] Thus we see the impact of the permanency planning movement's push to get older children adopted, a slackening off of that impact after 1977, but then a bolstering of permanency planning efforts by the AACWA, after 1980.

The New Jersey statistics indicate that the proportion of children placed in adoptive homes who were nonwhite was 42 percent in SFY 1974, 50 percent in SFY 1977, 51 percent in 1980, and 68 percent in 1985.[14] The American Public Welfare Association statistics indicate a substantial rise from FY 1982 to FY 1984 (from 30% to 42%) in the proportion of public agency finalized adoptions involving nonwhite children (Tatara et al., 1987, pp. 93–94). Thus, again the impact of the permanency planning movement and then of AACWA is evident.

Finally, in New Jersey, the proportion of public agency adoptive placements involving children with handicapping conditions (children with a physical handicap, mental retardation, severe emotional disturbances, and multiple handicaps) was 32 percent in 1982, and 37 percent in 1985.[15] The American Public Welfare Association data indicate that the proportion of public agency finalized adoptions involving children with "special needs" (including age, disability, and minority or sibling group status) rose from 38 percent in FY 1982 to 61 percent in FY 1983 and declined slightly to 57 percent in FY 1984 (Tatara et al., 1987, pp. 95–96). It rose again to 62 percent in FY 1985 (Tatara et al., 1988, p. 92).

We may conclude that the permanency planning movement halted the decline of public agency adoptions, by way of increased efforts to get older and nonwhite children adopted out of the foster care system, but lost some steam in the late 1970s. The faltering movement was then given a shot in the arm by the AACWA of 1980 (which itself was a result of the permanency planning movement).

The AACWA was then responsible for a sharp rise in the percentage of children placed for adoption who are older, minority, and handicapped. In New Jersey, more than two-thirds of the children placed for adoption in 1985 were nonwhite, over one-half were age six or more, and more than one-third were handicapped. The characteristics of children placed for adoption through public agencies have changed drastically.

A major mechanism by which such change was effected was the state adoption subsidy, and then federal participation in subsidies after 1980. The boost that was given to the permanency planning movement by the AACWA was primarily accomplished through that act's provision of federal money for adoption subsidies. In Illinois, for example, subsidized adoptions as a proportion of all public agency adoptions rose from 41 percent in SFY 1978 to 48 percent in SFY 1980, and then to 70 percent in SFY 1985 (Testa & Lawlor, 1985, p. 55). In Tennessee, subsidized adoptive placements as a proportion of all public agency adoptive placements rose from only 11 percent in SFY 1977 to 26 percent in SFY 1980, and to 42 percent by SFY 1985.[16] In New Jersey, this proportion climbed from 48 percent in 1977 to 61 percent in 1979, dropped to 52 percent in 1980, and then jumped to 83 percent in both 1984 and 1985.[17] Subsidies are often used to transform the same foster home in which a child had been residing into an adoptive home. In Tennessee, the proportion of adoptive placements that were with foster parents rose from 32 percent in SFY 1982 to 42 percent in SFY 1985, the same proportion of placements given adoption subsidies in that year.[18] In New Jersey, the proportion of adoptive placements with foster parents rose from 35 percent in SFY 1974, to 53 percent in SFY 1980, to 68 percent in 1985.[19] The impact of adoption subsidies, and federal participation in such programs, is clear.

ADOPTION DISRUPTIONS

The permanency planning philosophy, because it has been largely directed at children already in foster care, and because it has spurred a push toward adoptions as well as toward returning children home, may lead to increasing numbers of displaced children remaining where they are (since many of the children being adopted are being adopted by their foster parents), but now with adoption papers in hand and parental rights terminated. Despite this push toward adoption of children out of the foster care system during the 1970s and 1980s, whereas previously public agencies merely served as agents for transferring children (mostly infants) to be adopted directly from their birth parents to the adoptive parents, or perhaps with a temporary stay of weeks or months in a foster home, the foster care population has been rising again. That is, it is rising despite the fact that roughly 20,000 children per year are technically being moved (although many are not physically moving) from one displacement system (foster care) to another (adoption).

From one perspective—the one that is inherent in the permanency planning philosophy—the children transferred from foster care to adoption will now have the benefit of a permanent and stable home. From another point of view, we might expect that children who are older and/or mentally or physically handicapped, as are many of the children currently being adopted through public agencies, will be more difficult to deal with and raise than the healthy infants who constituted a large part of public agency adoptions in a previous era. Indeed, from this point of view, we might wonder why an older handicapped child would prove any less difficult to deal with in an adoptive rather than a foster home. We might anticipate that just like many children who are returned home from foster care enter the system again, many of the new adopted children may also become recidivists back into the foster care system.

There are recent indications that this might be the case, or at least that adoption disruptions might be rising. An early study found adoption failure, limitedly defined as the return of a child to the agency at any time between adoptive placement and legal adoption (finalization of the adoption) to be related to the age of the child at the time of the adoptive placement (Kadushin & Seidl, 1971). The failure rate varied from a low of less than 1 percent for children placed when under two years old to a high of 9 percent for children who were six or older at the time. The author of another early study suggested that the increasing rate of prefinalization adoptive placement disruption in California up until 1973, when the rate was 7.6 percent of those placed, probably reflected the increasing number of older children being placed (Bass, 1975).

A more recent study of adoption disruptions in several parts of the country found an average disruption rate for 1984–85 of 13 percent (Benton et al., 1985, Ch. 2, p. 11). A study at an agency that specializes in "hard-to-place" children, of 255 children placed for adoption over a five-year period, reported that 66 disrupted, for a disruption rate of 26 percent (Boyne et al., 1982). This prefinalization disruption rate increased with age, from 7 percent for children 5 years old or under, to 15 percent for children 6–8, 25 percent for those 9–11, and 47 percent for those 12–17.

The period until finalization of an adoption is usually up to one to one-and-a-half years. Thus compared with the recent overall recidivism rate of children who enter foster care, it can be said at best that recent adoption disruption rates are somewhat lower. However, in a small-sample follow-up study of children who had been discharged from foster care during a five-year period, Fein et al. (1979) found that the disruption rate (31%) for those who had been discharged to adoptive homes was roughly the same as the recidivism rate (33%) for those who had been returned to their natural parents.

Another study, of a sample of 187 children who left foster care in Connecticut between July 1, 1979 and March 15, 1980, found that only one disruption had occurred 12 to 16 months after the date of adoptive placement, among a total of 52 adoptive placements, compared with disruptions in home placements in 32 percent of the cases of 62 children who had been returned to their biological homes (Fein et al., 1983). However, no child in the sample was over 14 years old, and while 71 percent of the children in the adoptive placements were under 6 years old, 60 percent of those returned to their biological homes were 6 years of age or older. Thus, the two groups were not comparable, and the adoptive placement group did not reflect, agewise at least, the characteristics of the population of children currently being placed for adoption from the foster care system nationally. Similarly, although Block and Libowitz (1983)—in following up 311 children between 9 and 33 months after discharge from foster care—found no disruptions among the 32 who were placed for adoption as compared with a 27 percent recidivism rate among the total, the children placed for adoption were not comparable to the others, nor were they typical. We are told that they were considerably younger than the rest of the sample, and that many more were Jewish, in an agency in which already 40 percent of the children in foster care are Jewish.

Indeed, limiting the concept of adoption disruption to prefinalization disruptions, as almost all studies have done, is rather peculiar, given that the idea behind permanency planning adoptions has been to give children permanent homes. We should like to know the rate of adoption disruption when defined as the separation of the child from the adoptive family, or the child's return to foster care, at any time from the date that the child was initially placed in the adoptive home until the date that the child has reached the age of majority. No such study has yet been done, but given our knowledge of such high rates of prefinalization disruptions in recent years as have been reported above, we can expect the results to be very depressing.

In a recent study, the investigators did attempt to identify adoptive placements that had been disrupted by 1986, among a large sample of placements made of children three years old or more, from the beginning of 1980 through the middle of 1984, in 13 California counties (Barth et al., 1988). Defining disruptions as placements that end with the return of the child to the adoptive agency, they report a 19 percent disruption rate for placements made in 1980, but a rather steady decline in the rate to 6 to 7 percent of those placements made in 1983 and 1984. While acknowledging that this decline may have resulted from the greater passage of time during which disruptions could occur in placements made in the earlier years, they discount this explanation for the following reason. Of the total of 94 disruptions identified, only 16 occurred after legalization of the adoption, and these were distributed proportionately among each year's placements. Thus, disruptions did not continue at a substantial rate after legalization.

However, in addition to 94 disrupted adoptions and the 832 that were not disrupted, outcomes could not be identified in 229 cases. These 229 cases had significantly more previous adoptions per child than the remaining sample, a factor that is known to be related to an increased probability of disruption of the current placement. Furthermore, they had proportionately more cases in which parental rights had already been terminated. The latter difference raises the possibility that these cases belong disproportionately to the earlier years. What I am pointing to is a possible undercount of postlegalization disruptions, in addition to a likely underestimate of the disruption rates for all years' placements, which the investigators themselves acknowledge. In fact, in this study, cases in which the child was no longer living with the adoptive parents but was not returned to the agency were not counted as disruptions. Yet this outcome can be considered a disruption from the parents' and child's perspectives, and might be more likely to occur after legalization (because the agency is more out of the picture than before) and hence disproportionately more in earlier years' placements.

Be that as it may, this study found that overall, according to its definition of disruption, the disruption rate increased with age, from 8 percent for children 3–9 years old, to 21 percent for children aged 10–17. Even for children as young as 9–11, the rate was 17 percent. Moreover, disruptions were significantly more likely among children with behavioral problems, although not so among those with a physical disability or medical condition.

Some adoption experts have given impressionistic estimates of disruption rates that have ranged from 20 to 70 percent for recent years, with the higher part of the range applying to older children with special problems (*Child Protection Report*, 1984). Presumably, they were using an expanded definition of disruption to include postfinalization separations. More studies, using an expanded definition, are needed to give us a better grasp of the scope of the problem of adoption disruptions than we now have.

SUMMARY EVALUATION OF PERMANENCY PLANNING

Evaluated in terms of outcomes, the permanency planning movement, by shortening the median length of continuous time that children spend in foster care and thereby increasing the rate of exit from foster care, has reduced the size (one-day count) of the foster care population, when compared with that population in the mid-1970s. However, together with the child abuse crusade, it has turned the foster care system into a huge "revolving door" in which high numbers of children enter and leave foster care each year. The high numbers of children who experience foster care for some part of each year may not be much lower now than in the mid-1970s.

Permanency planning also has halted the decline in public agency adoptions, by changing the characteristics of children being adopted through public agencies. These children are increasingly older, non-white, and handicapped. At the same time, adoption disruption rates of public agency adoptions have increased, and these rises have been directly related to the increasing proportions of children placed for adoption who are older and mentally handicapped, although not to color or race. Indeed, it can be argued from the data already available that if full investigations of the full scope of adoption disruptions were to be performed, which they have not been as yet, we might reasonably expect to find that the disruption rates have reached intolerable levels by any standard.

We have seen that the permanency planning movement has not stopped the high rate of flow of children into foster care from their natural parents, and that recidivism-into-foster care rates are high for both children returned home from foster care, and children adopted out of foster care. Each year, thousands of children are being returned to foster care in this country from disrupted adoptions. These facts point to the simple conclusion that either that services to prevent initial foster care placement, as well as services to prepare families for the return of their children from foster care and to help adoptive parents to cope with their adopted children, are in sorely short supply in this country, or that the kinds of services currently being employed are ineffective.

In fact, we already know that not only is a relatively small "pot" of money devoted to the child welfare system in this country, but that the lion's share of the total child welfare budget continues to go for foster care. Even the portion going for adoption subsidies, while still relatively small, is increasing rapidly. In FY 1988, under the AACWA of 1980, 77 percent of the federal funding for foster care, adoption assistance, and child welfare services (which can be used for preventive services) combined went for foster care and adoption assistance combined, up from 67 percent in FY 1981 (see table in Children's Defense Fund, 1988, p. 216). Thus, money for preventive services continues to be sorely lacking. Yet even if the budgetary emphasis of the child welfare system could be shifted toward preventive services, would the services be effective?

We will take a brief look at this question of effectiveness shortly, at least in regard to services to the natural parents. But first, in preparation for this discussion, I wish to explore the complex relationship between poverty and adoption. The conclusion was drawn earlier that the reason for foster care placement is often that the natural parents, frequently due to poverty, do not have the resources to offset the impact of situational or personal problems, which themselves are often caused by poverty, and the agencies have failed to provide the needed supports. We have seen that the most predominant characteristic of parents whose children enter foster care, which has been regarded as a "temporary" arrangement, has been poverty. However, adoptions, important because they represent the ultimate form of parent-child separation, occur not only through the public child welfare system, but via other routes as well. What has been the general relationship between poverty and adoption?

POVERTY AND ADOPTION

Why would a mother relinquish her child for adoption? The answer to this question is complicated by the fact that, as we have seen, the sources of children for adoption have been changing. Little direct research, involving the interviewing of parents, exists concerning mothers in other countries who relinquish their children for foreign adoption, and the question might not even make sense in regard to mothers whose children have been more or less taken from them and sent on a convoluted route through foster care into adoption under the name of child protection and permanency planning.

Most such direct research that exists pertains to mothers who relinquished infants for domestic adoption before or during the 1960s and early 1970s, and many of the studies refer to white adolescent mothers who relinquished their children through private agencies. The factor that was found to be most strongly and consistently associated with relinquishment was the influence of the unwed mother's parents (see Pelton, 1987a, for a review of these studies). It would seem that the parents, and especially the mother, were the key transmitters, at least up through the 1960s and early 1970s, of the then-prevailing cultural values against unwed motherhood, and of the social stigmatization of that role.

These being the prevailing cultural values, social workers and other professionals at that time might have exerted influence in the same direction. In a questionnaire study of a narrow segment of relinquishers, those who were members of Concerned United Birthparents, a national organization formed in the 1970s, more than 300 respondents, the majority of whom apparently had relinquished during the 1960s, constituted the sample. The investigators found: "External factors, including family opposition, pressure from physicians or social workers, and financial constraints were cited by 69% of the sample as the primary reasons for surrender" (Deykin et al., 1984). A study of 22 mothers who had surrendered a child for adoption years earlier and known to the investigators through their psychotherapy practice, yielded this finding: "Most reported that social workers and counselors offered no options, (and) emphasized instead that others could provide better lives for their children . . ." (Millen & Roll, 1985).

It seems that, especially during the 1960s, the social conventions against illegitimate childbirth and single-parent motherhood were especially strong amongst the middle class, and many middle-class girls were threatened with being "cut off" from their embarrassed parents if they did not relinquish the child for adoption (see Pelton, 1987a). Not having anywhere else to turn, they succumbed to the influence of their parents and even internalized the prevailing social values against single parenthood. Thus, an interview study of parents who had relinquished a child for adoption years earlier revealed that two-thirds gave as the reason for relinquishment that they were unmarried and wanted the child to have a family (Pannor et al., 1978).

Current motives and factors related to adoption decisions among the smaller number of American mothers who relinquish infants for private agency and independent adoptions in the 1980s are not known, and this is a matter for further investigation. Currently, however, the majority of nonrelated adoptions are a combination of adoptions of children coming from the public agency foster care system, and foreign adoptions.

In country after country, of those previously mentioned that in recent years have supplied almost all of the foreign adoptions into the United States, several factors consistently keep cropping up that tend to lead to the relinquishment of children for adoption: poverty combined with rapid urbanization; lack of government assistance; and, somewhat less consistently, the social stigmatization of illegitimacy (see Pelton, 1987a, for a review).

From a study of South Korean parents whose children were adopted abroad (summarized by Kim, 1978), the researcher concluded that lack of financial capacity to raise the children was a major cause of relinquishment. However, it seems that this was one of several related factors, including the social stigmatization of illegitimacy and pressure from extended family members, that combined to restrict the mothers' alternatives (Kim, 1978). Indeed, such external factors probably served to cut off economic and social support, thus forcing the adoption decision.

If a South Korean mother is living in poverty, not much assistance is likely to come from the government. In 1981, less than 1 percent of the South Korean government budget went for all social welfare programs combined, and prior to that year, mothers with dependent children were ineligible for any government assistance, although it was established at that time that over 1 million children needed assistance (Alstein 1984).

Between 1945 and 1980, South Korea's urban population grew from 15 percent to 57 percent of the total population, mostly as a result of migration from rural areas (Seekins, 1982). The city of Seoul grew from under 1 million to more than 6 million during those years (Lee, 1980). Many commentators attribute to such change—in South Korea as well as other countries—the breakdown of stable extended family structures that were present in rural society, as people migrate to and fail to find jobs in the cities, or otherwise remain poor. Hence there is an increasing abandonment of children (e.g., Baig & Gopinath, 1976; Benet, 1976, pp. 121–22; Goriawalla, 1976; Joe, 1978; Kim, 1978; Goldschmidt, 1986).

In Colombia, street children roam the large cities (Joe, 1978; Goldschmidt, 1986). In Brazil, millions of abandoned and needy children are growing up in the city streets. Seven million Brazilian children have lost all or most links with their families. More than half of Brazilian children under the age of six years are undernourished. Family disintegration in Brazil is due to large-scale peasant migration from the impoverished northeast to urban slums in the south (Riding, 1985). Speaking of Latin America in general, Goldschmidt (1986) comments: "Because there is insufficient protection for mothers and too few measures to strengthen the family, women who are left on their own are often forced to abandon their children for economic reasons."

Indian commentators have likewise attributed the abandonment of children in their country to urbanization, together with lack of supportive services from the government to meet the needs brought about by the breakup of extended families (Baig & Gopinath, 1976; Sohoni, 1976). In India in 1971, 46 million of its 228 million children under 14 years were estimated to be living below the poverty level (Baig & Gopinath, 1976). In India, too, social stigmatization of the unmarried mother and the "illegitimate" child plays a role (Goriawalla, 1976; Kulkarni, 1976).

Relinquishment occurs when the poverty of rural areas is exchanged for the poverty of urban areas, where there is a concomitant severance of external sources of support for the mother and child. Relinquishment is also more likely to occur when unwed mothers are socially ostracized, because this again cuts off external sources of support.

In societies in which unwed motherhood is socially stigmatized, this stigmatization is likely to affect government welfare policy, so that public aid will not be extended to unwed mothers, leaving them in poverty and without support. In the United States, there was a time when "illegitimacy" was severely stigmatized. Young unwed mothers were threatened with isolation from their own parents if they did not relinquish their infants for adoption. They could have turned to public aid, and perhaps many did, because in the United States the stigmatization did not totally invade public policy (although locally established "suitable home" criteria that excluded "illegitimate" children were invoked for a time; see Bell, 1965). Perhaps the threatened cutoff of social support, ignorance of public aid, and the prospect of a greatly reduced material level of living were enough to frighten many young unwed mothers into relinquishing their children. They were not encouraged to understand that alternatives existed.

Although "illegitimate" births can certainly occur among middle-class women, poverty is related to "illegitimacy" in several ways. First, urban poverty creates the social conditions that cause births to be "illegitimate." Women who do not have their own resources are subject to the whims of men. If men, because of their own job instability, walk in and out of their lives without marrying them, then they are subject to "illegitimate" births. Second, where "illegitimacy" is stigmatized, it can cause poverty among young women by cutting them off from the financial support of their own parents and community. Third, where "illegitimacy" is stigmatized, it can cause the unavailability of public economic aid to unwed mothers, due to designation of such mothers as among the "unworthy poor" in social policy.

The most prevalent and general causes of relinquishment of children for adoption, then, are that the mother is or faces the prospect of living in poverty, is or faces the prospect of being cut off from previous family supports, and new sources of support are not available or not sought. In this general form, these principles apply equally as well to the American mothers who relinquished children for adoption back in the 1960s, as they do to foreign adoptions today.

No wonder, then, that the low number of Swedish children available for adoption has been attributed to relative lack of discrimination against women in the job market, the absence of stigmatization of the unmarried mother, and governmental economic and social supports for mothers (Benet, 1976, pp. 92–93). On the other hand, where poverty is found, due to sex discrimination or any other factors, and where supports are not available to offset it, the relinquishment of children is fostered.

On the one side are the pressures of poverty. On the other is the narrow range of alternatives imposed and structured by others, namely, support for the child only under condition that the mother allow the child to be permanently separated from her. The mother's response options are limited to watching her child starve, or relinquishing all rights to the child, never to see him or her again. In South Korea, as in other countries, the only recourse for some mothers was to abandon the child to an institution (Benet, 1976, pp. 124–25).

The clearest documentation of the flow of *domestically* adopted children from indigent parents to those who are economically better off is found in Israel. Data available on domestic adoptions for the period of 1970–77 in Israel indicate that 71 percent of the children adopted by nonrelatives were relinquished by Sephardi mothers, while most adoptive parents were Ashkenazi (Jaffe, 1982, pp. 202-3). The socioeconomic significance of this fact is that in 1975–76, 56 percent of the families in the lowest net-income decile in Israel were Sephardi Jews (i.e., of Asian and African background) while only 6 percent of families in the highest decile were Sephardi. In contrast, 70 percent of the families in the highest income decile were Ashkenazi (of European and American background), while only 11 percent of the families in the lowest decile were Ashkenazi (Jaffe, 1982, pp. 83–84).

What makes the situation in Israel especially interesting is that the Sephardi Jews tend to be of darker skin complexion than Ashkenazi Jews. The fact that the Sephardis, like the Ashkenazis, are Jews, apparently has overridden, in many cases, any reluctance to adopt due to darker skin. Blacks in American society have held a comparable economic position to that of Sephardis in Israeli Jewish society. Yet in the United States, for a variety of reasons, few black children had been adopted in the past. This fact contributed to a weak relationship between adoption and prior poverty of the natural mother in the United States. In Israel, however, the relationship between poverty and adoption has been clearly visible.

In capsule form, in Israeli society, we see a similar pattern of adoption flow that is going on in the world at large today in regard to foreign adoptions: from the disadvantaged to the advantaged. It was the dwindling of the supply of white infants for adoption in the United States and the European countries that led to a turn toward Third World countries, particularly in Asia and Latin America, for children to adopt. While this has necessitated looking to children of darker skin complexion (Oriental children and, in the case of Latin American countries, children of mixed European and Indian origin), very few children come from Africa. As we have seen, however, due to the permanency planning movement in the United States, increasing numbers of American black children are now being adopted.

The source of children for adoption through the permanency planning movement is foster care, and we know that most of the children in the foster care system were placed there from impoverished families. We have already alluded to studies in New Jersey indicating that in the 1980s, homelessness and inadequate housing have been frequent reasons for foster care placement, and that the families of a very large proportion of the children in placement had experienced homelessness or severe housing difficulties at some time (see Chapter 3). Such, then, are the circumstances of the pool of families and their children in foster care from which the permanency planning policy is currently extracting children for adoption. The direct link between poverty, adoption, and lack of preventive support is illustrated, for example, by the fact that in New York City in 1981, adoption was the discharge objective for 29 percent of the children for whom inadequate housing had been at least one of the reasons for placement in foster care, and for 32 percent of the children for whom inadequate finances had been one of the reasons.[20]

Throughout most of the twentieth century, the stated commitment of American child welfare policy has been to preserve families. The tone was set by the proclamation of the 1909 White House Conference on the Care of Dependent Children that children "should as a rule be kept with their parents, such aid being given as may be necessary to maintain suitable homes for the rearing of the children" and that "except in unusual circumstances, the home should not be broken up for reasons of poverty" (in Bremner, 1971, p. 365). This commitment has been reinforced by the "reasonable efforts" clause of the AACWA of 1980.

When homelessness and poverty figure so prominently among the exceptions to the rule, we must wonder whether the policy cannot be more diligently implemented. Ironically, as we have seen, the permanency planning provisions of the AACWA have given a boost to the most extreme form of severance of parental ties for many children. This might not be a cause for concern if we could be confident that all reasonable efforts are being made to prevent the separation of children from parents in the first instance.

Surely, once children have been broken from their families for whatever faults or shortcomings of their country's economy or social system, or of their government's provisions for those in need, there is nothing inhumane about others taking it upon themselves to care for such children. But the humane response of individual adoptive parents to children in need of care is preceded by an inhumane collective response to the needs of destitute families that first denies them necessary resources, and then offers only an extreme alternative. At present, the entire public and professional discourse on adoption is marked by a glaring unconcern with the "front end" of the institution of adoption, with the parents who give birth to the children, and the circumstances that cause them to relinquish their children.

The humane care given to adopted children by adoptive parents comes after the fact that reasonable efforts were not made to prevent the need for separating children from their natural parents—whether we speak of children being adopted from foreign countries, or children being adopted within our own country out of the foster care system.

Collectively, efforts must be redoubled to implement the stated child welfare policy of preserving families. Insofar as possible, this policy should be applied to concern for children in foreign countries as well as in the United States. The child welfare establishment and social work profession should intensify their concerns with international child welfare and focus on the prevention of the need to separate children from parents. They have the obligation to research more fully the sources of foreign adoptions, and to contribute to the shaping of American foreign policy in a direction that includes a greater focus on child and family welfare in other countries.

POVERTY, FOSTER CARE, AND PREVENTION

Studies have indicated, not surprisingly, that the reunification of a child with his or her parents after the child has been placed in foster care is more difficult to achieve than the prevention of placement in the first instance (Frankel, 1988). Once the child is placed in foster care, a host of changed circumstances affecting the child, the parents, and their relationships tend to develop and impede successful reunification (Magura, 1981). Thus, if family preservation is to be achieved, it will be less likely done paradoxically through separation, than through prevention of placement in the first instance, which more closely conforms to the true meaning of preservation.

But how effective have preventive service programs proved to be in preventing the need for placement? Over the past 15 years or so, a number of preventive-service demonstration projects have been implemented. While they have been varied in their approaches, most have tried to provide clients with more intensive and/or comprehensive services than they ordinarily would have received. Several of these projects have reported considerable success. For example, the Comprehensive Emergency Services model implemented in Nashville included emergency caregiver and emergency homemaker services, and an around-the-clock emergency intake that enabled swift delivery of such services to families in crisis situations. An approximately 50 percent reduction was reported in the number of children who entered foster care in Nashville during the year preceding the inception of the program, compared with the number who entered during the first year of the program (Burt & Balyeat, 1977).

The New York State Preventive Services Project operated in several localities in the state and provided a wide array of services. Chief among them, in addition to counseling, were financial assistance, medical services, and help with housing. Family life education, education in home management and nutrition, remedial education, recreational services, vocational services, and homemaker services were also provided to a greater extent than ordinarily would have been received. The project was limited to "high-risk" families in which it was considered that a child was likely to have been placed in foster care within the next six months. Within the project, cases were randomly assigned to the experimental preventive services group, or to the control group in which they would be subject to ordinary agency procedures. Six months after the original one-year intake period of the project, it was found that only 8 percent of the children in the experimental group had entered foster care, as opposed to 23 percent of the children in the control group (Jones et al., 1976).

Although other programs have also reported seemingly impressive results, methodological shortcomings in the evaluations of most of these projects do not permit a conclusive verdict on effectiveness (see

Magura, 1981; Stein, 1985; and Frankel, 1988, for critical reviews). For example, most projects did not include control groups (the New York State Preventive Services Project was an exception), thus ruling out the possibility of assessing effectiveness with any certainty. The fact that there are still other programs that have been tried, whose initial findings did not point to any promise of success, does not negate the promise that some programs have already shown, nor the possibility that new ones will yet be developed. The evidence to date permits the conclusion that some preventive service programs developed thus far show signs of effectiveness, but that further evaluative research will be necessary before any definitive conclusions can be drawn. How much time, energy, and resources we will wish to invest in the search for effective prevention will reflect, of course, the extent of our society's commitment, as well as the child welfare establishment's commitment, to the goal of family preservation.

A follow-up evaluation of the New York State Preventive Services Project was performed five years after the initial year of the project (Jones, 1985). By that time, 34 percent of the children in the experimental group were found to have entered foster care, as opposed to 46 percent of the children in the control group. Thus, while the difference was statistically significant, the results were more modest than at the time of the previous evaluation, especially in that such a high percentage of the children in the experimental group had eventually entered foster care. However, many of the experimental group children who entered foster care did so long after their cases had been closed in the preventive unit, and very few cases (including those in which children had not been placed) were ever reopened in the preventive unit after having been closed there.

If we are to limit our child welfare services to crisis-oriented, ameliorative services of a secondary prevention nature aimed merely at preventing foster care placement (as the services in the programs referred to here essentially are), then it should not be surprising that one "fix" of such services—even if applied for an average of one-and-a-half years, which at least is the average length of time that cases remained open in the New York project—does not necessarily last for several years after. I am not arguing against the provision of crisis-oriented, prevention-of-placement services (I am in favor of them), but we must expect that when we go this route, additional reapplications will be necessary as the families in question drift from crisis to crisis.

Indeed, the establishment of a simple and inexpensive statewide emergency cash fund within New Jersey's state child welfare agency was shown to have obvious links, when looked at on a case-by-case basis, to the immediate prevention of harm to children as well as the immediate prevention of the need for foster care placement (Pelton & Fuccello, 1978). Individual cash grants prevented eviction, turned utilities on, and provided for the emergency purchase of food. Moreover, the start of a decline in the number of children entering foster care in New Jersey coincided with the initiation of the fund in the beginning of 1978, and an acceleration of the decline during 1980 and 1981 in the number of children *in* foster care coincided with the increased availability and use of money in the fund (Pelton, 1982a). Of course, we could expect that an emergency grant would have only temporarily and minimally interrupted the flow of stresses of poverty, and that additional grants or other services at later irregular intervals would have been needed to continue to stave off harm and placement.

As stated before, it is largely poor children who populate the foster care system. In her 1967 paper on foster care, after reviewing some of the evidence on the high incidence of poverty among families whose children are placed in foster care, Bernice Boehm (1970, p. 222) wrote:

It is more than half a century since the tenet was first enunciated that "no child should be separated from his family for reasons of poverty alone." It is unforgivable that in more than half a century this basic principle, to which there is such strong commitment, has not been implemented. It may be true that in many instances we do not place for poverty alone, because poverty seldom comes "alone."

Now, more than three-quarters of a century have elapsed, and Boehm's statement still holds true. It is as though some minimal quota of children from poor families is still being sent into foster care, but for different stated reasons. Before the turn of the century, poverty itself would suffice as the reason, although there was the implicit assumption that poverty itself was an indication of the unfitness and immorality of the parents. Later, when poverty was identified as a force outside of parents, and it was held that children should not be removed for reasons of "poverty alone," it was incumbent upon the child removers to make separate "findings" of the unfitness and immorality of impoverished parents. In more recent times, the parents are not perceived as immoral, but as psychologically defective in some way. If poverty can no longer be located in the parents, then at least the effects of poverty on parents and children can be located there, and children would not be removed for "poverty alone." The behavioral effects of poverty would now call forth the attribution of motives and personality characteristics indicative of psychological deficiencies. Thus, the reasons would be couched in the modern benevolent language of psychology, but the results would be the same: The victims of poverty would be blamed, and the children would be removed.

The number of related children under the age of 18 years living in families below the poverty level, as well as the poverty rate for such children, for selected years from 1960 to 1982, are shown in Table 1 in Chapter 1 (U.S. Bureau of the Census, 1982, p. 21). The poverty rates for children are also plotted in Figure 2 in Chapter 1. It can be seen that the child placement rate bears no apparent relationship to the poverty rate. For example, during the period of 1960–75, the poverty rate declined and then rose, but the child placement rate rose throughout.

On the other hand, we must keep in mind that the children *in* foster care, by and large, come from families living in poverty. Indeed, it is somewhat misleading to calculate placement rates based on the total child population of the nation, since the "pool" from which foster children are drawn more closely corresponds to the smaller "pool" of children who live below the poverty level. Poverty placement rates (i.e., the number of children in foster care per every 100 children living with their own families below the poverty level) for selected years from 1961 to 1983 are presented in Table 1 and plotted in Figure 2 (in Chapter 1). We see that trends in the poverty placement rate parallel those in the original placement rate, although at far higher levels. If foster care population estimates could be taken at face value, we would be able to say that in the 1980s, about two children reside in foster care for every 100 children residing with their own families below the poverty level.

When AFDC recipient families on the caseload of New Jersey's state child welfare agency for alleged abuse and neglect were compared with AFDC families not known to that agency, the former were found to be the poorest of the poor (Wolock & Horowitz, 1979). It is possible that the "pool" from which foster care children are drawn is even smaller than the one we have just indicated: They may be drawn from an underclass of families most deeply submerged below the poverty level. This might explain why the fivefold increase in the number of children covered by AFDC benefits between 1955 and 1975 did not serve to stem the rise in the placement rate ("Current Operating Statistics," 1985, p. 74). That is, foster children might largely come from a harder-core subset of impoverished families who have always availed themselves of AFDC support.

We may conclude that the child placement rate is not related to the poverty rate, but rather to how our society has treated or dealt with the children of families living in poverty, and especially of those most deeply submerged in poverty. There has always been a sufficient "pool" of impoverished families available to supply large numbers of children to the foster care system. The crucial variable affecting child placement rates has been the nature of the social interventions engaged in by society, not the fluctuating size of the poverty population. One hesitates to say that the crucial factor has been "social policy" in regard to child welfare, for the stated policy through much of this century has been to strengthen and preserve families. Rather, we must look to the social programs implemented, sometimes in the name of that policy, and often misguidedly, which have reflected deep-rooted attitudes toward poor people and toward approaches needed for the protection of children.

In recent years, perhaps a cyclical pattern has been set in motion in which periodic concerns over child protection will push up the foster care placement rate, until alarm is again expressed over the rising foster care population. The perception of the value of child abuse prevention as seemingly in conflict with the value of separating as few children as possible is, however, only a product of particular conceptions of child abuse, based on the psychodynamic medical model of child abuse originated by C. Henry Kempe and his colleagues back in the early 1960s. The abiding and prevalent inclination in our society to seek the causes of harm to poor children in the supposed personality deficits of their parents, whether couched in terms of moralistic or psychological shortcomings, rather than in socioeconomic conditions and forces, will continue to create imagined conflicts between child protection and family preservation.

Under these dynamics, we may expect no sustained reduction in the child placement rate below recent levels. Child welfare officials will continue to respond merely to the immediacy of events, such as a rise in the foster care population, without any significant reform occurring. This pessimistic conclusion is premised on the belief that the social awareness of our society that does indeed find expression in many of its social policies is nonetheless underlain by a deep-seated suspicion of the poor, and that this suspicion will continue to guide the manner in which our programs are carried out and, in effect, the way we deal with the poor.

NOTES

1. Immigration and Naturalization Service, Statistical Analysis Branch, Table IMM 2.5. Immigrant orphans admitted to the United States by country or region of birth: Fiscal years 1981–85 (hereafter referred to as Table IMM 2.5).

2. Immigration and Naturalization Service, Table IMM 2.5.

3. Immigration and Naturalization Service, Table IMM 2.5.

4. Immigration and Naturalization Service, Table IMM 2.5.

5. Adoption placement statistics for 1963–85 for New Jersey were provided (in the form of tables) to the author by Mary Lou Sweeney, Supervisor of the Central Office Adoption Unit, New Jersey Division of Youth and Family Services, Trenton, New Jersey (hereafter referred to as Adoption placement statistics for 1963–85 for New Jersey).

6. Adoption placement statistics for 1963–85 for New Jersey.

7. Annual adoption placement statistical reports for state fiscal years 1970–85 for Tennessee were provided to the author by Joyce N. Harris, Program Manager, Adoptions, Tennessee Department of Human Services, Nashville, Tennessee (hereafter referred to as Annual adoption placement statistical reports for 1970–85 for Tennessee).

8. Adoption placement statistics for 1963–85 for New Jersey.

9. Adoption placement statistics for 1963–85 for New Jersey.

10. Adoption placement statistics for 1963–85 for New Jersey.

11. Annual adoption placement statistical reports for 1970–85 for Tennessee.

12. Adoption placement statistics for 1963–85 for New Jersey.

13. Annual adoption placement statistical reports for 1970–85 for Tennessee.

14. Adoption placement statistics for 1963–85 for New Jersey.

15. Adoption placement statistics for 1963–85 for New Jersey.

16. Annual adoption placement statistical reports for 1970–85 for Tennessee.

17. Adoption placement statistics for 1963–85 for New Jersey.

18. Annual adoption placement statistical reports for 1970–85 for Tennessee.

19. Adoption placement statistics for 1963–85 for New Jersey.

20. CWIS/CCRS Special Report Series, New York City, Series A, Status date 3/31/81, p. 6, Table 13 and pp. 36–37, Table 34.

5

An Analysis of the Dual Role
Structure of the Child Welfare System

In this book, I have documented the trends in the foster care population from 1910 until recent years using the best available data and have shown that the foster care population in proportion to the total child population in this country is no less now than it was near the beginning of this century (see Table 1 and Figure 2 in Chapter 1).

In retrospect, it can be argued that child removal has survived as a major strategy in regard to child welfare problems among poor people in this country despite a long-standing policy of family preservation; that there has been a persisting discrepancy between policy and reality despite the best intentions of child welfare professionals and advocates; and that the child welfare system has proved itself to be incapable of implementing the child welfare policy first enunciated at the beginning of this century.

I will propose here that a key factor in this failure has been the dual role structure of the system, due to the incompatibility of the investigative/coercive/child removal role and the helping/supportive/family preservation role of that structure. I will review this dual role historically, examine its dynamics, and maintain that it is dysfunctional from the point of view of preserving families and protecting children.

THE STAFF SIZE HYPOTHESIS AND THE DUAL ROLE

If the dual role were conducive to the implementation of a family preservation strategy, we might expect to find that when more resources are put into the child welfare system and staff size is increased—allowing intervention into a greater number of cases—then the greater amount of family preservation work would lead to declines in the foster care population. On the other hand, if the dual role were somehow inherently obstructive to policy, inclined toward child rescue responses, then we might expect increased staff size to lead to increased rates of foster care placement. There is evidence that the latter has been the reality. In the next chapter, I will propose a restructuring of the child welfare system to eliminate the dual role.

As we saw in Chapter 1, by the turn of the twentieth century, child rescue work in regard to dependent, neglected, and abused children was being carried out by private agencies. Prominent among them were the Societies for the Prevention of Cruelty to Children, or SPCCs, scores of which had been formed around the country beginning in the 1870s. By the 1910s and 1920s, the juvenile courts had become the primary child welfare agencies. Although a move toward more specialized public child welfare agencies had begun as early as the 1910s, it was the Social Security Act of 1935 that paved the way for their future development. It was not until the 1950s that state public child welfare agencies as we know them today began to appreciably grow and expand.

Through these changes in administrative structure for child welfare services, the functional structure in this century, at least, remained constant: The agency would both investigate the family and try to help it. This dual role structure, whether vested in one and the same worker, as it was in the probation officer of the juvenile courts, or in different workers within the same agency, characterizes public child welfare agencies at the present time.

The dual role in casework with families dates back at least as far as the 1870s, when the Charity Organization Societies began to be formed in this country. They deployed paid agents and volunteer friendly visitors to the homes of poor people who had applied for relief or who had been reported to the agencies. The primary role of the paid agent was to investigate the application or report to determine whether or not the client was "worthy" of services or relief, and that of the friendly visitor was to offer advice, friendship, and moral exhortation. Although the roles sometimes overlapped, with the paid agent taking on some of the functions of the friendly visitor and vice versa, there is no doubt that the agency itself, if not the individual agents and visitors themselves, had a dual role: to investigate and to help (Hancock & Pelton, 1989).

Investigation, ideally, was to include a study of the entire history, character, and resources of the whole family, and a gathering of information from every available source, including the children, relatives, physicians, school teachers, truant officers, and the police, all for the purpose of helping (Birtwell, 1895). Given the facts that the Charity Organization Societies, especially in their early days, were notorious for being very stingy in their relief-giving and for having a tendency to perceive poor people as "unworthy," the statement of Mary Richmond, a Charity Organization administrator and the mother of modern social casework, that "we should never cease repeating that we investigate applicants not to find them out, but to find out how to help them" (Richmond, 1900), has a ring of too much protestation about it. And although the Charity Organization Society movement is regarded as one of the precursors of the social work profession, there is a real question as to whether, more precisely, it was the paid agent or the friendly visitor who was the true forerunner of the modern social worker, whose work not infrequently involves a combination of investigatory and helping roles (Hancock & Pelton, 1989).

As we have seen, child rescue was a major strategy for dealing with dependent and neglected children during the nineteenth century. No bones were made about it then. It was widely believed that dependent and neglected children should be saved from the "bad" influence of their parents, whose poverty was seen as due to their own immorality. The SPCCs acted in a quasi-legal capacity, as an arm of the courts, and tended to focus on child removal. They served case-finding and investigatory functions for the courts (Giovannoni & Becerra, 1979, pp. 47, 59, 66). Yet, gradually being influenced by the new family preservation policies of the twentieth century, they also began to profess to try to help families stay together, thus taking on a dual role.

Paralleling the development of the SPCCs, children's home societies and aid societies also proliferated at the turn of the century, and they often circumvented the courts in their child-placing activities (Tiffin, 1982, p. 104). Moreover, as Giovannoni & Becerra (1979, p.

64) state: "The 'friendly visitors' judgment about parental fitness and the denial of aid could be just as effective as the SPCC in stimulating the removal of children, albeit without the legal and criminal sanctions."

During the 1910s and 1920s, all types of agencies involved in casefinding—private relief agencies, children's home and aid societies, and SPCCs—as well as the juvenile courts themselves (to which many of the cases were brought and that would investigate and make decisions on the cases) gradually came to embrace, in rhetoric at least, the family preservation philosophy enunciated at the 1909 White House Conference.

It is ironic, then, that despite this new emphasis on family preservation, the child placement rate in the United States actually *increased* between 1910 and 1933 (Pelton, 1987b). This increase occurred despite the fact that, beginning with Illinois in 1911, 40 states had passed mother's pension laws by 1920 (Abbott & Breckinridge, 1921, p. 5), and the express intent of these laws was to avert the breakup of families for reasons of poverty alone, by giving financial aid, to "deserving" mothers at least, so as to allow them to keep their children (Thompson, 1919, p. 11).

The probation officer of the juvenile court, according to the new court's advocates, was to be "a friend to the child and the family, going into the home, studying the surroundings, and remedying detrimental influences" (Tiffin, 1982, p. 222). As one historian has noted, while this "rehabilitation was supposedly carried out through a relationship of trust and understanding, it is obvious that coercion was part of the probation officer's armory." The chief probation officer in the Chicago Juvenile Court "could advise probation officers to enter a family almost as one member of it and immediately follow this by urging them to use threats if parents refused to cooperate" (Tiffin, 1982, p. 225).

The family preservation strategy afforded the opportunity to "more closely monitor children," and "sanctioned rather than challenged the state's intrusion into the relations between parents and children" (Katz, 1986, p. 129). "Entering families as helpers or friends, probation officers backed up their advice with the authority of the state. No more than the agents of charity organization could they separate friendship from power" (Katz, 1986, p. 136).

Under the dysfunctional dynamics of the dual role, it is not surprising to find that the increase in the foster care population from

1910 on was paralleled by the growth of probation officer staff in juvenile courts, as well as the proliferation of SPCCs and other agencies and societies involved in child welfare.

It appears that under the policies of family preservation and not removing children for poverty alone, increasing numbers of dependent children were being redefined as neglected children. Given long-standing inclinations to find fault with impoverished parents and to use child removal as a "solution" to their problems, the investigative role was incompatible with a family preservation role when the two roles were placed within the same individual or under the same administrative roof. Investigation would soon take on a psychodiagnostic coloration, making the dual role appear more benign (Hancock & Pelton, 1989), and the child placement rate continued to rise.

As suggested in Chapter 1, the subsequent decline in the child placement rate, from the mid-1930s until about the mid-1950s, paralleled a contraction of agencies and decline in personnel due to the Depression and World War II. This was a period of transition to specialized public child welfare agencies, but these new programs did not begin to expand appreciably until the 1950s.

The new public child welfare agencies continued the dual role of their predecessors. Child-placing activities continued amidst the rhetoric of family preservation (Rosenthal, 1983, pp. 351–52). Thus, increased money available to hire more employees simply meant that more placements would be made. Again, in the 1950s and early 1960s, as in an earlier part of this century, rises in the rate of child placement coincided with increases in the staff available to investigate families and to do the rescuing.

There was a veritable explosion in the child placement rate from the early 1960s until the 1975–77 period. It may have been due, in part, to the "discovery" of child abuse by C. Henry Kempe and his colleagues in the early 1960s (Kempe et al., 1962). As it happened, social services spending increased enormously in our country during this period, and a good deal of it went for child welfare.

Once again, under the dynamics of the dual role structure, an increase in staff led to an increase in child removal, despite a strong bias, in policy, at least, toward prevention and family preservation. The child abuse crusade provided the reports to be investigated and the rationale for child removal; the resources that became available provided for more caseworkers to be hired who could investigate more reports and remove more children. The rationale of child abuse and neglect cloaked the fact, under a myth that child abuse and neglect are not related to economic class, that the children being removed were, as such children have always been, among the poorest children in our society (Pelton, 1978a).

In recent years, there has been a break in this link between changes in staff size and changes in the size of the foster care population. There was indeed a decline in the child placement rate between 1977 and 1982, and this decline is attributable to conscious efforts on the part of child welfare agencies to decrease the size of the foster care population by getting children out of foster care more quickly (Pelton, 1987b). But the number of children *entering* foster care did not decline; in fact, more children entered foster care in FY 1983 than in FY 1982, and the foster care population was on the rise again by FY 1983 (Tatara et al., 1985, p. 39). It can be concluded, then, that there is a continuing failure to deal with the "front end" of the foster care system, namely, prevention of foster care placement in the first instance. Indeed, the foster care population, in proportion to the total child population in this country, was no lower in 1983 than it was in 1910 (Pelton, 1987b). It has been argued here that a key factor in this failure has been the dual role structure of the child welfare system. Due to the inherent inability of the dual role to serve a policy of family preservation, policy continues to be discrepant with reality.

Gordon (1988, p. 4) has argued that from about 1880 on, it has been the women's rights movement that has been most responsible for mobilizing action against family violence. She claims that "concern with family violence grew when feminism was strong and ebbed when feminism was weak." Although she acknowledges that agencies' responses to family violence have often been antifeminist, she views agency responses as being particularly antifeminist (by emphasizing child neglect and defining it as a female crime) during periods (particularly 1920 to 1960) when the feminist movement was dormant (Gordon, 1988, pp. 4, 289–99).

Although family violence can certainly be seen as a feminist issue, it can be argued that an issue even worthier of feminist concern has been the removal of children from their parents under the guise of various forms of child abuse and neglect. Indeed, it is surprising how seldom child removal has been construed as a feminist issue, and how little attention has been paid to it as such. It has been, after all, most often the mothers from whom the children have been taken. Moreover, it has been impoverished women who have been most frequently accused of some form of "immoral" behavior (often defined in terms of a double standard of behavior for men and women), or who have been denied necessary supports to maintain their families, and then have had their children removed. In addition, it is mostly women who have been implicated in "neglect" cases, the most prevalent form of alleged child maltreatment. In 1986, for example, a woman was the alleged perpetrator in 70 percent of all child neglect reports nationwide (AHA, 1988). Single-female-headed families were involved in 51 percent of all neglect reports (AHA, 1988). Although men were implicated in 47 percent of all maltreatment reports combined (AHA, 1988), it is very often the mother from whom the child is eventually taken because the father has long since been gone from the household, and this circumstance has not changed from 1880 to the present time.

Even during periods in which child abuse was emphasized over child neglect in rhetoric, such as from the 1960s on, neglect cases predominated in numbers over abuse cases in terms of actual interventions. The important variable in terms of the rate of child removal has been the growth or decline of agencies' capacities to make child welfare interventions. Thus, ironically, if the rises and declines of feminism have truly been responsible for the waxing and waning of concern with family violence, as Gordon (1988) suggests, then the feminist movement has also contributed to increases in the rate of child removal. As we have seen, it was the child abuse crusade during the 1960s that led to the greatest rise in the foster care population. If the child abuse crusade grew in part due to the rising feminist movement at that time, then the feminist movement indirectly contributed to the increased rate of child removal, even though this result was obviously contrary to its intentions. But if this were so, then it is only attributable to the staff size hypothesis and the dysfunctional dynamics of the dual role. That is, under these dynamics, concern for family violence leading to increased child welfare staff would result unfortunately in increased child rescue as opposed to family preservation work.

THE DYNAMICS OF THE DUAL ROLE

Let us now examine this dual role more closely. In most child protection cases, it is the investigative regulator/coercive role with which the parents are first confronted. School or hospital authorities, the public welfare agency, other government agencies, relatives, and in many cases an anonymous neighbor, files the initial complaint, and it is the caseworker's task, on behalf of the public child welfare agency, to investigate that complaint. Not only is the agency charged with the responsibility of investigating suspected child abuse and neglect, but it is vested with considerable power to initiate proceedings to remove a child from the home of his or her parents, and in fact has used this power in many cases in the past. In most cases, the parents are aware that the investigation might result in removal of the child. In most cases, also, the parents do not want to give up the child. Thus the nature of the parent-agency interaction, right from the beginning, can best be characterized as one of social conflict: The will of the suspected parents to keep their child is in opposition to the potential threat represented by the agency through its responsibility to investigate suspected child abuse and neglect and its power to obtain the removal of children from their homes.

Yet the agency is also charged with the task of attempting to help to preserve families, by offering treatment and services. These dual functions constitute different modes of influence, each of which tends to obstruct the other at certain points of intervention. They entail a juxtaposition of persuasion and coercion, assistance and control, advocacy for and advocacy against, and firmnesss and conciliation, which might often work at odds with each other. Dual role conflict arises when actions taken in pursuit of one objective, stemming from one role, interfere with the realization of other objectives stemming from the other role. Dual role conflict occurs both at the agency level and at that of the individual caseworker. Dual role conflict, together with the conflict dynamics of parent-agency interaction engendered by the investigatory/coercive role, presents several inherent difficulties for both the investigative and helping tasks, or a mutual interference.

First, the caseworker's attempt to form a positive, trusting, and cooperative relationship with the parents for the purpose of helping might inhibit her or him from asking investigative questions that might be offensive to the parents. The worker represents the agency, and whether or not the same worker will continue to handle the case after the initial investigation, this worker is aware that his or her initial actions may set the tone for the longer-term relationship between the agency and parent. The desire to form a positive relationship might also inhibit the worker from taking the child for a medical examination when severe child abuse is suspected, from questioning neighbors for fear of antagonizing the parents, and for similar reasons, from making unannounced home visits, which for obvious reasons, would be preferable to announced visits for investigative purposes. Furthermore, the attempt to form a positive relationship may inhibit the worker from being firm with the parents, and optimally clear and explicit with them as to the purpose of the investigation, the agency's mandate and policies, the realities of the present situation, the obligations of the parents, the agency's possible actions, and the possible consequences. In addition, a confusion of helping and investigative roles can easily blur the reality that a police-type action is taking place, and that therefore the parents' procedural rights vis-à-vis the agency should be clearly explained to them if the investigative role is to be carried out properly.

This confusion of roles might, in part, be responsible for such findings as those of my Mercer County study (Pelton, 1977a), which indicated that many parents who had had children in placement did not even have clear conceptions of why the agency had sought the placement of their children to begin with, and that many had faulty or vague conceptions of when and under what conditions their children would be returned.

Indeed, it seemed that information about such matters had not been clearly articulated to the parents in the first place. The fact is that many parents are not given a clear understanding of what standards they may be violating, what actions they must perform in order to prevent child removal, what the agency regards as their responsibilities or, if the child is in foster care, exactly what conditions they must meet in order to have the child returned. This situation can only generate uncertainty and confusion on the part of parents who must deal with the agency. As Mandell (1973) has said: ". . . social workers empowered to investigate neglect complaints are often vague and ambiguous in their dealings with 'neglectful' parents and 'neglected' children. This increases parents' anxiety and works against an honest relationship between parents and social workers."

Second, and conversely, asking investigative questions of the parents, questioning the neighbors, taking the child for a medical examination, and making unannounced home visits might antagonize the parents and harm the development of a positive and trusting relationship. Moreover, removing a child from the home against the parents' wishes may engender hostility that will mitigate against being able to work effectively with the parents toward the goal of returning the child. Also, the investigatory/coercive role of the agency severely limits parents' self-referrals for services, out of their fear of becoming targets of investigation and coercion. Most importantly, the child welfare agency's mandate to investigate child abuse and neglect complaints lodged against the parents isolates the agency's responsibility toward the child from its responsibility toward the family as a whole, including the parents. This investigatory role leaves the parents with no advocate, and inhibits efforts of the agency to become an advocate of services for the family.

Finally, the conflict dynamics of parent-agency interaction engendered by the investigatory/coercive role promotes the formation of inaccurate negative perceptions of the parents, which, in turn, can lead to inappropriate actions and the delivery of inappropriate services on the part of the agency.

There is ample research evidence to show that there is a pervasive tendency among people in general to attribute the causes of others' behavior to personality characteristics more than to situational factors (see reviews by Ross, 1977; Wills, 1978). Moreover, we have already seen in Chapter 2 how the influence of the psychodynamic medical model in child welfare has encouraged the tendency to emphasize the role of personality factors in child welfare problems, while minimizing the importance of the socioeconomic context in which these problems arise. But another process influencing the personality traits attributed to parents in abuse and neglect cases derives from the fact that the attributions are based on observations of parents made while they are involved in a *conflict situation* with a child welfare agency.

Because of the conflict nature of the parent-agency interaction, it would not be surprising to find the parent suspected of child maltreatment to be hostile toward the agency and suspicious of its intent. In her study of child abuse and neglect case records, Young (1964, p. 127) said of the reaction of severely abusing parents to caseworkers: "Suspicious, secretive, hostile, they did not discuss anything personal if they could avoid it." She also found that they "did not like to have people talk to their children when they were not present" (1964, p. 65). Through omission of any discussion of the possibility that these observations are the product of the agency-parent conflict, the implication is left that they represent pervasive characteristics of abusing parents. "This suspiciousness seemed to be common among parents like these" (1964, p. 65). In their psychiatric study of abusing parents, Steele and Pollock (1968) found "evidences of suspiciousness, distrust, and feeling victimized, but in only one case were they significant enough to be classified as truly paranoid." The implication here is that the personalities of these parents *do* approach the paranoid, and that their fears are irrational.

It has often been reported that abusing and neglectful parents resist medical help for their children. Of severely neglecting parents, Young (1964, p. 27) said: "If a child was ill, they were more likely to seek a remedy from the drugstore than to take him to a hospital or clinic." She found that: "Three quarters of the severely abusing families failed . . . to secure medical care for their children" (1964, p. 65). These reports, as do those by caseworkers, often convey the contemptuous implication: How can parents be so unbelievably cruel? Young (1964, p. 65) stated that "even" when a social agency sought to provide medical care, severely abusing parents refused permission. She found in such parents "a tendency to ridicule the importance of physical injuries or illness in children. It was, in fact, a way of saying that their lives were not very important" (1964, p. 66).

Such attributions of negative attitudes and paranoid tendencies are misleading and unfair since no consideration is given to the context of conflict. Young (1964, p. 65) said of abusing parents: "Their suspicious attitude implied that any offers of help for the children were an excuse to indict them." Polansky and coworkers (1972, p. 17) suggest the "unreasonableness" of parents who resist medical care for their children. Nowhere is acknowledgement made of the fact that medical care in suspected abuse and neglect cases does include medical examinations, one of whose purposes is to find any evidence of parental abuse and neglect. Physicians, in fact, *do* act as informers, and the seemingly benign "offers of help" from the agency are thus realistically suspect. Given the often-expressed strong desire of these parents to keep their children, their fears are quite *reasonable*, and do not necessarily reflect either paranoid tendencies or low regard for the welfare of their children.

We have here an instance of the self-fulfilling prophecy, often observed by social psychologists to be a property of a conflict situation: Party A's suspicions lead it to take certain actions toward Party B; these actions elicit certain reactions from Party B, which, in turn, are taken as confirmation of the original suspicions. In this case, the initial referral of the family to the agency arouses suspicion of abuse and/or neglect, as do the observations of the caseworker. Whatever else might be the purposes of attempting to have the child medically examined, the attempt is also part of the investigation that has been launched. The parent's resistance to this action is then taken as further evidence of our emerging image of cruel and negligent parents.

Several social psychologists have noted the recurrent rise in conflicts of the diabolical enemy image and the virtuous self-image. "The adversary comes to be viewed as unmitigatingly evil, cruel, unfair, unjust, and out for its own interests at the expense of others. By contrast, we (view) ourselves as kind, virtuous, just, and humane" (Pelton, 1974, p. 195).

The agency's virtuous image of itself is shared by social scientists who study child abuse and neglect, as well as by its own representatives. In their book about child neglect, Polansky and coworkers (1972, pp. 16–17) state that "immature mothers often have poor judgment about others. They may trust charlatans blithely, while suspecting those dedicated to their welfare." The agency proclaims itself to be wholly beneficent. It regards itself as a benevolent protector of citizens and altruistic dispenser of social services. It regards separating children from their parent only as "a last resort," although it does so in many instances.

The diabolical enemy image is similarly evident. "The caseworker who faces abusing parents cannot be afraid of them. They exploit fear and deride weakness. . . . [T]hey can be very convincing and remarkably adept at saying what the caseworker wants to hear. . . . Primarily they respect power, and there is substantial indication that they evaluate any caseworker, or anyone else for that matter, in terms of how much power over them that person has. It is a frightening personality type. . . ." (Young, 1964, p. 95).

In conflict, dehumanization is a well-known phenomenon. Regarding the adversary as subhuman is a step beyond the enemy image already discussed. Abusing and neglecting parents have not been described as subhuman, but in the more sophisticated special vocabulary of psychiatry and psychology, as psychopathological in some way, as we saw in Chapter 2.

The parent-agency interaction represents a particular *type* of conflict, one in which—far from the two parties having more or less equal power—one party is vastly more powerful than the other. The agency has on its side the police, the law, and public opinion. The caseworker has emergency legal power to remove a child from his home on the spot. When the agency goes to court, it has an abundance of reports containing interpretations according to its own lights, the product of vast investigatory resources. The case record is embellished with reports in sophisticated language with opinion freely expressed, from school officials, psychologists, and representatives of other agencies. It contains the results of psychological tests and medical examinations, not to mention the allegations of neighbors. Confronted with this array of power, the parent may see little means at her disposal, except to "clam up," become secretive, pull her shades down, avoid the social worker and neighbors, prevent her children from talking with anyone, lie, and "say what the caseworker wants to hear." (Of course, from the agency's point of view, there are "rational" responses that the parent can make, but this view does not take into account the parent's perceptual reality, and the threat and fear that she feels.)

No one is advocate for the allegedly abusive or neglectful parent. No one investigates and collects evidence on *her* behalf, presents *her* side of the story, presents results of psychological tests commissioned by *her* rather than the government, nor bears witness on *her* behalf. Pathologized by psychiatrists and victimized through her interaction with the agency, she stands isolated and alone. As cruel as her actions toward her children might appear, she deserves an advocate. Her hostility, which has often been observed within the context of her interaction with the agency, may stem at least in part from her utter powerlessness within the situation, having no advocate.

Until now, I have been speaking mainly of the images that the agency holds of itself and of the parent. But students of social conflict have noted the phenomenon of mirror images (Pelton, 1974, p. 195). By this they mean that *each* party views itself as virtuous and the other as evil.

Unfortunately, there is a lack of information as to the nature of the images that the parent holds. Studies of abusive and negligent

parents more often concern psychological factors thought to characterize such parents, the prior psychological development of the
parents, and the sociological variables operating upon them, rather
than their subjective realities. Thus, the parent is studied as object
rather than as subject. Case records, too, contain more discussion
about the parents than they do reports of the parents' cognitive constructions of reality.

It would be important to learn, for example, whether abusive and
neglectful parents tend to regard the agency as "child-snatchers." It
does seem that many mothers are frightened by any mention of
foster care for their children and that they often voice the opinion
that their children are just about all they have in the world. These
factors may be the source of their often-observed hostility and suspiciousness in regard to the agency.

Likewise, it would be fruitful to explore the virtuous self-images
that these parents may hold. The mother who reacts to the agency
in the ways already described may view herself as attempting to "preserve the family and protect the child." In fact, it has been observed
that in social conflict each party believes itself to be upholding the
same values as the other party believes itself to be upholding (Pelton,
1974, pp. 2, 42).

In many cases in which a child has been put under foster care, the
caseworker later observes that the biological parent never visits and
has dropped all contact with the child. The belief system that representatives of the agency have already formed of abusive and negligent
parents directs them to interpret these new facts as further proof
that the mother, who was visibly hostile about giving her child up,
really did not have a strong love for, or attachment to, the child after
all. (See Pelton, 1974, pp. 42–52, for a discussion of the dynamics of
striving toward cognitive consistency.) An alternative interpretation
is that the mother, who in many cases is a person who has been victimized and defeated throughout her life, has now suffered the ultimate defeat. Dejected, despondent, and having lost all hope, she tries
to completely escape from her defeats or any reminders of them.

The deceptiveness, manipulativeness, distrust, and hostility claimed
in the literature to be personality characteristics of parents in child
protection cases (e.g., Young, 1964, pp. 64, 95, 127; Steele & Pollock, 1968; Polansky et al., 1972, pp. 16–17), and frequently by
caseworkers, very likely are situationally rather than dispositionally
determined. The behaviors observed might really reflect responses to

a conflict situation by the least powerful party to that conflict (Pelton, 1976). When we take into account the parents' subjective reality, part of which is the threat and fear they feel when confronted by the agency, we understand why they might react with hostility and suspicion, and we recognize that such reactions may be conflict-specific and not indicative of pervasive personality characteristics. Yet, based on such erroneous inferences and negative personality attributions, the agency may conclude, and often does, that the parents need "treatment" and will prescribe psychotherapy. When the parents "resist" or prove "uncooperative," the conclusion may be reached that their children must be removed. The focus on the person promoted by the conflict dynamics of the situation deflects attention from the larger day-to-day situational context of poverty in which most parents reported to the agency live.

A rapidly descending and accelerating spiral of distrust is difficult to stem once it originates from the initial source of conflict. The issue of harm or danger of harm to the child, the agency's only legitimate concern, easily spreads to the relationship between the parents and the agency's representatives. Thus, the parents' "uncooperativeness" might evoke punishment in the form of child removal. Indeed, it is difficult for any worker not to get drawn into the conflict dynamics. The worker, in a sense, has been "set up" by the dual role structure of the child welfare agency designed by others. Due to the conflict dynamics, the worker can easily become fixated on process, such as whether or not the parents are hostile to the agency or have "cooperated" with the agency by attending scheduled therapy sessions, rather than focusing on results, in terms of whether or not the risk of severe harm to the child has been reduced, regardless of whether or not the parents have "cooperated."

ATTEMPTS TO AMELIORATE THE DYSFUNCTION OF THE DUAL ROLE STRUCTURE

Research studies show that the types of services that child protection agencies most often have the resources to offer, and most frequently want to recommend, are those of a psychotherapeutic and educative nature, designed to change the person in some way, such as mental health services, instruction in money management, and parent education courses. On the other hand, the types of services that the parents on their caseloads most prefer to receive, are those of a concrete and supportive nature directed at altering the clients' situation, such as housing assistance, day care, and financial assistance (Sudia, 1981; Pelton, 1982b). These discrepancies in preferences between the agencies and parents reflect the fact that the caseworkers tend to attribute the causes of the families' problems to the parents' functioning, while the parents tend to attribute them to situational and environmental circumstances (Pelton, 1982b).

Although there is no *a priori* reason to accept one perspective as more valid than the other, there is considerable evidence that the great majority of families in child abuse and neglect cases live in poverty. In addition, there are reasonable theories and an abundance of case illustrations to suggest that the stresses of poverty and the conditions of poverty, such as health and safety hazards in the home, are often responsible for the harms and risks of harm to children that are seen in child protection cases (e.g., Pelton, 1977a, 1978a; Gil, 1970; Wolock & Horowitz, 1979; Horowitz & Wolock, 1981). On the other hand, it is likely that both economic and personal factors contribute to child maltreatment (Pelton, 1982b).

I have argued that very often the true reason for placement is that the family, frequently due to poverty, does not have the resources to offset the impact of situational or personal problems, which themselves are often caused by poverty, and the agencies have failed to provide the needed supports (Pelton, 1982b).

From this perspective, one can advocate for many modifications of the current child welfare system that might allow it to better fulfill its mission of protecting children while preserving families, that might minimize dual function problems, and that might improve its ability to respond to the needs of families reported to it.

It can be argued, as this author and many other advocates have, that public child welfare agencies must enhance their helping role by more fully developing a range of services to deliver (through direct service delivery, or coordination with other agencies) in significant quantity aimed at preventing the need for foster care placement, with a greater emphasis on concrete services than in the past. In light of scarce resources, this would require a shift in the budgetary emphasis of public child welfare agencies from foster care placement to prevention-of-placement services.

Ideally, it can be envisioned that the greater availability and use of preventive services by public child welfare agencies will reduce the need for child removal and push its coercive role to the background.

Through more effective development of the helper role, the coercive role will diminish in terms of need for implementation. Thus, also, the perceived threat of the coercive role to clients will become less salient. As the helper function thereby comes to the fore, it will play an increasingly greater role in shaping the image of the agency. It can even be envisioned that the greater development of attractive services of a preventive nature that clients say they want, in accordance with the research studies alluded to above, would increase self-referrals and reduce the "uncooperativeness" of clients, and reduce the need to exercise the investigative/coercive role. The resulting more limited or less frequent use of the coercive role will itself contribute to more self-referrals and preventive intervention, which will further reduce the coercive role. The enhanced helping image of the agency, in turn, will promote a spiral of trust whereby more self-referrals will be made, more people will be helped, and less coercive intervention will be needed.

In reality, long-standing and repeated attempts by child welfare advocates to shift the resources of public child welfare agencies from placement to preventive services have met with considerable budgetary intransigence. Large proportions of these budgets continue to be tied up in foster care placement functions. While one of the more recent attempts, the Adoption Assistance and Child Welfare Act of 1980, states that "reasonable efforts" will be made to prevent the need for child removal and provides fiscal incentives for the development of prevention-of-placement services, such efforts continue to be lacking. Further, it is not clear that the directives handed down through the courts in recent class action suits will succeed any better than the legislation in getting state and local governments to make such efforts.

Amidst these difficulties in trying to budge the budgets, this author as well as other advocates have also looked to cost-free approaches to at least minimizing dual role problems and narrowing the hitherto too-broad focus on placement and coercion. These have included new approaches to casework procedures and training.

Among the proposals offered have been that minimal child welfare standards should be developed that focus narrowly and specifically on severe harm and risk of severe harm to the child, under the assumption that society has the responsibility to prevent severe harm to children, but it has no right to coercively invade the privacy of the family beyond that point. Agency standards focused on severe harm would help to chart a course that would safeguard the family from arbitrary and overzealous intrusion on the part of the state while assuring some minimal level of care and safety to the child (Wald, 1976). Minimally, no child should be allowed to suffer, or be exposed to the risk of suffering, the following severe harms:

1. life-threatening injury;
2. severe impairment of physical, bodily, or behavioral functioning;
3. disfigurement;
4. severe emotional damage, evidenced by extreme and enduring anxiety, depression, or withdrawal;
5. severe cognitive damage, evidenced by extreme deficiencies in logical reasoning ability and/or learning ability; and
6. injuries that do not fall into any of the above categories but are extremely painful, either physically or emotionally, and occur frequently.

A special note regarding sexual abuse is in order here. Except in the rarest case, there is no immediate physical harm or risk thereof in sexual abuse incidents. Any immediate emotional damage might be difficult to detect, and any long-term effects may be due more to the victim's reactions to and internalization of the negative conceptions of adult-child sexual relationships shared by the society at large, rather than to the experience itself. For these reasons, it is difficult to justify intolerance of sexual relations with children on grounds of harm alone. According to Finkelhor (1979), sexual relations between adults and children are wrong because informed consent is lacking, since a child is not capable of giving such consent and does not have the freedom to say yes or no. A child cannot give informed consent because he or she lacks information about sex and sexual relationships that would allow him or her to make an informed decision, and the child is the far weaker party to a lopsided power relationship when an adult is the other party to that relationship. The wrong, as conceptualized by Finkelhor, is not contingent upon a harmful outcome. Indeed, according to this formulation, perhaps sexual abuse is best characterized as a form of child exploitation, and wrong or even criminal for that reason. Furthermore, it will be recalled from Chapter 2 that in most sexual abuse reports, the alleged perpetrator is someone other than a parent or stepparent. Indeed, the child is entirely unrelated to the alleged perpetrator in 35 percent of such reports (AHA, 1988). For all of the above reasons, I would suggest, as part of the proposal being presented here, that sexual abuse matters not be dealt with by public child welfare agencies. Rather, after developing standards to determine what types of incidents we consider serious enough to call sexual exploitation, such standards should be incorporated into law only, and the cases should be handled by law enforcement agencies and the courts only.

Continuing our discussion of the child welfare standards focused on severe harm described above, the state should not, and cannot effectively, use its investigative/regulatory/coercive function toward any semblance of a goal of optimal child care. If we were to attempt to hold parents to one or another conception of ideal or optimal care, we would incur a considerable risk, as we do currently, of imposing personal, class, and cultural biases upon others, of making arbitrary judgments of parents' life styles and personal characteristics, and of violating parents' rights. Besides, the state is in no position to offer optimal child care, as we have already seen in this book, and it could end up doing more harm than good to the child (Wald, 1975). We can agree, however, that society has the responsibility to prevent severe harm to children. This the state has the realistic capacity to do.

At present, there is the reality that in most cases white middle-class workers make judgments upon the child care of lower-class, often minority, families. The results for the children are disastrous when, as is still currently the case, these workers are encouraged to address themselves to parental life styles and presumed personality characteristics and personal deficits in making decisions on the use of coercion, rather than to the common concern of prevention of severe harm to the child, a value that transcends all class and racial lines.

It is important to note that the proposed standards do not utilize the terms abuse and neglect, and do not refer to parental characteristics, conduct, or fault, or to household conditions. The standards pertain to severe harm, no matter what the cause.

Coercive intervention would be *prohibited* in any case that does not fall below the minimal standards. On the other hand, coercive intervention would be used in only some of the cases that do fall below minimal standards, and even in such cases would be limited to child removal and medical examination and treatment. All other services would be administered on a *voluntary* basis.

The proposed process would work in the following manner in cases that fall below the standards. The standards would be clearly articulated to the parents, as well as the specific circumstances that might be causing the below-standards situation. The parents would be informed that the standards must be achieved in order that the family be out of danger of child removal. The agency would be obliged to offer specific services that address specified risks, on a *voluntary* acceptance basis, but the parents would be under no obligation to accept such services. Their only obligation is to come up to standards, with or without the agency's assistance.

Even if finally child removal must be contemplated, after all reasonable services have been offered to protect the child while preserving the family, a "least detrimental alternative" analysis would have to be performed. That is, the agency would be obliged to make the case, based on all available evidence of alternatives, taking into account the known facts about foster care placement in general, the particular placement to which the child in this particular case will be removed, the current risks in the natural home and the feasibility of other alternatives, that child removal in this instance will have a reasonable chance of least harming the child's welfare. Such placement should then be made through the court.

Thus, it is proposed that an *absolute* standard should take precedence over a relative standard. This absolute standard, the risk of severe harm to the child, should be a *minimal* standard forming a floor below which coercive action can be considered in the context of a least detrimental alternative analysis, but above which no coercive action can be contemplated. Narrow limits must be placed on the potential of government for coercive intervention, for reasons already discussed.

To repeat, the minimal standards, by focusing on severe harm itself or the risk thereof, make no reference to intention, motivation, personal characteristics of the parents, blame, or responsibility, or indeed to acts of abuse or neglect. The primary concern is to protect the child from severe harm, no matter what its origins. In many cases in which the child is in danger of severe harm, and in which child removal has been contemplated, the least detrimental alternative would prove to be, upon analysis, the remediation of certain poverty-related safety and health hazards existing in the household, or the offering of other concrete services.

It is the belief of this author that in many cases even in which risk of severe harm has existed, the child could have been protected through less disruptive and less detrimental alternatives than placement in foster care, if only public child welfare agencies would get down to the business of offering the more realistic services that their impoverished clients want and need. But in their psychologizing about poor people they overlook such simple and straightforward remedies as repairing the health and safety hazards of the home, and tend to blame one victim (the parent) and punish both victims (the parent and child).

The public child welfare agency would be concerned with finding the least detrimental alternative for preventing severe harm in the future, and not with abuse and neglect per se. The agency would contemplate coercive intervention only when the minimal standards have been violated, and the factors responsible for this situation have not been rectified. The position would be that the welfare of all children must meet the minimal standards. When they are not met, corrective steps would have to be taken that are the least disruptive to family life as possible. Any agency intervention must be clearly demonstrated to be, based on all available evidence of alternatives, the least detrimental alternative for protecting the child. The violation of minimal standards would constitute grounds for child removal, *provided that the conditions causing the violation have not been and cannot be remedied by other means.*

It has also been proposed that decision-making *guidelines* be developed for making decisions in reference to the standards (Pelton, 1977a). Such guidelines would aid in determining the presence of risk of severe harm as defined by the minimal standards, in the individual case, and in selecting the most appropriate services to offer on a voluntary acceptance basis. Some factors, such as abandonment of the child, or lack of shelter, practically insure the risk of severe harm. Other factors (pertaining to safety, sanitation, and even to certain characteristics of the parents) may present risk of severe harm to the child with varying degrees of frequency. Therefore the existence of risks of severe harm would have to be established in the individual case, and evidence would have to be gathered to identify the specific potential harms and to determine the specific factors that might be causing or contributing to the risks in the particular case.

Such factors as certain parental characteristics or conduct, or household conditions, which were excluded from our standards, become relevant only when there is reason to believe that one or another of these factors is specifically tied to risk of severe harm in a particular case, and when we are trying to determine what services to offer to reduce that risk. For example, the alcoholism of the parent by no means always causes risk of severe harm to the child. Evidence would have to be gathered in the particular case to show that the parent's behaviors are causing the risk of severe harm. Few alcoholic parents severely abuse their children. But if we found that the parent severely beats the child every time he or she drinks heavily, then dealing with the parent's alcoholism might become our top priority.

While the establishment of certain factors as the probable causes of risks of severe harm in a particular case would call for action, they would not, with few exceptions, call for child placement. Even the extreme case of a mother who has abandoned her child may not require placement. The mother may be found, and her actions may have resulted from panic due to utter poverty and depression due to having no place to live and no way to care for her child. Even *she* can be helped to preserve her family.

On one or another occasion over several years, various agencies, including the state child welfare agency, reported that Ms. M.'s household was "a shambles"; the floors were filthy and littered; the mother was "morally loose"; the beds were unmade and the bedding was urine-stained; the children were filthy and wearing wet underwear; piles of dirty clothing were in the corner of one room; dirty dishes were piled on the table and in the sink; there was no heat; there was no hot water and the children were nude; and the floors were "full" of excretion from the cat and dog.

During most of this period, no medical problems were noted. Then one child was hospitalized with pneumonia. A few months later, two of the children were reported to have severe rashes on their bodies, and the public health nurse said that one child appeared to be suffering from malnutrition. A few weeks later, however, the caseworker reported that the children appeared well nourished.

Several months later, after another referral was made by an anonymous caller, the children were placed in foster homes. Apparently, they were placed largely on the weight of accumulated reports over the years indicating a chronic state of disorder and filthiness in this household, although one child might have been suffering from a life-threatening respiratory infection at the time of placement.

The primary focus in this case should have been on the health status of the children rather than on "dirty dishes." For example, when one child "appeared" to be suffering from malnutrition, she should have been taken immediately for a medical examination to confirm or disprove this suspicion. If risk of harm could be established, then the caseworker should have tried to determine the specific conditions contributing to that risk, and then offered services to address those circumstances. In this case, no services appear to have been offered until the time of placement. There was more judging than helping. In this particular case, it can be contended that the fact that the children remained minimally healthy over the long run constituted strong evidence against a relationship between the filthy conditions and the risk of harm.

Eventually in this case there was a question of malnutrition and dangerous respiratory infections, although the answer was not well documented in the case record. Yet, over the years, no attempts were made to help Ms. M. to address the obviously dangerous condition of lack of heat, or to provide a homemaker or other service that might have helped this low-income mother to feed her children properly.

Ms. M.'s children were returned to her after three-and-a-half years and several foster home moves. It is not clear what was accomplished. The conditions that were set for return were that Ms. M. "work on" certain areas by, among other things, getting involved in the parent-school relationship and getting involved in "groups." Provisions so vague and so remotely related to any of the more important questions of need in this case should never have been set as conditions for anything. Services, if needed, addressing specifically identified dangerous factors in this case should have been offered *before* placement.

Many of the so-called "reasons" for placement commonly recorded in the past, such as "parents unable to cope," "inadequate housing," "parent's drug and alcohol abuse," "parent's physical illness," and "hospitalization" are not sufficient reason for placement. If it is indeed established that risk of severe harm exists, then good practice would address such questions as: What, exactly, is the parent unable to cope with, and how can we help her or him to cope with it? What is inadequate about the housing, and can we get it repaired? If not, how can we help the family to obtain other housing? How, precisely, is the parent's substance abuse resulting in harm to the child? If the mother is temporarily hospitalized, can we provide substitute care for the children within the home? Many children have been placed in foster care because the family did not have the resources to offset the impact of situational or personal problems and to overcome family crises without outside assistance. The proposed standards and guidelines would provide a sound framework for helping such families in a nonpunitive manner.

It has also been proposed that informational booklets should be developed that would be given to parents who come into contact with the agency. Such booklets would apprise parents of the minimal standards, their responsibilities as parents, the responsibilities of the agency to ensure that minimal standards are met and to provide appropriate services, and their procedural rights in dealing with the agency (Pelton, 1977a).

In addition, training approaches have been developed that instruct caseworkers in how to transform, insofar as possible, the initial conflict interaction with the parents into a cooperative relationship, thereby reducing the parents' fear, suspicion, and hostility; that advise caseworkers to ascertain and respect the parents' perspectives and to be honest with the parents at all times, clearly explaining to them their rights and responsibilities vis-à-vis the agency; and that instruct the workers in selecting services to offer that address specific risks of harm (e.g., Pelton & Bricker-Jenkins, 1988).

For example, this author has developed a "harm-oriented case management approach" for caseworkers to be trained in (Pelton & Bricker-Jenkins, 1988). The workers are instructed that a pattern of multiple causation often underlies child protection cases, and that the elimination of even just one element from the combination of causes often can prevent harm from occurring. They are told that their *main* task is not to place blame, but to take effective action to reduce the risk of harm, and that this can be done by assessing the combination of factors involved and deciding which one or several factors, if addressed, could defuse the dangerous situation. They are instructed to operate within a framework of minimal standards and decision-making guidelines, to establish that risk of harm exists, to identify the specific risks involved, and to determine the specific factors that may be causing or contributing to these risks. They are cautioned that malnutrition, for example, may be caused by the mother's ignorance of nutrition, inadequate financial income, or a host of other factors. One factor requires a different service than another, and so the probable causative and contributing factors must be carefully identified, lest inappropriate services be offered. Resources must be garnered that best *fit* the specific risks and factors identified, as a first priority.

The workers are also advised to seek common ground with the parents in identifying and focusing upon actual harms and risks of harm to the child in a nonaccusatory and nonblaming manner. We must seek to establish with the parents that we and they share a common goal—prevention of harm to the child—and that we can work together to achieve that goal. The workers are instructed to evaluate progress in a given case not in terms of process, but in terms of results, that is, in terms of the goal of elimination of specific risks of harm. Just because a parent has attended all scheduled therapy sessions and has cooperated with the caseworker in all ways does not necessarily mean that the risks have been reduced. On the other hand, it is possible that a parent has refused all services, and yet the dangers observed at the beginning of the case are now no longer present. It would be foolish, the workers are told, and dangerous for the child, for the caseworker to be obsessed with process while losing sight of the goal. The workers are also instructed in decision making and case management, and in developing case plans and case records that are consistent with the overall harm-oriented approach.

Admittedly, this overall approach is a "minimalist" one, but given public child welfare agencies' notorious dearth of resources and high caseloads, the crisis-orientation position into which they are forced, and the multiple-problem nature of the families that arrive at their doorstep after falling through all other "safety nets," the approach offered here—with its relatively modest and limited goals and its emphasis on a few specifics—is designed to make the caseworker's difficult job less confusing, and at least reasonable, manageable, and feasible, while allowing the achievement of limited but important results.

The measures enumerated in this section, as well as other measures, have been offered to make the dual role more workable, less confusing to both the workers and parents as well as the agency, less potentially capable of destroying clarity and honesty in worker-parent interactions, less potentially violative of parents' procedural rights, and better capable of allowing the worker to be firm in regard to the issue of preventing severe harm to the child, while being helpful and conciliatory toward the parents, eliciting their cooperation.

Some of the measures proposed have indeed been implemented in one form or another by various states within the past decade or so, together with some increased provision of concrete services. Several states have revised their laws concerning child abuse and neglect in the direction of being more specific, less "moralistic," and more narrowly focused on harm and danger of harm to the child. A few state child welfare agencies, for example, in Illinois and Rhode Island (Fandetti & Ohsberg, 1987), have developed some version of standards, decision-making guidelines, and risk assessment scales. The New Jersey child welfare agency has developed informational booklets that it distributes to parents with whom it comes in contact. Many public child welfare agencies have promoted a case management approach to casework practice and have expanded their training programs. In New Jersey, this author aided the public child welfare agency to institute a statewide emergency cash fund (mentioned in the previous chapter) to address concrete needs in child protection cases in order to prevent the need for placement. Cash grants to families from this fund have been used for the emergency purchase of food, the payment of rent, rental security deposits on new apartments, rent arrears, utilities payments, and the purchase of furniture such as cribs and beds (Pelton & Fuccello, 1978).

In order to overcome a "catch-22" of foster care (whereby the public child welfare agency will not return children home because the parents' apartment is inadequate, but the parents do not have the means to remedy the situation because the public assistance agency will not make AFDC payments until after the children are returned), this author formulated a return-from-placement amendment to the New Jersey Division of Public Welfare's Emergency Assistance regulations. This amendment, now on the books in New Jersey for several years, permits the Emergency Assistance program to be used to prepare the way for the return of children to their natural parents by enabling the parents to pay the security deposit and first month's rent on a new apartment before the children are returned. Just recently, New York State followed suit by passing legislation that would make a family with children in foster care eligible for up to $300 per month in rent subsidies for a maximum of three years, in cases in which inadequate housing is the only remaining barrier to returning the children to the natural parents (Barbanel, 1988).

In addition, all states have implemented case review systems for the periodic review of every child in foster care, as required by the AACWA of 1980. This act, through a complex system of fiscal incentives to states for improvements in the child welfare system, also called for case plans to be developed for every child in foster care and, as we have seen, for "reasonable efforts" to be made to prevent the need for placement and to make it possible for children already in foster care to be returned home. In fact, the regulations proposed under the act, which were suspended by the Reagan administration, had been excellent in specifying that preventive services include, at minimum, procedures and arrangements for access to available emergency financial assistance, as well as 24-hour emergency caretaker and homemaker services, day care, respite care, and crisis counseling; and that each state child welfare agency should develop guidelines to assist the worker to make appropriate case assessments, to determine appropriate services, and to determine when a child should be removed from the home while specifying the factors to be considered in making such a decision. The proposed regulations also included procedures for increasing the clarity of communication with parents, and for safeguarding the parents' procedural rights. In fact, these proposed regulations, now defunct, had incorporated a good deal of the suggestions made by this author and other critics of the child welfare system during the preceding years.

THE DUAL ROLE STRUCTURE
IS FUNDAMENTALLY FLAWED

While all of the efforts enumerated above that *have* been instituted, albeit in a patchwork fashion among the states, no doubt have been worthwhile in that they have benefited many families, foster care placement continues to be a dominant response in our country in regard to child welfare problems, and there has been no sustained reduction in the foster care population.

This situation cannot simply be blamed on the Reagan administration. This administration left the philosophy and goals of the AACWA of 1980 essentially intact (Burt & Pittman, 1985, p. 35). While it did attempt to reduce federal funding for child welfare programs, *overall* federal funding did not decline due to the opposition of Congress. Yet Congress' influence led to complex results. Federal funding that could be used for preventive services (Title IV B monies under the AACWA, and Title XX monies) declined slightly between FY 1981 and FY 1984, while federal funding for foster care and adoption assistance (Title IV E under the AACWA) increased substantially (Burt & Pittman, 1985, p. 35, Table 4). The AACWA of 1980 had provided for a cap to be placed on federal funding for foster care when federal funding for Title IV B child welfare services reached specified "trigger" levels. The idea was that as state child welfare agencies would begin to provide more preventive services, the need for foster care would decline. But because Title IV B monies declined slightly during the first Reagan administration, the cap on foster care spending was not triggered. Interestingly, when the Reagan administration sought to cap federal funds for foster care anyway, Congress blocked it (Burt & Pittman, 1985, p. 36).

Federal funding for child welfare services under Title IV B did increase during the second Reagan administration, from $165 million in FY 1984 to $239.4 million in FY 1988, although Title XX funding, a far larger source of money for child welfare, did not increase appreciably (Children's Defense Fund, 1988, p. 216). Federal funding for foster care under Title IV E, however, more than doubled from FY 1982 to FY 1988, from $321.6 million to $703.2 million, and federal funding for adoption assistance increased more than twenty-one-fold from $5 million in FY 1984 to $108 million in FY 1988 (Children's Defense Fund, 1988, p. 216). As already noted in the previous chapter, federal funding for foster care and adoption assistance combined, under the AACWA of 1980, increased as a proportion of federal funding for child welfare services (Title IV B), foster care, and adoption assistance combined, under that act, between FY 1981 and FY 1988, from 67 percent to 77 percent (Children's Defense Fund, 1988, p. 216). Incredibly, this proportion increased to 81 percent in FY 1989 under this "reform" act (*Child Protection Report*, 1989). A federal act under which more money, and increasingly more money, is pumped into placement rather than prevention-of-placement services can hardly be considered a reform.

Thus the AACWA failed, as have all efforts in the past, to shift the budgetary and operative emphases of child welfare agencies from child rescue to family preservation. Even if the Title IV E monies for foster care had been capped, there is no assurance that the foster care population would not have risen. As we saw in Chapter 2, much "social services" (eventually under Title XX) money has been used for foster care in the past. In the 1960s and 1970s, state child welfare agencies, as we saw in Chapter 3, circumvented the courts in many of their foster care placements, thereby not even bothering to collect AFDC-FC monies that could have been available to them, and the foster care rolls rose anyway. The important matter here is what the public child welfare agencies do with the money they already have. In state fiscal year 1988, for example, 76 percent of the service dollars spent by New Jersey's state child welfare agency by its district offices (on their caseloads) went for placement. There is some primary prevention that is already done by the states, in the form of social services such as day care, through Title XX monies, to individuals and families other than those on the public child welfare caseloads, but it is the children on these caseloads who are most in danger of placement. There is a substantial amount of money already in the child welfare system that can be potentially used for prevention-of-placement services, although it can always use more, but much of this money continues to be tied up in foster care, and we have still not gotten this system to shift its budgetary emphasis from placement to prevention.

This intransigence cannot be attributed to one or another presidential administration because it has persisted through all of them. I have already indicated that the foster care placement rate in this country is no lower today than it was near the beginning of this century. If I have done anything in this book, it is to show, by taking the long historical overview, that the problems of the child welfare system are largely endemic to that system and are not caused by one or another relatively brief political, social, or economic swing. No. There are apparently factors even more primary than external funding patterns that are affecting the operations of the child welfare system.

A major reason why foster care placement continues to be a predominant response to child welfare problems is that the dual role structure is *fundamentally* flawed, no matter how we might tinker with it to improve its functioning. One indication of the dysfunction of the dual role is that role conflict and role ambiguity have been identified as among the chief causes of the high rate of burnout and job turnover among child protection workers (Daley, 1979; Harrison, 1980; Jayaratne & Chess, 1984; Drews, 1980). In addition, dividing up the role among different units or caseworkers, as some agencies have done, may reduce burnout and turnover (Fandetti & Ohsberg, 1987), but does not resolve the issue, for it still leaves the *agency* with a dual role structure. The roles are still under the same administrative roof. The agency that investigates families with the outcome of placing many of their children away from home is the same agency that tries to preserve the home. These efforts are contradictory and compel the agency to choose between allocating scarce resources to foster care or to preventive services, with foster care winning out in the crisis atmosphere in which the agency operates. There is a question of contradictory operative goals, if not official goals, and contradictory agency tasks.

There is something fundamentally wrong with an approach that requires an agency to work at odds with itself. The caseworkers, along with the agency itself, are put in an untenable position in which they try to gain the parents' trust and cooperation in order to help the family at the same time that they are viewed by the family as a potential threat. Indeed, they do resort to coercion at the same time that they try to offer help.

In speaking about alternative ways to deal with a criminal, Mohandas Gandhi (1961, pp. 351–52) once said: "You cannot expect to touch his heart and win his confidence, if at the same time you are prepared to go to the police and inform against him. That would be a gross betrayal of trust. A reformer cannot afford to be an informer." In regard to dealing with parents suspected of child abuse and neglect, we are faced with the same basic truth. The same agency that investigates and threatens parents, that encourages informers to come to it, and that itself puts an emphasis on informing upon the parents to other agencies, cannot expect to fully gain the parents' trust nor be very successful at reform.

However, in the vast majority of child protection cases, we are not even confronted with criminal behavior. Moreover, in most cases, the parents do not stand in need of being "reformed." Impoverished and socially isolated, they need modifications in their situations and environments through the supply of additional specifiable resources and supports. These families need advocates.

Yet by adopting a reporting law strategy as discussed in Chapter 2, our nation, in effect, has encouraged an informer approach to child welfare problems. Such an approach can only increase hostility and suspicion on the part of parents that the child welfare system should be reaching. The presence of informers always generates suspicion, fear, and distrust. Parents with serious child welfare problems are likely to become more secretive and withdrawn than ever.

Each year, for many years now, as the reporting systems increased their efficiency in eliciting complaints from other public agencies and the general public, the number of reports of alleged child abuse and neglect in this country has climbed dramatically (AHA, 1987). In retrospect, it may not be unfair to suggest that the informer approach has contributed to the development of what can best be characterized as greatly expanded bureaucracies of investigators. Looking ahead, we may predict that the informer approach may result in a nation of informers, but that this unsavory end is not likely to solve the serious and widespread child welfare problems that do exist in our country.

Indeed, it can be legitimately claimed that our public child welfare agencies, as currently structured, and under the weight of an avalanche of reports, do more investigating than helping. But as helping agencies, these agencies have peculiar "eligibility" requirements for services if, in fact, only families reported for suspected child abuse and neglect will receive services. The most recently available reporting statistics indicate that currently about 2 million complaints of suspected child abuse and neglect flood American public child welfare agencies each year, and more than half of these reports are found to be unsubstantiated by caseworkers (AHA, 1988). It can be questioned whether the investigation of all of these complaints for the purpose of verifying child maltreatment, and the discarding of half of them (in some cases in which the report is unsubstantiated, the families may be offered services anyway, but these families receive a low priority in the distribution of what little services are available), is the most effective way to serve the children and families involved. Should not *all* families experiencing child welfare problems be helped, and must that help be delivered under suspicion that the problems have evolved from parental wrongdoing?

There are indeed many harms occurring to the children seen by our public child welfare agencies, and the desperate plight of the children and their families is real and not imagined. They face many dangers all around them. Our current system, fueled by an inclination to "investigate" parents to find "evidence" that they are to "blame" for the harms and dangers befalling their children, promotes the likelihood that child protection issues will be "resolved" through child removal rather than through the offer and delivery of services that will reduce the dangers and allow the family to be preserved.

The dual role structure creates a conflict between family preservation and child rescue. Reflected in the dual role is our ambivalence toward poor people in trouble. We do not know whether to help them or to punish them. Our policies tug in one direction, but the actual administration and day-to-day tactics, underlain and guided by a deep-seated suspicion of the poor, go in another. When both aims, those of helping and punishing, are under the same auspices, the balance inevitably tips toward punishment, given our "blaming the victim" impulses that underlie our behavior, despite stated public policy.

In criticizing the home visiting practices of the Charity Organization Societies at the beginning of this century, Jane Addams—one of the leaders of the other precursor of the social work profession, the settlement house movement—stated: "The only really popular charity is that of the visiting nurses, who by virtue of their professional training render services which may easily be interpreted into sympathy and kindness, ministering as they do to obvious needs which do not require investigation" (Addams, 1915, p. 26). In fact, it was the settlement house workers who, by living among the poor and ascertaining their subjective realities, were able to adopt a more purely helping role than their counterparts in the Charity Organization Societies. While the Charity Organization workers tended to view their clients as responsible for their own poverty and in need of moral rehabilitation, the settlement house workers regarded their clients as normal individuals coping with a dysfunctional environment. Seeing their clients' problems in this light, they were able to become advocates for them, and saw no need to investigate or threaten them.

Our current emphasis in child welfare on the constructs of "abuse" and "neglect" promotes an inclination to blame parents for their child welfare problems and a disinclination to appreciate the ways in which the circumstances of poverty might give rise to these problems. Such an emphasis has sustained the dysfunctional dominance of the investigatory/coercive role in public child welfare agencies, to the detriment of its family preservation role.

Social workers are trained to help. That is what they go into the profession to do, and that is what they do best. The investigative role is not even taught in social work schools. We must create an agency structure in which social workers, when going into the home in child welfare cases, can say "I'm here to help," and truly mean it, with the resources to do it, and without the nagging overtones of role conflict and role ambiguity. The discovery, investigation, and judgment of individual culpability and wrongdoing is another matter entirely, and is the province of law enforcement agencies and the courts. By entangling the two distinctly different roles, we have not only diminished our ability to deal firmly and effectively with true unlawful behavior, but have tied the hands of social workers in their efforts to effectively serve the child welfare policy of family preservation enunciated at the beginning of this century.

6

Restructuring the Public Child Welfare System

The catalog of harms associated with child protection cases known to public child welfare agencies is staggering. In my Mercer County, New Jersey study (Pelton, 1977a), in a sample of just 60 cases (each case corresponding to one child), there were seven known deaths among these children's siblings. The suspected causes included pneumonia (three children), being hit by a truck, asphyxiation, Sudden Infant Death Syndrome, and one boy being shot by his brother while both were living in a foster home. Only one of these deaths (asphyxiation) was alleged to be due to abuse or neglect. Among the 60 children and their siblings, there were four who had fallen out of a second-story window. Two such children sustained cerebral concussions and another, a broken leg. One child, as a result of hanging on to a moving car, suffered a fractured skull, a brain contusion and hemorrhage, and paralysis of an arm. Illnesses included pneumonia, iron-deficiency anemia, bronchitis, asthma, and respiratory infections. Other harms included malnutrition, dehydration, extreme retardation in physical development, "failure to thrive," severe emotional disturbance, brain damage, diabetic coma, unconsciousness due to drinking vodka, burns, and hot water scalding. Injuries from beatings included black-and-blue marks, bruises, welts, strap marks, lacerations, scars, black eyes, and internal bleeding. One infant was severely battered, sustaining over a period of time two skull fractures, a fractured spine, and an untreated broken arm.

What are we to make of this? Besides the actual harms, risks of harms included inadequate food in the house, lack of heat, the use of the stove for heating the home, fires in the home, and other health and safety hazards, with the dangers often heightened by children being left alone in the home without adult supervision. But not all of the harms listed above can be attributed to abusive behavior or negligence. Many harms and risks of harms occur to children known to child welfare agencies, but the causes are varied and multiple. As previously noted, less than 3 percent of reported *abuse and neglect incidents* involve major physical injury (AHA 1988). Elmer (1981), comparing abused, accidentally traumatized, and nontraumatized children from the lower social classes, found poverty to be the most powerful adverse influence upon their development, and chronic illness to be prevalent among these children, with little difference between the groups. Horowitz and Wolock (1981) found severe health problems to be prevalent among children in child maltreatment cases, but most prevalent among the poorest of the poor families. Severe physical illness also abounded among the caretakers of these children, yet was most prevalent among the parents living in the most deprived circumstances (Horowitz & Wolock, 1981). Elmer (1981) noted that the mothers of both the abused and accidentally traumatized children, although fairly young, suffered from conditions that included high blood pressure, chronic arthritis, diabetes, and renal disease.

Child abuse and neglect do not occur in isolation from other family problems. They are often embedded in a context of poverty and poverty-related problems, such as unemployment, poor education, alcoholism, extreme family disorganization, chaotic living conditions, household safety and health hazards, and other physical, psychological, and social problems. Many of the families seem to exist in the the twilight fringe of civilized society, beset by almost every problem of living imaginable, while generating others. At the same time that we become outraged at the parents as perpetrators of child harm, we find indications that they, too, are victims.

Indeed, these impoverished families are submerged in such a morass of living problems, and the negative consequences to their children are the result of such an entanglement of multiple causes and situations, that it is often difficult to determine if the dangers to the children are attributable to lapses in parental responsibility or societal responsibility, and the question of who is to blame becomes a moot one. Too often, the assessment of blame has been the basis for social responses toward poor people. The conditions of poverty pose greater dangers to children than does child maltreatment. Elmer (1981, p. 212) questions "the singular, intense focus on abuse without regard for the matrix in which it flourishes." She comments: "It is paradoxical that families suspected of abuse or neglect should receive a ticket to comprehensive social services while other families, equally in need, go unserved because they express their difficulties in ways that do not include the maltreatment of their children" (1981, p. 213).

Unfortunately, in the past and present, "comprehensive services" have frequently amounted to foster care placement and little else. Moreover, impoverished families in need of services have been caught up in the net of child protection under questionable allegations of abuse or neglect that have led to the removal of their children to foster care.

NONINTENTIONAL INJURIES

Accidental injuries are the leading cause of death for every age category of children from one through 19 years old in the United States (National Center for Health Statistics, 1988, Table 1–25). In 1985, 16,200 children from birth through 19 years of age died from accidental injury (National Center for Health Statistics, 1988, Table 1–25). Accidental injuries accounted for almost half of all deaths to children from one through 19 years old in 1985 (National Center for Health Statistics, 1988, Table 1–25). Of course, far greater numbers of children suffer severe injuries, other than death, due to accidents.

About half of the accidental deaths to children from birth through 19 years old in 1985 occurred while they were occupants in motor vehicles, but other leading accidental causes were drowning, pedestrian–motor-vehicle accidents, and fire, in that order. Additional causes included firearms accidents, bicycle–motor-vehicle accidents, suffocation, falls, and poisoning, respectively (National Center for Health Statistics, 1988, Tables 1–25 and 5–2).

The leading causes of accidental fatalities in the home in 1984 among children from birth through the age of 14 were fires, suffocation, drowning, firearms accidents, poisoning, and falls, in that order (National Safety Council, 1985, pp. 80–81). In fact, most of the fatalities in this age group due to each of these factors except drowning occurred in the home (National Safety Council, 1985, pp. 6–7, 80–81). These factors along with electric shock, burns and scalds, animal hazards (such as the presence of rats in the home), toys, and other common objects in the home cause tens of thousands of severe injuries to children each year in the homes in our country.

There is much evidence that heightened risk of severe accidental injury to children is strongly related to low socioeconomic status (see also Rivara & Mueller, 1987; Roberts & Brooks, 1987). The physical home and neighborhood environments of children from low-income families are far more dangerous than others. For example, studies have confirmed that the rate of residential fires as well as the fatality rate from such fires is far greater in low-income areas than it is in middle-class neighborhoods (Gunther, 1981; Mierley & Baker, 1983).

In a study of all deaths to children aged 8 days through 17 years old in Maine during the years 1976 through 1980, it was found that children from low-income families (defined as children who were participants in the Medicaid, Food Stamps, and/or AFDC programs at the time of death) had died, from all causes combined, at a rate that was 3.14 times greater than children from other families (Nersesian et al., 1985). Their rate of accidental death was 2.58 times greater than that of children from other families. In terms of more specific accidental causes, children from low-income families were five times more likely to die from fire and four times more likely to die from drowning than other children. They were even more than twice as likely to die from motor-vehicle accidents.

In a study of AFDC-recipient families in northern New Jersey, about one-third of the families interviewed reported having seen rats in their homes (Wolock & Horowitz, 1979). The highest rat complaint areas in New York City in one recent year, according to that city's Department of Health, were the lowest-income neighborhoods, such as East Harlem and Bedford-Stuyvesant.

Other hazards are also greatly elevated for children in low-income families, often due to the deteriorated state of the housing in which many such families live. Lead poisoning, for example, is a particular danger in old tenement buildings built prior to 1950, in which the walls may have layers of paint with high lead content underneath newer coats of paint. Each year, tens of thousands of young children are found to be poisoned by lead, which can lead to mental retardation and even death (Center for Disease Control, 1975). In New York City, where there were 1,538 cases of lead poisoning in children in 1981, almost 90 percent of which involved children between the ages of one and five years old, just the Bedford-Stuyvesant, Bushwick, and Fort Greene sections of Brooklyn accounted for 43 percent of the entire city's cases.

Children's falls from windows are also related to socioeconomic status. In New York City, it was found that about half of all such falls occurred in families receiving AFDC (Spiegel & Lindaman, 1977). In 1971, 23 fall-related deaths of children 15 years or younger occurred in the South Bronx alone, one of the poorest sections of the city (Spiegel & Lindaman, 1977).

Even pedestrian injuries to children due to pedestrian–motor-vehicle accidents are more likely to be suffered by children in low socioeconomic areas. In a study of all pedestrian injuries to children from birth through the age of 14 years reported to the police in Memphis in 1982, it was found that those census tracts in which such injuries had occurred had lower household incomes, more children living in female-headed households, more families living below the poverty level, greater household crowding, and greater housing-unit density than census tracts in which no such injuries had occurred (Rivara & Barber, 1985).

It is highly probable that the risks of severe accidental injuries and fatalities are even further concentrated among children known to public child welfare agencies (Pelton, 1983).

In their study of window falls in New York City, Spiegel and Lindaman (1977) found that a majority of the falls occurred in single-parent households and that, in 1975, about 60 percent of the families in which the falls occurred had been receiving social services. They note: "There is an association between incidence of falls and the economically disadvantaged since it is this group that resides in substandard housing under circumstances of overcrowding, family instability, tensions, and pressures."

In their evaluative study of a program to reduce foster care placement, Jones et al. (1976) found that the caseworker perceived inadequate housing to be one of the problems that had created the need for protective service in 36 percent of the cases. Young (1971), in her study of child abuse and neglect, found that few of the families lived in adequate housing. She stated: "Poorly heated, vermin-ridden, in various states of disrepair, much of the housing was a hazard to health."

Such conditions are likely to increase the chances of accidents occurring. Poor physical health, and mental and emotional handicaps, of both children and parents, are factors that are heavily concentrated among families on child protection caseloads and may increase the risks of accidents. Inadequate supervision may also increase the risks. Patterns of financial hardship, physical and emotional problems of both children and parents, large single-parent families, inadequate housing, family tensions, social isolation, and inadequate supervision of children add up to tremendous stress on the parents and great risk of accident for the children.

The conditions of poverty not only impose stresses on the parents, but more directly, provide an extremely dangerous environment for children to be raised in. The context of inadequate housing drastically beset with health and safety hazards multiples the dangers of inadequate supervision.

In many cases, the parent is actually forced to take a dangerous course of action because of impoverished living conditions and lack of child-care supports and other alternatives. A low-income mother may be forced to leave her children alone, or in the care of the oldest child, who may not be old enough or mature enough to handle such responsibility. While she is away, a small child may crawl up onto the window sill and fall out, or wander into other dangers. If a fire starts, there is no adult to rescue the child. When the impoverished mother leaves her children unsupervised, or even in the next room, the deficiencies of poor housing may lead to severe injury, and sometimes death.

We can see now why the dangers of accidental injury to children in their own homes may be much greater in child welfare cases than for other children, and why accidental injury may really be the chief danger in child welfare cases. Accidents are multiply caused and often occur within a context of other family problems.

First, as we have seen, there are the increased health and safety hazards associated with the deteriorated housing of low-income families. While even middle-class physical home environments contain certain hazards, these are multiplied and intensified for children living in poverty. Broken stairs, chipping lead-based paint on walls, rats, and frayed electrical wiring are just a few of the heightened physical dangers.

Secondly, inadequate supervision is present in many child welfare cases. This can take the form of a mother actually leaving her children alone, for whatever reason, but can also be due to the mental, emotional, or physical problems of the nonabsent mother. These latter factors may inhibit her ability to provide adequate supervision without help. Inadequate supervision is a major contributing factor to injuries to children.

Thirdly, there are the physical, mental, and emotional handicaps of the children themselves in many child welfare cases. These handicaps increase the risks of injury, and handicapped children require *greater* supervision than other children. A physically handicapped child might have more trouble than other children in escaping from a fire in the home. A retarded child may be more likely to inadvertently overturn a pot of boiling water, or perhaps ingest a poisonous substance. A child with emotional problems might set fires in the home.

We come to this conclusion: What one observer might call an "accident," another might call "neglect." As discussed previously, patterns of multiple causation often underlie child protection cases and the risk of harm to children. Thus, looking at the harm through the lens of "neglect," shaped by the research and literature on child abuse and neglect, we may find reason to blame the parents; but looking at the harm through this different lens, that of "accident," shaped by the research and literature on children's injuries, we may find reason to change aspects of the environment. Indeed, it is recognized by those who study nonintentional injuries that the most effective way to reduce injuries is not through attempts to change individual behavior, but through environmental changes and passive measures (such as guardrails on windows) (e.g., Dershewitz & Williamson, 1977; Pless & Arsenault, 1987; Wilson & Baker, 1987).

What used to be called "accidents" are now termed "nonintentional injuries" in the relevant research literature (Roberts & Brooks, 1987). The latter term perhaps best describes the injuries that occur in child protection cases, for even those who wish to ascribe some of the injuries that do occur to "neglect," in the child abuse and neglect literature, admit that the injuries are nonintentional.

Every nonintentional injury is multiply caused. Prevention is a matter of analyzing the causal patterns and removing or reducing as many causal elements as possible. The removal of even one causal element might prevent or reduce the risk of the injury occurring. A five-year-old child falls from a second-story window. If the child had not been left alone in the room, this incident might not have occurred. If the child had been instructed not to play near open windows, this incident might not have happened. If guardrails had been installed on the windows, this incident would not have occurred.

Any of the several measures might have reduced the risk of harm to this child. And so it is for all hazards. However, some *types* of preventive measures are more effective than others. In the above example, assistance from the child welfare worker (who might have previously noted the hazard) in securing window guardrails might have most assuredly prevented the incident.

It serves no purpose, after the fact of a window fall, to say that the mother *should* not have left the children alone and was instructed not to do so. The placing of blame will not erase the fact that the child was severely injured. Besides, the mother's behavior might have been due to a lack of alternatives. In any event, the modification of human behavior is not easy, although for the reduction of some hazards, it will be the only strategy available, and it has been found to have positive effects (Wilson & Baker, 1987; Pless & Arsenault, 1987). For example, it is only possible to verbally instruct parents never to leave a bathroom while a small child is in the bathtub. A child welfare worker can only advise parents to keep small children away from the stove, or to teach their children not to use electrical equipment around water. Attempts at modification of both the children's and parent's behavior are necessary.

But the relative safety of children in child welfare cases is often a matter of alternatives. Poverty and its correlates limit alternatives. A mother living on public assistance might not have the means to purchase needed safety devices or to otherwise modify her home situation. A mother without heating in her apartment may have as her only alternatives having a cold apartment or using unsafe substitute heating mechanisms.

It is possible to view the child welfare agency's roles, and those of the caseworkers, as that of garnering, providing, and advocating for alternatives, or supports, for individual families, while at the same time counseling and instructing them toward the end of reducing risks of harm to the child.

Child welfare agencies can neither enter the housing industry nor raise clients' welfare benefits. But they can seek to remedy many of the health and safety hazards that attend poverty and that, in combination with parental factors produced in part by those very hazards, place children in danger of harm. The child welfare worker can help a client to secure needed repairs and safety remedies or devices that will make the home safer and protect the child. The worker can work with the parents to modify both behavior and the situation.

The foregoing discussion might appear rather mundane and unexciting. But if we truly wish to focus on the most important issue, that of preventing harm to children, which can be realistically addressed within the prevailing larger economic and social welfare context, which is more resistant to change than are child welfare agencies, then these are the directions in which child welfare agencies must go. Seeking ways to blame parents and entertaining esoteric constructions of child abuse and neglect seem far less constructive in this regard.

In my experience, child welfare agencies are not really oriented in these directions at the present time. Caseworkers are sent into homes primarily to investigate child abuse and neglect, not to detect health and safety hazards that can be corrected. Workers may walk in and out of homes in which there are nonfunctioning heating systems, peeling lead-based paint, rats, no guardrails on the windows, etc., and merely report back on dubious indications of child abuse and neglect, such as that the dishes were piled high in the sink and the beds were unmade. There is more judging than helping.

I do not blame the workers for an obsession with reporting that there is or is not a possibility of child abuse or neglect, while ignoring all else. The agency has oriented and trained them toward this narrow perspective and has not equipped itself to advocate for the family. I have found it exasperating, for example, in sitting on a foster care review board, to be confronted time after time with cases in which a child had been placed in foster care because of the inadequate housing or homelessness of the parents, and being told of the psychological problems of the parents, or listening to insinuations of child neglect. The mother is depressed, I might be told, but most of us would be if we were homeless with two children to care for. The roots of depression, as well as other psychological problems, can often be found in the environment rather than in the inner psyche.

"What has the agency done to help the family to obtain adequate housing?" I would ask. "That's not our job," was often the answer. "But the mission of your agency is to protect children and preserve families," I would retort, knowing full well that the day-to-day operations of the agency are not guided by its stated mission, so much as by an implicitly agreed upon division of labor between bureaucracies, whereby the state child welfare agency's domain is the investigation of child abuse and neglect, the provision of foster care, and as far as preventive services go, the provision of counseling, some arrangements for day care and a few other services, and little else. Mistakenly and foolishly, of course, I would sometimes take out my upsetness on the caseworkers. The agency is not geared to deal with the fact that inadequate housing places the children in danger of severe harm and the family in danger of disintegration, even if no overt maltreatment by the parents has been alleged, and the agency is not prepared to take steps consistent with its stated mission in such cases. The result is foster care placement that may harm the children and that is surely counter to family preservation.

In 1984, the Oregon Court of Appeals decided that proof that a mother left her two young children alone at home for several hours while she attended a party, during which time the children were killed in a fire of unknown origin, was insufficient to support her conviction for child neglect (*State* v. *Goff*, 1984a). The court concluded that under the Oregon child neglect statute, the state must show that there was a "dangerous condition" in the home from which a "substantial and unjustifiable risk" could be inferred. The Oregon Supreme Court later reversed this decision and reinstated the conviction. This court argued that "the fact that the children died indicated that the risk was substantial" (*State* v. *Goff*, 1984b).

There is little doubt that poverty is associated with "dangerous conditions" in and around the home. Moreover, poor people may not be able to afford baby-sitters and, as was noted previously in this chapter, the rate of residential fires as well as the fatality rate from such fires is far greater in low-income areas than it is in middle-class neighborhoods. These well-known facts imply that poverty is dangerous to children, and that to minimize these dangers, impoverished parents, if left only to their own devices, may need to be *more* diligent than middle-class parents in the supervision of their children. In a sense, we can say that middle-class parents have more leeway for irresponsibility than do impoverished parents, or that while occasional lapses in responsibility are normal for most parents (since there are few perfect parents), they are more dangerous when committed by impoverished parents (Pelton, 1978a).

Granted these conclusions, should different standards of *behavior* be applied by law to middle-class and impoverished parents? And are they? Should impoverished parents, by law, be compelled to exercise *greater* diligence than middle-class parents, in order to guard their children against the dangers of poverty? And is that what the neglect laws, in effect, demand of such parents? Put another way, should incidents involving injury to children caused simultaneously by the dangerous conditions of poverty and the failure of parents to exert the utmost care, be attributed by law solely to the behavior of the parents, by dint of neglect laws aimed at personal behavior and not at the conditions of poverty?

On a November evening in 1974, in Salem County, New Jersey, Lucille Lewis walked out of her apartment with the intention of getting some cigarettes (*State of New Jersey* v. *Lucille Lewis*, 1978). She left her oldest child, a boy aged 12 or 13, in charge of her four younger children. Before she departed, she turned on the top burners of the electric stove as well as the oven, leaving the oven door open, in order to generate heat. She did this because her apartment, provided by Salem County welfare officials, was unheated.

While Ms. Lewis was out, she met some friends and accompanied them to a tavern. During the time that she was in the tavern, a wire leading to the electric stove in the apartment shorted out, a fire started, and her three youngest children, girls aged 2, 4, and 5, died in the fire. The two boys managed to escape.

The trial judge, upon guilty pleas to charges of neglect, abandonment, and cruelty, sentenced Ms. Lewis to three concurrent six-month jail terms. Ms. Lewis appealed her sentences, but the Appellate Division upheld them. A dissenting judge, however, stated that: "The statute proscribing, in the most general terms, criminal neglect of children, . . . does not condemn as criminal leaving children in the care of a 12 or 13-year old youngster" (*State of New Jersey* v. *Lucille Lewis*, 1978).

She indicated that the *result* of this conduct was not, or should not have been, at issue: "By acceptance of the plea, the trial court and my colleagues obviously accept the proposition that any mother who leaves her children in the care of a 12 or 13-year old youngster is guilty of a criminal act by virtue of that conduct alone and irrespective of results" (*State of New Jersey* v. *Lucille Lewis*, 1978).

The New Jersey Supreme Court, upon further appeal of this case, suspended the sentences, but did not address the conviction itself (McMahon, 1979). The defendant's lawyer criticized the court for not having "the courage to say why" the jail term should be suspended (McMahon, 1979). He had urged the Supreme Court to adopt the dissenting judge's viewpoint, but was rebuffed. He claimed that the Supreme Court, by refusing to address the conviction, implied that parents who leave their children with a teenage baby-sitter may be committing a crime. He further claimed that the Supreme Court's action was a perfect example of an "all-white, middle class male court being unable to understand the problems of a poor, black single woman," and asserted that the court's order was "the most classic example of a separated society based on class and race" (McMahon, 1979).

Indeed, the original trial judge in this case who sentenced Ms. Lewis said that she might not have been guilty if she had "discovered that she needed some milk for her children and had gone over to the corner store . . . and had left the children unattended." He said that that was a different situation from one of "a mother walking off and leaving five children . . . so that she could indulge herself in traveling from bar to bar and forgetting entirely about the fact she had children." This judge said that he was imposing the jail term to set an example to other parents and "hopefully deter others from being neglectful of their children" (McMahon, 1979).

It is obvious that this case of a mother leaving her children under the supervision of a 13-year-old baby-sitter never would have come to the attention of a court if it were not for the fact that three children died in a fire. It is equally apparent that the fire was at least partially related to the fact that the mother's substandard apartment lacked adequate heating. Indeed, there is a real question as to whether or not the mother could have saved the children from the fire even if she had been present.

The dissenting judge erred in one part of her opinion when she stated: "Fires of domestic origins are democratic in the victims they claim . . . " (*State of New Jersey* v. *Lucille Lewis*, 1978). Such fires are by no means democratic; they occur far more frequently in impoverished homes. To be sure, this case is an explicit example of the relationship between poverty and fires: a concomitant of poverty (lack of an adequately heated home) caused a sequence of events (turning to a dangerous method of heating as the only alternative) that led to a fire.

When middle-class parents engage in the same exact conduct as this mother, that is, leaving their children with a 13-year-old baby-sitter, a fire is far less likely to start when they are out (or when they are in, for that matter) because middle-class homes are not so beset with health and safety hazards as are impoverished homes. Moreover, we view such middle-class parents as going out for a perfectly innocent evening of entertainment, while the impoverished mother, as depicted by the trial judge in this case, "walks off" so that she can "indulge" herself in "traveling from bar to bar." The middle-class parents take a brief respite from their children, while the impoverished mother "forgets entirely about the fact she had children." The judge, by his words, creates the image of an irresponsible evil parent, and he sets the impoverished parent up nicely for her scapegoat role. The middle-class parents' conduct carries a presumed innocence: They need account to no one as to the purpose they had in going out. The impoverished mother's behavior, on the other hand, carries a presumed lack of innocence, redeemable only if her purpose in going out was to buy milk for her children.

Children were killed in a fire. The judge wants to hold someone responsible. It is satisfying to find the culprit readily available, in the form of an impoverished mother, and to punish her as an example to others. It would be less satisfying to hold responsible the abstract social forces that result in poverty. Yet, in a real sense, it was poverty that killed the children, and another of the victims of that poverty was blamed.

The law need say nothing about leaving children alone in "dangerous conditions." Of cases involving the same exact conduct, only those in which children have been seriously injured usually come to court, and these are the precise cases in which poverty has produced "dangerous conditions." Thus the "dangerous conditions" and, in effect, poverty, are the *de facto* reasons for finding the parent neglectful, even if there is no mention of "dangerous conditions" in the law. Thus, different standards of *behavior* are applied to middle-class and impoverished parents, and no responsibility is attributed to poverty and society. To conclude that, to eliminate the double standard, we should "go after" middle-class parents as diligently as we do impoverished parents would be counterproductive, for such ventures would serve no constructive purpose.

It has been argued here that often a combination of poverty-related conditions and less-than-optimal behavior on the part of the parents are responsible for many of the serious injuries to children that do occur. Child abuse and neglect laws focus our attention on blaming the parents in such cases. While child abuse and neglect laws may be necessary, an overemphasis on blaming the parent has led to the all-too-frequent separation of children from lower-class parents, the placement of such children in foster care, and an underemphasis on directing our society's energies and resources toward remedying dangerous conditions of poverty that cause severe harm to children. A focus on what society can do to prevent dangerous conditions should replace the focus on who is to blame; the latter practice helps no child.

RESTRUCTURING THE SYSTEM

On the one hand, we see that public child welfare agencies are not prepared to deal with and prevent the vast majority of severe injuries and fatalities that do occur to children in low-income families, and particularly to children in child welfare cases. Few severe injuries occur in reported child abuse and neglect incidents, yet many severe injuries occur in these families. The agency's orientation to child abuse and neglect obstructs its ability to prevent injuries.

On the other hand, we have seen that public child welfare agencies do not respond effectively to the rarer cases of severe child abuse and neglect, of the kind that sometimes result in fatality, due to the parents' blatant negligence or severe abusive behavior.

In addition, we have seen that public child welfare agencies are quick to respond to perceived problems with foster care placement, and that they frequently do so in cases in which it would have been possible to protect children by preserving families, while *not* placing children for the *wrong* reasons in cases in which placement should have been made.

These malfunctions are endemic to the *system* itself. Therefore, what is proposed here is a restructuring of the child welfare system, in which the investigative/coercive roles are shifted to law enforcement agencies, and decisions of child removal to the family court. The foster care system would be monitored and controlled by the court, although special social workers would be attached to this system to serve solely as foster care workers. The public child welfare agency would be freed to pursue its helping role, with the goal of preserving families, unencumbered by investigatory functions and child removal decisions.

Importantly, child abuse and neglect laws would be made far more specific than they are now, to insure that police intervention is limited to serious charges of severe child abuse and neglect that can stand up in court. Too often in the past, children have been removed from parents under circumstances that could best be described as societal rather than parental neglect, and child welfare agencies, in making these decisions, have circumvented the courts. Then, too, even the courts, operating under vague, ambiguous, and moralistic laws (Mnookin, 1973) have made similar decisions. Child-exploitation laws to include serious charges of extreme sexual abuse, would also be made specific, and such matters as sexual abuse (as already proposed in the previous chapter), would also be investigated by law enforcement agencies and taken out of the hands of the public child welfare agency.

It might be argued that ultimately the dual role remains under the same administrative roof, that of the state government. But the important thing is that the agencies assigned different parts of the dual role have different mandates and their own budgets. They can pursue their separate aims, of investigation of possible violation of laws, and of helping, unencumbered by internal contradictions.

Very importantly, the helping agency will not have the role of judging, which it does now, and therefore will not provide the opportunity for blaming-the-victim inclinations to be played out. For example, a nurse's role is to help the patient, even if the patient is a criminal. There is nothing in her job description that would permit her to act upon her private judgment of the patient's behavior, or to deny services on the basis of her judgment of the patient's character.

Under this proposal, state child protection laws would be narrowed to focus on severe harm to the child, in accordance with the minimal child welfare standards described in Chapter 5. In addition, the laws would specify that such harm, or danger to the child of such harm, must be due to clearly deliberate harmful acts or gross abdication of responsibility on the part of the primary caretakers while the child is under the supervision of those caretakers.

Allegations of such severe child abuse and neglect would be investigated by the police. Special police units would be developed to investigate severe child abuse and neglect as well as other forms of family violence (police currently do investigate spouse abuse charges). Police in such units would receive special training in family crisis intervention (Schuchter, 1976, pp. 5–6, 121). Such units would have the capacity to respond immediately to serious complaints, bring the child for medical examination and emergency medical treatment, gather evidence, and refer the cases, if warranted, to the coroner and/ or to civil court or criminal proceedings.

The primary goal would be protection of the child (and/or other children in the family), not punishment of the parents. Thus, a case might be referred by police to civil court for the placement of the child or children, or the public child welfare agency might be called in to provide emergency caretakers in order to avert the need for placement. A foster care worker from the family court would gather information that would allow the family court judge to determine whether placement or continued placement would be necessary. Rare cases of the severest abuse and neglect may be referred to the district attorney for criminal proceedings against the parents.

I do not relish the idea of expanding the police role in child welfare situations, nor even that of the family court. My primary objective here is to clear the way for the public child welfare agency to become a nonpunitive, noninvestigatory, nonplacing agency that will be a true advocate for and "friend" to families experiencing child welfare difficulties, by virtue of offering an attractive array of services wanted and needed by such families. Unencumbered by the other roles that I am proposing to shed from it, the hope is that such an agency—in an unconflicted manner and by devoting its entire budget to preventive services—will be able to develop a broader array of preventive services than it now possesses, in greater quantities than it now possesses, and that it will reach, and more effectively reach, on a voluntary acceptance basis, more families than it had been previously able to on coercive intervention premises.

In actuality, the restructuring that would be required to make this happen is not all that drastic and would make good sense even in terms of the investigatory and foster care components. First, in order to deemphasize, reduce, and reverse our society's child abuse and neglect reporting and blaming "mania," which has been aided and abetted by vague child abuse and neglect laws, and the adoption of a "reporting law strategy," state child abuse and neglect laws would be narrowed in a manner already indicated, and the reporting laws would be narrowed in a consistent manner. Currently, the encouragement of overzealous reporting to state central registry "hot lines" given by reporting laws and reporting campaigns have created systems, as Douglas Besharov has indicated, which cannot distinguish serious dangers from an act such as littering (quoted in Hechler, 1988, p. 132). Reporting campaigns should be curtailed, or at least, as Besharov (1985, p. 572) has suggested, fashioned to emphasize what should not be reported as well as what should.

Second, in addition to greatly attenuating the inundation of complaints into "hot lines," the "hot lines" would be moved from state child welfare agencies to police departments. The public would be encouraged to report suspicions of severe child maltreatment in accordance with the newly narrowed and specific definitions provided in child abuse and neglect laws. Truancy from school and "dirty" homes, for example, would not be reported. Thus, the recipient of reports—and now with only reports of a serious nature being encouraged—would be changed from state child welfare agencies to police departments. Even at present, many of the reports of a serious nature initially come to the police. But with specially trained police units, investigation might be more efficient when done by the police than by caseworkers. Moreover, police have a better capacity to respond on an around-the-clock emergency basis and on weekends, when a large proportion of child maltreatment reports are received.

Third, the foster care system, with all the functions related to it, such as home finding, and most importantly, decisions about child removal, would be placed under the family court system. The foster care system would be monitored and controlled by the court. Foster care workers attached to the court, and specially trained for this purpose, would operate this system. Very importantly, judgments in the form of recommendations to the judge, in regard to initial placement of a child, continued placement or return home, and/or termination of parental rights and placement for adoption, would no longer be made by the public child welfare agency, but by the foster care workers under the court. The foster care workers would gather the information that would allow the family court judge to make decisions.

Furthermore, in order to expand the vision of the court beyond blaming the parent, the foster care workers as well as the judges would be trained in applying "reasonable efforts" and "least detrimental alternative" criteria to case determinations. They would be encouraged to use the power of the court to press the public child welfare agency as well as public welfare and other social agencies to use their resources to provide concrete services to clients as alternatives to removing children.

It is interesting that under a New Jersey statute (N.J.S.A. 9:6–8.51) governing child abuse and neglect cases, one of the dispositions available to the court is to require that the parent accept therapeutic services, but there is no alternative disposition available under that law to require public agencies to provide housing assistance, child care, or other concrete services.

According to one set of commentators:

By focusing on psychological aspects of parental behavior, the social agencies and the courts continue to reinforce traditional notions of individual culpability on the part of parents while couching their concerns in terms of the interests of children. . . . While the potential exists for the courts to press for needed concrete remedial services for families, so far there have been no general attempts to use the courts in this way. (Rosenthal & Louis, 1981, pp. 84–85)

In recent years, in part due to the "reasonable efforts" clause of the AACWA of 1980, this situation has changed somewhat, partly in the form of class action suits (Pelton & Rosenthal, 1988). For example, in a class action suit against the state of West Virginia, a consent decree (a decision worked out between the parties) issued in federal District Court in 1981 mandated, in part, that the state must provide reasonably available supportive services as an alternative to removal in cases of alleged abuse or neglect (*Gibson et al.* v. *Ginsberg et al.*, 1981). Such services, the court declared, will include housing location assistance to avoid child removal merely because of the parents' inability to locate suitable housing; day-care services; homemaking services; economic assistance for immediate needs over and above regular income maintenance allowances; emergency caretakers within the home; family shelter care; and "financial assistance up to amounts which may be provided foster families when the primary reason for an anticipated removal is that the family lacks sufficient resources to adequately care for a child."

In 1985, in an individual case, the District of Columbia Superior Court ordered the District to provide housing to a mother charged with abuse, in order to reunite her with her children (*Family Law Reporter*, 1985). The mother had complied with all conditions of a rehabilitation plan set forth for her to have her children returned, except for obtaining adequate housing, which she could not afford.

The family court itself should be encouraged to apply the expanded horizons of recent federal and state "reform" laws in individual cases, to expand the family court's focus from who is to blame to who is responsible. Judges should be encouraged to recognize that society is in part responsible and thus has the obligation to provide services that might reasonably prevent the need for separation of children from parents. Under this perspective, hopefully, family court judges will begin to order other agencies, including the public child welfare agency, to fulfill their responsibilities to provide concrete services in individual cases.

It is argued here that the three restructuring measures outlined above—the reformation of state child abuse and neglect laws, reporting laws, and reporting campaigns; the transfer of the responsibility of receiving reports and of the investigative role from the public child welfare agency to the police; and the transfer of the foster care system to the court—would free the public child welfare agency to vastly improve its capability to provide such concrete services and to be advocates for families.

The public child welfare agency caseworkers would no longer have a dual role. To date, some states have attempted to disentangle the dual role by establishing separate investigative units, which operate much as the police units would that have been proposed here, except that they are housed within the child welfare agency (Fandetti & Ohsberg, 1987). But such an arrangement splits the dual role in only a quite limited fashion. Thus, the investigative unit worker does the initial investigation, but if the case is now transferred to a social services worker within the same agency, that worker will be called upon, somewhere down the line, to make judgments regarding continuing abuse or neglect, the need for "voluntary" placement, or referral for court-ordered placement. In effect, we have only a separate intake unit that receives, screens, and investigates initial reports. Yet dual role problems are not limited to intake. Under current arrangements, the social services worker will continue the monitoring and control of the case, is responsible for continued ongoing investigation, represents the agency's ever-present threat of child removal, may judge upon the parents' "cooperativeness" in receiving services, and may represent other more subtle forms of coercion, all while at the same time trying to help the family as a unit.

Under the new proposal, the public child welfare agency workers would not have a dual role because, and most importantly, the agency itself would not have a dual role. The agency will be able to pursue a mission of attempting to preserve families and protect children through family advocacy and the provision and coordination of *helping* services in an unconflicted manner. For the conflict that such an agency experiences at present is not, as has often been claimed, inherent in the supposed duality of the goal of protecting children and preserving families, but rather in the *means* used to pursue the protection of children. Helping services do have the potential to protect children while preserving families, or by preserving families. Only in some of the most severe instances of child abuse and neglect is child separation the only means possible to protect the child. But such means should not be the function of a helping agency with the mission just described. In all but such rare cases, advocating for children cannot truly be done apart from advocating for families, and the admittance of the investigatory, coercive, and child removal functions into the helping agency inevitably interferes with the agency's capacity to carry out its role of advocating for *families*, and of protecting the child and preserving the family by providing helping services, as testified to by much of the evidence presented in this book.

With the dual role of the agency eliminated, the agency could devote its entire budget to the provision of helping services without having that budget drained off, and indeed the largest parts of that budget drained off, by resources for foster care placement, and increasingly in recent years, by resources for investigative functions. To be sure, having been divested of these other functions, the agency might now be forced to begin with a smaller budget. Like any agency, it—or its advocates—will have to begin to fight to increase its budget. However, the entire restructuring framework proposed here calls for a narrowing of the transferred investigative function as well as a narrowing of the transferred foster care function, in that under revised laws, far fewer cases will be deemed appropriate for coercive intervention. The immediate savings, it is proposed, would be retained by the newly structured public child welfare agency. The agency would still begin with a small budget, but one that is larger than that portion of the budget that was devoted to preventive services under the old structure. With the autonomy of a budget devoted solely to prevention, and with administrators freed to, and charged with the task of, devoting their intellectual energies to the sole task of developing preventive service strategies and programs, the agency will have a greatly increased capability, even with a modest budget, to begin to fulfill the obligations of the state to make "reasonable efforts" to prevent the need for child placement.

By a "bootstrap" procedure, through proving its own worth by reducing the number of foster care placements that need to be made even further, and having the savings transferred to its own budget, the agency would gradually expand the array and increase the quantities of the services that it is able to offer.

All services would be offered on a voluntary acceptance basis. The agency may be ordered by the court to offer to provide certain services to a particular family, but in that case, the foster care worker from the court would monitor the case. The child welfare agency worker's obligation on behalf of the agency would be solely that of coordinating and offering services. Upon request from the police, the agency would offer emergency services to certain families, but the police would be responsible for referring the case to the court if necessary.

However, the agency would provide services to other families far beyond such cases, on a voluntary acceptance basis. Many such families would be self-referrals. "Outreach" to families who might need such services, even approaching families on reports of neighbors and relatives that such services might be needed, would not compromise the agency's new orientation, since the agency would receive such referrals solely for the purpose of offering services.

The public child welfare agency would offer both emergency and preventive services. For the first time, the agency would be freed, in a realistic sense, to expand beyond its crisis orientation to primary prevention. Through the development of its own direct service programs, the development of purchase-of-service contracts with private agencies, and the facilitating of the coordination of services with other public and private agencies, the public child welfare agency would become a focal point for the coordination and provision of such emergency and preventive services as: emergency caretakers and homemakers; housing assistance (including gaining needed structural repairs for the family's current housing, and eliminating certain household health and safety hazards, as well as helping the client to locate new housing); emergency cash assistance; installation of window guardrails and smoke detectors; rodent control; lead-based paint testing and removal of the danger; in-home baby-sitter services; enuresis treatment; day care and night care; instruction in parenting skills and in safety supervision; provision of cribs and playpens; parent aides; visiting nurses; child home-safety instruction; self-help support groups; assistance in gaining access to substance abuse treatment, health care, and welfare benefits; transportation (e.g., for medical appointments); instruction in money management; respite care; crisis intervention counseling; and other forms of counseling.

A primary role of the public child welfare agency caseworker would be that of case management, which includes several functions. The worker would provide direct services from the agency, refer clients to appropriate community resources, facilitate coordination and collaboration among several service providers, monitor the services being provided, and negotiate the delivery of services and respective roles with the various agencies and individuals that are involved, or should be involved, in the case (Maluccio et al., 1986).

The worker might also act as counselor/educator by instructing the parents in child-discipline methods, instructing the parents in how to initiate change in the conditions of their environment, and by providing advice, encouragement, and support (Maluccio et al., 1986). In a client interview study, it was found that parents in child protection cases gave much credit to their caseworkers for helping them to achieve greater self-confidence and for demonstrating how to increase their coping capacities in various spheres of life. "This counseling was considered important (by the parents) both for the emotional support it provided and for the practical advice it afforded" (Magura, 1982).

Very importantly, the caseworker would also act as an advocate for the family. On a case basis, he or she would take action to protect the rights and entitlements of the family, to establish the eligibility of the family to receive certain services, and to press all agencies and systems (including public welfare, housing, mental health, education, medical, and the worker's own agency) to provide or create necessary services for the child and family (Maluccio et al., 1986).

By no means would the public child welfare agency's main functions be limited to casework. This agency would be in a better position than any other government agency to learn about, understand, and collect data on the needs of families and, freed from the dual role, would be in the best position to *advocate* for *families* on community and statewide levels. The agency would conduct research and advise legislators on the problems and needs of families, especially impoverished families. It would advocate for new legislation, such as in the areas of health, safety, and welfare benefits, aimed at protecting children from harm and preserving families. It would initiate interagency negotiations and agreements for the coordination of programs and service delivery toward these same goals. The agency would develop its own policies and creative new programs focused on protecting children and strengthening families. Many programs might entail service delivery on a case-by-case basis, but others, such as educational campaigns or the development of day-care centers, would not.

EXPECTED BENEFITS

Let us look at the benefits of a public child welfare agency that is freed to pursue the helping role without investigative, coercive, or child-placing responsibilities. Without the task and mandate to judge (all child separation issues will be handled by the court), the worker and agency will both be cast in the role of helper and *advocate* for the family. The agency could devote its full resources and energies to developing an array of services that are highly *attractive* to parents with child welfare problems and that simultaneously serve to achieve the agency's goal of preserving families and protecting children from harm.

Such an agency could no longer be perceived as a threat to families, and thus could attract families with potential as well as existing child welfare problems. In other words, it could begin to serve a truly *preventive* function and could attract self-referrals. For example, the public welfare assistance agency does not need informers to find people to whom it can deliver its services. It dispenses a highly attractive service—money—that people come for voluntarily and that simultaneously helps to achieve the goal of the agency, namely, ameliorating the effects of poverty. Analogously, if the public child welfare agency were to dispense services that parents with child welfare problems want and need, parents would seek them out voluntarily, and such services would serve the goal of preserving families and protecting children.

The aim of developing services that the parents want and need would lead the public child welfare agency to make efforts to understand the parents' perspectives and their subjective realities for the purpose of helping. An appreciation of their subjective realities will allow the agency and its workers to become true advocates for the parents as well as the children. Under the present dual role structure, the investigative/coercive role works against the agency becoming an advocate for the family. With no coercive role, advocacy on behalf of the children would not be incompatible with advocacy on behalf of the parents. The new structure of the child welfare system proposed here would allow public child welfare agencies to become advocates for the families who are the poorest of the poor, giving clients the services they want and need.

The expected results of such interventions might include a reduction in physical injuries to children within the state, improvement of family functioning, the removal of certain immediate threats to children's well-being through the increased availability of concrete services, reduction in the placement of children in foster care due to improved housing conditions, and the relieving of parents of certain poverty-related barriers to caring for their children.

Neugeboren (1985, pp. 268–86) has cataloged a variety of social care, or situation-changing, human-service technologies that emphasize the provision of concrete and environment-modifying services. Concrete services, in terms of effectiveness, often have a "face validity" that is agreed upon by all, because the cause-effect relationships are believed to be known (Neugeboren, 1985, pp. 253, 259–62). For example, the provision of adequate housing or food to a family who lacks these has an obvious client benefit. Such provision contributes in a readily apparent way to reduction of the risk of harm, which in any event, would not be difficult to independently measure. Yet because there is an apparent "fittingness" between the means and ends, it may suffice to simply know, in terms of evaluating program success, whether the client has received the adequate housing or not. These notions are in accordance with suggestions that some advocacy as well as concrete services can be judged on the basis of "mundane" measures of performance: "If they are supplied to the client, then the goal of the social service program has been accomplished" (Handler, 1973, p. 153). In reality, we can say that the success of any such service program could be evaluated in terms of the *quantity* of families in need of such service that it reached. More abstract services, such as those of an educative nature, designed to change the person in some way rather than the person's situation, are more difficult to evaluate. Some of the ultimate results expected of the entire thrust of this proposal, however, will be easily measurable, such as a reduction in physical injuries to children and child fatalities within the state, and a very large reduction in the foster care population.

In fact, under the current proposal, we would anticipate that the foster care population would be reduced due to two reasons: We would no longer be sending an army of investigators out to "substantiate" questionable charges of child abuse and neglect and to make placements for which there is questionable need; and that same army, now turned into an army of advocates and helpers, would actually provide tangible benefits that would reduce the real need for foster care placement.

The agency will focus on harm and will have the mission of preventing harm, rather than focusing on the investigation of child abuse and neglect. All services will be offered to families strictly on a voluntary acceptance basis.

Currently, the public child welfare agency is the agency of last resort for the state's most extremely deprived children and families. It is the flimsy "safety net" that society provides for families that have fallen through all other safety nets, such as public welfare. By the time the path of deterioration has led a family to the public child welfare agency, given that agency's limited resources, little can be done that would be of positive value for the family, and all options have their dangers and drawbacks. Ironically, because of its role of agency of last resort, this agency easily becomes the scapegoat and whipping boy for the ills of society when it fails to "save" a child or family. Currently, there is probably no public child welfare agency in the country that does not have a serious ongoing "image" problem, and that is not battered in the news media on an almost periodic basis. When a child dies at home, the agency is blamed for not having placed the child in foster care. If too many children are removed to foster care, the agency is blamed. The agency is accused of over-zealous overintervention and, alternatively, of underintervention. When a child dies in foster care, the agency is blamed for not having accurately judged all of the foster families it was obliged to recruit. Although social science has failed to generate solid knowledge of practical value in meeting the kinds of social problems faced by such agencies, and has been unable to provide predictors of danger and dangerousness, the news media have operated with amazing twenty-twenty hindsight. The agency is viewed as callous and incompetent. Increasingly, individual caseworkers are being held liable for deaths that occur (Besharov, 1983).

The fact that a poor agency image is so widespread among such agencies indicates that it is, to a large extent, not a function of more or less competent management—indeed, there are many dedicated and competent managers, administrators, supervisors, and caseworkers in such agencies—but of structural problems inherent in the system. It is contended here that the dual role structure is unworkable and that the image problem is one of the symptoms of its unworkability.

The restructuring proposed here will not eliminate all of the ingredients of this problem. The ability to predict danger will remain just as difficult as ever. The target of blame may merely be shifted to the police and courts. But the public child welfare agency, in an unconfused and unconflicted manner, not having to decide between help and coercive intervention, will be able to focus upon the provision of services in an unrestrained way. No doubt, grounds to criticize it will still be found, but the inherent inability of the agency in its present form to even respond to criticism by constructively modifying itself will be eliminated.

Under the new proposal, a family would have the right to refuse all services. If ongoing child abuse and neglect exists as defined by the new laws, it would be dealt with through the police and courts. Only medical examination, medical treatment, and child removal could be forced upon a family, but this would be handled by the police and courts. The public child welfare agency would not be responsible for investigating child abuse and neglect, nor would it be responsible for detecting child abuse and neglect and reporting it to the police anymore than any other party in society. The public child welfare agency workers would merely be subject to the same limitations on confidentiality in their relations with clients as are psychiatrists, psychologists, social workers, and clergymen. Such limitations, exercised in rare instances in practice, when a third party is threatened with severe harm through a criminal act, have not altered the image of these professional groups from helpers to that of coercive informer-investigators. In practice, only in rare instances, when the public child welfare agency worker, in the course of delivering services, might directly observe or be informed of a threat of imminent severe harm to a child, would he or she make a report to the police. Even in such cases, the worker would not have the responsibility of investigation, nor of taking a child for a medical examination. These would be the functions of the police and court.

Since the worker would not make unannounced home visits and would deliver services for the most part of a concrete nature (not involving extensive probing of the parent's psyche), it is anticipated that he or she would only rarely be faced with the obligation of reporting. We can debate to what extent, under the restructuring proposed here, the new agency might merely fall back into a coercive-like informer-investigator role. But many of the benefits envisioned by this proposal are really empirical questions: Under the restructuring, to what extent are perceptions of the public child welfare agency as "child-snatchers" reduced? Does the new agency tend to evolve a greater array of services, available in greater quantities than before? Does the agency attract a far greater number of self-referrals for preventive services? Does the agency's work actually result in a reduction of severe harm to children within the state, whether attributable to child abuse and neglect or to nonintentional injuries? Does the foster care population decline? Under the restructuring, are law enforcement agencies found to deal effectively with severe child abuse and neglect, and do fatalities in such cases decline? Does the new public child welfare agency, through its offering of services on a voluntary acceptance basis, sufficiently reach all families in which children are at risk of severe harm, regardless of whether it is attributable to child abuse and neglect or nonintentional injury, and at least, does it reach more such families than under the old system?

ADDITIONAL CONSIDERATIONS

Under the proposal for modification of the current public child welfare agency that I presented but then discarded in Chapter 5, in favor of the restructuring proposal I have presented in this chapter, I suggested that while services would be voluntary, the family would still be responsible for coming up to standards focused on severe harm to the child without regard to fault, by availing itself of the services or in some other way. If all else failed, the agency would have the option to refer the case for child removal. For example, under this scheme, it is conceivable that a homeless family, although homeless through no fault of its own, but not willing to accept housing assistance, might have its children removed on the grounds of danger of severe harm to the children due to the situation of homelessness. Under the restructuring plan, the new public child welfare agency would not have such power. Theoretically, the police might refer such a case to the court on the grounds of child neglect. The court then would be able to remove the children if it could make the case, under the law, that refusal to accept help, which would allow the family to leave the situation of homelessness and thereby avoid the risk of severe harm to the children, constituted neglect. Thus, theoretically, the separation of coercion (in this case, in the form of child removal) from service delivery may not be able to exist in a "pure" and complete form. I would contend, however, that in actuality, the separation would be complete enough to far better protect the rights of parents than under the old structure, and that the offer of such services on a voluntary acceptance basis through the new public child welfare agency proposed here will sufficiently reach all families in which risk of nonintentional severe harm exists, without the need for coercive intervention by the police and courts.

At the very least, even in such rare cases as the example suggested above, the agency engaged in service delivery would not be the same agency engaged in investigation, child removal, and law enforcement. And in all other cases, as Hoshino (1971) argued in regard to an earlier and different but related issue, (the separation of income-maintenance programs from the delivery of social services), "although some individuals will choose not to accept services that clearly would be beneficial to them, paternalism, intrusion, and coercion are far more dangerous."

In retrospect, under the proposal discarded in Chapter 5, it would probably not have been possible, in actuality, to keep the delivery of services on a voluntary acceptance basis while at the same time having the same agency enforce minimal child welfare standards, through child removal, if necessary. In fact, the frequent practice, in public child welfare agencies currently, of deciding that children should be placed because of the parents' "failure to cooperate" in receiving services already proves the point that in an agency with a coercive agenda regarding child protection, it is difficult for the worker to regard the refusal of services as a separate issue and to divorce coercion from service delivery. It is hoped that under the proposed restructuring, the new public child welfare agency would be able to more closely approximate, in practice, the ideal of service delivery on a voluntary acceptance basis.

As alluded to a moment ago, the issue of separation of services was debated in the 1970s, in the form of separation of AFDC payments from social services. A major rationale for separation was to increase client discretion in rejecting services (Hoshino, 1971; Handler, 1973; Piliavin & Gross, 1977). That is, so long as AFDC and social services are administered under the same agency or program, the client is in danger of being coerced, subtlely or otherwise, into accepting services as a condition for receiving AFDC payments.

As it turned out, after such separation was effected, much of Title XX monies for social services served to fund child welfare in separate public child welfare agencies, and much of this very money went for foster care and child protective services, in addition to preventive services such as day care. Thus, although services were separated from AFDC payments, they were never separated from child protection investigation and the threat of child removal. (As we have seen in this book, they never had been previously. But in the 1960s and 1970s, monies for social services increased dramatically, much of it fueling the child welfare system and allowing the threat of child removal to be made to, and carried out with, more and more poor families.) While poor people would not have to accept services as a condition of receiving AFDC benefits, some poor people, those reported to public child welfare agencies for alleged child abuse and neglect, might still be forced to accept services under the threat of child removal. It is this second separation, of course, that the restructuring proposal presented here is designed to achieve.

A key rationale presented here for the restructuring is that, in separating the helping function from the investigative/coercive function, the helping agency would offer services on a truly voluntary acceptance basis, and in doing so would be freed—and obliged to—develop an array of services that are highly attractive to parents with child welfare problems, and that such parents want and need. Such services would attract self-referrals, and the agency would thereby serve a truly preventive function by reaching a broader range of families with potential as well as existing child welfare problems. Moreover, the agency could focus on reducing harm to children, including harm due to nonintentional injuries, without assessing blame or responsibility as a criterion for service.

However, Handler (1973) has interestingly argued that the more that the services developed are those that poor people want and need, such as services of a more concrete nature, the less free they will be to reject them, and the less able will they be to resist submitting to coercive conditions in order to obtain those services. ". . . [I]f social services have something to offer, then poor people will be forced to participate; they simply do not have that many options" (Handler, 1973, p. 13).

If, as under the restructuring plan proposed here, child abuse investigation and the threat of child removal are taken from the new helping agency, what possible conditions might officials of such an agency coercively impose upon their clients? As Handler (1973, pp. 139–41) has suggested, when workers for a social services agency hold a pathological perspective of their clients' problems, they may view their clients' stated needs only as the "presenting problems," which mask deeper psychological problems to be analyzed and cured. Under this psychodynamic medical model orientation, as I described it in Chapter 2, the workers may deliver concrete services to their clients only as a means of getting them to accept people-changing services, such as therapy, and may be inclined to withhold concrete services from those who do not "respond to treatment," or who do not "cooperate" with the workers' own agendas or case plans. The workers' agendas, if focused on psychological problems, may differ quite significantly from that of their clients', who tend to view their problems as social and environmental in nature (Pelton, 1982b). Thus, by having command over scarce resources, the workers may condition the delivery of certain services upon the acceptance by clients of intrusions into their lives that the clients did not ask for nor want, but might feel forced to accept (Handler, 1973, pp. 65–67, 80–83, 139–41). So although, under the restructuring proposed here, workers for the new helping agency could not employ the threat of child removal, it is conceivable that, if they subscribed to people-changing agendas at odds with the clients' own agendas, they would be tempted to promise or withhold certain needed services on condition of the clients' compliance with other aspects of the workers' "case plans."

We have already seen in Chapter 2 that ironically, although the intent of the Public Welfare Amendments of 1962 and 1967 was to "strengthen family life," they served to provide the resources for a child abuse crusade whose thrust was to detect psychological defects in impoverished parents rather than to provide them with concrete services. According to Handler (1973, pp. 138–39), such vague, people-changing goals (or at least, goals that can be interpreted in terms of people-changing, i.e., rehabilitation, objectives) open the door to all kinds of arbitrary intrusions into individual and family life.

Handler's arguments are well-taken here. But what can be done? It is of the utmost importance that the new child welfare agency proposed here not be shaped in accordance with a psychodynamic medical model orientation. Such an orientation must be avoided in the statutes establishing the agency, in the policies and philosophy developed within the agency, in administrative rules and in the direction given to the agency by the administrators, and in the training of supervisors and caseworkers. I suggest that minimal goals that are clear, specific, and limited, focused upon preventing harm to children, rather than vague optimalist goals such as "enhancing family life," be mandated for the new agency. Moreover, as an alternative to the medical model, this agency would operate under a conception of the multiple causation pattern of injuries and the risk of harm to children, described earlier in this chapter. In accordance with this conception, it is recognized that specific harms are due to a combination of factors, that the removal of even just one of these factors can prevent or reduce the risk of the harm occurring, and that very often the most effective way to reduce the risk is not through direct attempts to change individual behavior, but to remove one or more of the causative factors through environmental changes and passive measures that can be accomplished through the delivery of certain concrete services. This conception or orientation would be implemented within the agency through statutes establishing the agency; through administrative direction; through the nature of the policies, programs, and services that are developed; and through the training of workers.

Under this conception, it would be against administrative rules, and specified as such, for the agency or caseworker to offer or withhold one service to a family on condition of acceptance of another. The sole criterion for offering a service, or the sole eligibility requirement for a service, would be that it has the potential, on its own merits, to reduce the risk of harm to the children in the family, and the family cannot afford to purchase the service on its own. To intentionally withhold such a service, or to impose any service upon the family against the parents' will, would be against the agency policies, and the implementation of those policies would be closely monitored.

Rehabilitation, or people-changing, technologies, such as parent education programs or services of a psychotherapeutic nature, would not be ignored by the new agency, but they would be made available, as would all services, on a strictly voluntary acceptance basis and would not be coercively imposed in any manner. It should not be impossible to get an agency to operate on the basis described here, in which each service is seen as having its own value, not dependent upon the delivery of other services. Indeed, even in the current traditional public child welfare agencies, a proportion of the caseworkers view their clients in similar ways to those described here and operate in accordance with orientations similar to the one developed here. There are workers who eschew the medical model and who give aid without conditions (Handler, 1973, p. 82). Under the restructuring proposed here, such an orientation would be made explicit and institutionalized within the new agency.

Under the current structure, the development of purchase-of-service contracts with private nonprofit agencies has become a widespread practice among public child welfare agencies. Thus, it may be argued that the separation of the coercive, investigative, and child removal role from that of the helping role, as advocated here, has already been accomplished to some extent, in that these private agencies, in effect, perform only the helping role. But this is not the case. The private agency is beholden to the public child welfare agency that grants it the contract; it makes recommendations to the public agency in matters concerning child removal in individual cases; it accepts clients who are under coercion by the public agency to receive such services as the private agency has to offer; and it monitors and reports back to the public agency in regard to the attendance and "cooperativeness" of the clients.

In addition, many such contracted private agencies operate under a medical model orientation and offer few, if any, concrete services. Moreover, the orientation proposed here, with its emphasis on concrete services and advocacy, would be best implemented by a public agency in that it is largely government that is responsible for addressing the needs of poor people, as it already does to some extent through the provision of welfare benefits; it is largely government that has the resources to make other concrete provisions available to poor people; and since much of the advocacy will have to be directed toward other government agencies, it is the public agency—as part of the government and thus backed by the power of government—that would have the most leverage to advocate successfully. Finally, the adequacy of purchase-of-service contract arrangements, both in terms of the quality of the services being provided and the adequacy of monitoring such contracts, which is currently being performed by the public child welfare agencies, has still not been researched very much. Despite all of these misgivings, it should be noted that the proposed restructuring allows for the continuation of the purchase-of-service-contract approach as one of several means that would be available to the new public child welfare agency for the provision of services.

There are some parallels between the restructuring being proposed here and the proposal developed by Schuchter (1976) several years earlier, but there are also many important differences. Besides his focus on child abuse in contrast to child neglect, which has been a greater and more frequent alleged source of risk of harm to children than child abuse, and in contrast to other types of child welfare problems that might put children at risk of harm, perhaps the greatest difference is the emphasis placed, in the restructuring proposal described here, on the creation of an expanded helping agency that would provide both emergency and primary prevention services, on a nonjudgmental and voluntary acceptance basis, to families experiencing all sorts of difficulties that put children at risk of harm.

Such an agency would become a true advocate for families. Under current arrangements, a primary difficulty presented to social work practice within a public child welfare agency is that the client cannot even be clearly identified. Who is the client? It can be said that the client is the child, who is claimed to be in need of protection, although aside from foster care, few services are specifically directed to the child, as critics have often pointed out. What services there are, are usually directed toward the parents, and in this sense it can be said that the parent is the client. But then again, if the parent is investigated and accused, and if actions are taken against his or her will, such a person can hardly be called a "client." If we were to take literally one of the professed goals of the agency, that of family preservation, then we might say that the family is the client. Yet we have seen throughout this book that a predominant response of the child welfare agency has been child rescue, that the agency has often separated children from their parents, and that the agency has, in many cases, contributed to rather than prevented the disintegration of families. Finally, it can be said that the true client has been the community at large who, egged on by simplistic accounts in the news media, and already inclined toward victim-blaming, calls out for the punishment and control of poor people through the removal of their children. Yet, to judge by the sorry reputation that the agency has among the general public, we can say that if the community is the client, then it has not served nor satisfied the client very well.

Under the proposed restructuring, the public child welfare agency would be freed to clearly identify the family as the client and would have the opportunity to develop services to be provided directly to the child with the consent of the parents, to the parents themselves, and to the family as a whole. The community would be served by the overall reduction of harm to children within the society and would be served as well as satisfied by the anticipated better and more efficient investigation and handling of occasional severe child abuse and neglect cases by the police and courts.

While "conservative" critics (I refer to them as conservative only in the sense of wanting to improve and modify the present dual role structure within its current framework, perhaps along the lines I proposed but then rejected in Chapter 5) might argue that this proposal goes too far, radical critics would claim that it does not go far enough. I have already addressed the conservatives' arguments in the course of explicating this proposal, and here I will address the radicals.

It can be said that what is presented here is just another organizational restructuring of which, we have seen, there have been several over the years, with none appreciably affecting overall child welfare outcomes. Indeed, I myself have been skeptical generally about administrative restructurings, believing that they often amount to merely shifting "boxes" around on the organizational chart, while creating the illusion that significant problems have been addressed. However, the restructuring proposed here would be the first in the history of child welfare in this country that separates the dual role, and thus addresses what I have argued are *fundamental* problems of the system, as I have analyzed them here.

But the radicals would argue that the really fundamental problems of child welfare in this country do not lie within the child welfare system, but within the larger economic and social welfare systems of our society. The issue that must be addressed is poverty itself, not merely some of its by-products. Anyone who documents the relationship between poverty and child welfare problems, as I have done in this book, can hardly disagree that the issue of poverty itself should be addressed on a societal scale. Radicals might suggest a restructuring of our capitalist system, but regardless of the merits and drawbacks of whatever system it is to be restructured to, we can agree that no such fundamental change of the economic system is anywhere in sight.

Short of such revolutionary change, radicals, joined by some liberals, have advocated changes within the prevailing social and economic systems. Child welfare advocates themselves have recommended such measures as: the creation of a full-employment economy or an unconditional right to employment at wages compatible with an adequate level of living; a guaranteed minimum annual income, perhaps set at one-half the national median income, or at least setting AFDC benefits at or above the poverty level and indexing them to cost-of-living increases; a universal national health-care system; and a universal day-care system (e.g., Horowitz & Wolock, 1981, pp. 172–73;

Gil, 1981, pp. 319–23). Although even these measures may not be foreseeable in the near future, I do believe that ongoing advocacy on their behalf is important and necessary.

Speaking in regard to the low levels of cash benefits to families provided by income maintenance systems—and the consequent need of poor people for services to overcome crises and emergencies, and for housing, health care, advocacy, and other in-kind benefits—Handler (1973, p. 136) argued: "In a significant sense . . . the debate as to whether the poor need money or services is largely academic. We may agree that the basic problem of the poor is lack of money, but society will not give them enough money; therefore, they will continue to have a whole host of needs not met by the income maintenance system." Although Handler believes that this is unfortunate, and that wherever possible, "cash benefits should be substituted for in-kind benefits," (1973, p. 152) because cash benefits lessen and make more difficult efforts to control recipient behavior, the reality is as he stated it.

The new public child welfare agency as envisioned here, by being in a unique position to document the needs of families and by demonstrating the value of its own programs, would become a major force in the advocacy for the development of such expanded benefits as a universal health-care system, or specified family support systems, such as day care, on a universal basis, and increased cash benefits in income maintenance programs. Perhaps it would document the need for and demonstrate the value of many of its own programs to the extent that the general public and politicians will come to appreciate the desirability and benefits for the society as a whole of expanding such programs, and will be willing to support them. With few major exceptions, most social welfare policies in our country today have been established and implemented in a rather incremental fashion. Through a "bottom-up" method of changing social policies, the agency proposed here can become a force for the gradual change of the overarching social welfare policy context in our nation.

In the meantime, it is anticipated that the proposed restructuring and the new public child welfare agency will improve the public child welfare system's capacity to go about its daily business of attempting to alleviate immediate human suffering and allow it to far more closely approximate in reality than it has at any other time in its past, the long-standing policy of family preservation, and of not removing children from parents for reasons of poverty.

Bibliography

Abbott, E., & Breckinridge, S. P. (1921). *The administration of the aid-to-mothers law in Illinois.* U.S. Department of Labor, Children's Bureau, Legal Series No. 7, Bureau Publication No. 82. Washington, DC: U.S. Government Printing Office.

Adams, J. E., & Kim, H. B. (1971). A fresh look at intercountry adoptions. *Children, 18,* 214-21.

Addams, J. (1915). *Democracy and social ethics.* New York: Macmillan.

Alstein, H. (1984). Transracial and intercountry adoptions: A comparison. In P. Sachdev (Ed.), *Adoption: Current issues and trends* (pp. 195-203). Toronto, Canada: Butterworths.

American Humane Association. (1977). *Statistics for 1975.* Denver, CO: Author.

American Humane Association. (1978). *National analysis of official child neglect and abuse reporting.* Denver, CO: Author.

American Humane Association. (1979). *National analysis of official child neglect and abuse reporting.* Washington, DC: U.S. Department of Health, Education, and Welfare, DHEW Publication No. (OHDS) 79-30232.

American Humane Association. (1981). *National analysis of official child neglect and abuse reporting. Annual report, 1980.* Denver, CO: Author.

American Humane Association. (1983). *Highlights of official child neglect and abuse reporting: Annual report, 1981.* Denver, CO: Author.

American Humane Association. (1987). *Highlights of official child neglect and abuse reporting, 1985.* Denver, CO: Author.

American Humane Association. (1988). *Highlights of official child neglect and abuse reporting, 1986.* Denver, CO: Author.

Antler, S. (1981). The rediscovery of child abuse. In L. H. Pelton (Ed.), *The social context of child abuse and neglect* (pp. 39-54). New York: Human Sciences Press.

Antler, J., & Antler, S. (1979). From child rescue to family protection: The evolution of the child protective movement in the United States. *Children and Youth Services Review, 1*, 177-204.

Ashby, L. (1984). *Saving the waifs: Reformers and dependent children, 1890-1917.* Philadelphia, PA: Temple University Press.

Axinn, J., & Levin, H. (1982). *Social welfare: A history of the American response to need* (2nd ed.). New York: Harper and Row.

Bachrach, C. A. (1986). Adoption plans, adopted children, and adoptive mothers. *Journal of Marriage and the Family, 48*, 243-253.

Baig, T. A., & Gopinath, C. (1976). Adoption—The Indian scene. *Indian Journal of Social Work, 37*, 135-140.

Barbanel, J. (1988). Rent aid is enacted for families with children in foster care. *The New York Times*, August 18, p. B1.

Barth, R. P., Berry, M., Yoshikami, R., Goodfield, R. K., & Carson, M. L. (1988). Predicting adoption disruption. *Social Work, 33*, 227-233.

Bass, C. (1975). Matchmaker-matchmaker: Older-child adoption failures. *Child Welfare, 54*, 505-512.

Bell, W. (1965). *Aid to Dependent Children.* New York: Columbia University Press.

Benet, M. K. (1976). *The politics of adoption.* New York: Free Press.

Benton, B., Kaye, E., & Tipton, M. (1985). *Evaluation of state activities with regard to adoption disruption.* Final report. Washington, DC: Urban Systems Research and Engineering, Inc. Prepared under Contract no. 105-84-8102, Office of Human Development Services, U.S. Department of Health and Human Services, November 12.

Besharov, D. J. (1983). Protecting abused and neglected children: Can law help social work? *Family Law Reporter, 9*, 4029-37. August 23.

Besharov, D. J. (1985). "Doing something" about child abuse: The need to narrow the grounds for state intervention. *Harvard Journal of Law and Public Policy, 8*, 539-89.

Biaggi, M. (1973). Statement of Hon. Mario Biaggi, a U.S. Representative from the State of New York. In *Hearings before the Subcommittee on Children and Youth of the U.S. Senate on the Child Abuse Prevention Act* (pp. 125-27). Washington, DC: U.S. Government Printing Office.

Biller, H. B., & Solomon, R. S. (1986). *Child maltreatment and paternal deprivation.* Lexington, MA: Lexington Books, D.C. Heath & Co.

Billingsley, A., & Giovannoni, J. M. (1972). *Children of the storm: Black children and American child welfare.* New York: Harcourt Brace Jovanovich.

Birtwell, M. L. (1895). Investigation. *The Charities Review, 4*, 129-36.

Bixby, A. K. (1981). Social welfare expenditures, FY 1979. *Social Security Bulletin, 44,* 3–12.

Block, N. M., & Libowitz, A. S. (1983). *Recidivism in foster care.* New York: Child Welfare League of America.

Blutstein, H. I., Edwards, J. D., Johnston, K. T., McMorris, D. S., & Rudolph, J. D. (1977). *Area handbook for Colombia* (3rd ed.). Washington, DC: U.S. Government Printing Office.

Boehm, B. (1970). The child in foster care. In H. D. Stone (Ed.), *Foster care in question: A national reassessment by twenty-one experts.* New York: Child Welfare League of America.

Bonham, G. S. (1977). Who adopts: The relationship of adoption and social-demographic characteristics of women. *Journal of Marriage and the Family, 39,* 295–306.

Boyne, J., Denby, L., Kettenring, J. R., & Wheeler, W. (1982). Log-linear models of factors which affect the adoption of "hard-to-place" children. *Proceedings of the American Statistical Association,* Social Statistical Section.

Bremner, R. H. (Ed.). (1971). *Children and youth in America: A documentary history* (Vol. 2). Cambridge, MA: Harvard University Press.

———. (Ed.). (1974). *Children and youth in America: A documentary history* (Vol. 3). Cambridge, MA: Harvard University Press.

Burt, M. R., & Balyeat, R. R. (1977). *A comprehensive emergency services system for neglected and abused children.* New York: Vantage Press.

Burt, M. R., & Pittman, K. J. (1985). *Testing the social safety net.* Washington, DC: Urban Institute Press.

Center for Disease Control. (1975). *Guides for state Title XIX directors for assurance of laboratory quality performance in lead poisoning prevention programs.* Washington, DC: U.S. Department of Health, Education, and Welfare, Public Health Service. May.

Child Protection Report. (1984). High rate of failures reported in adoptions of special needs children; services lacking. *10* (13), June 29. Washington, DC: Author.

———. (1989). Budget FY 90—Special report. *15* (1), January 9. Washington, DC: Author.

Children's Defense Fund. (1988). *A children's defense budget, FY 1989: An analysis of our nation's investment in children.* Washington, DC: Author.

Child Welfare League of America. (1983). *U.S. foster care population for 1980: Final estimate.* New York: Author.

Claburn, W. E., & Magura, S. (1977). *Foster care review in New Jersey: An evaluation of its implementation and effects.* Final report. Federal grant no. 18-P-90257/2-01, Social and Rehabilitation Services, U.S. Department of Health, Education, and Welfare.

Cohen, S. J., & Sussman, A. (1975). The incidence of child abuse in the United States. *Child Welfare, 54*, 432–43.

Current operating statistics: Monthly tables. (1985). *Social Security Bulletin, 48*, July.

Daley, M. R. (1979). 'Burnout': Smoldering problem in protective services. *Social Work, 24*, 375–79.

Dershewitz, R. A., & Williamson, J. W. (1977). Prevention of childhood household injuries: A controlled clinical trial. *American Journal of Public Health, 67*, 1148–53.

Derthick, M. (1975). *Uncontrollable spending for social services grants.* Washington, DC: Brookings Institution.

Deykin, E. Y., Campbell, L., & Patti, P. (1984). The postadoption experience of surrendering parents. *American Journal of Orthopsychiatry, 57*, 271–80.

Dillon, K. M. (1987). False sexual abuse allegations: Causes and concerns. *Social Work, 32*, 540–41.

Doe v. *Downey*, 146 N.J. Super. 419 (1976).

Doe v. *Downey*, 74 N.J. 196 (1977).

Drews, K. (1980). The role conflict of the child protective service worker: Investigator-helper. *Child Abuse and Neglect, 4*, 247–54.

Dullea, G. (1987). Child sex abuse charged in more divorces. *New York Times*, January 19, p. A14.

Eisenberg, L. (1962). The sins of the fathers: Urban decay and social pathology. *American Journal of Orthopsychiatry, 32*, 5–17.

Eliot, M. M. (1955). A twenty-year perspective on services to children. *Children, 2*, pp. 123–26, 160.

Elmer, E. (1981). Traumatized children, chronic illness, and poverty. In L. H. Pelton (Ed.), *The social context of child abuse and neglect* (pp. 185–227). New York: Human Sciences Press.

Emlen, A., Lahti, J., Downs, G., McKay, A., & Downs, S. (1978). *Overcoming barriers to planning for children in foster care.* Washington, DC: DHEW Publication No. (OHDS) 78–30138.

Family Law Reporter. (1985). Housing must be provided to reunite mother with children in foster care. *11*, 1367–368. June 4.

Fandetti, K. M., & Ohsberg, L. A. (1987). Rhode Island's child protective service system. *Child Welfare, 66*, 529–38.

Fanshel, D., & Grundy, J. F. (1980). CWIS/CCRS special report series, New York state reports. Child Welfare Information Services, Inc., June 30.

Fanshel, D., & Shinn, E. B. (1978). *Children in foster care: A longitudinal investigation.* New York: Columbia University Press.

Fein, E., Davies, L. J., & Knight, G. (1979). Placement stability in foster care. *Social Work, 24*, 156–57.

Fein, E., Maluccio, A. N., Hamilton, V. J., & Ward, D. E. (1983). After foster care: Outcomes of permanency planning for children. *Child Welfare, 62,* 485–558.

Ferguson, T. (1966). *Children in care—and after.* London: Oxford University Press.

Festinger, T. (1983). *No one ever asked us: A postscript to foster care.* New York: Child Welfare League of America.

Finkelhor, D. (1979). What's wrong with sex between adults and children? Ethics and the problem of sexual abuse. *American Journal of Orthopsychiatry, 49* (2), 692–97.

——— . (1984). *Child sexual abuse: New theory and research.* New York: Free Press.

——— . (1986). *A sourcebook on child sexual abuse.* Beverly Hills, CA: Sage Publications.

Frankel, H. (1988). Family-centered, home-based services in child protection: A review of the research. *Social Service Review, 62,* 137–57.

Friend, F. E. (1971). Memo from Fred E. Friend, Commissioner, to regional, county and area offices. Nashville, TN: State Department of Public Welfare, November 30.

——— . (1972). Memo from Fred E. Friend, Commissioner, to regional, county and area offices. Nashville, TN: State Department of Public Welfare, November 16.

——— . (1973). Memo from Fred E. Friend, Commissioner, to regional, county and area offices. Nashville, TN: State Department of Public Welfare, November 30.

Gandhi, M. K. (1961). *Non-violent resistance.* New York: Schocken Books.

Gelles, R. J. (1973). Child abuse as psychopathology: A sociological critique and reformulation. *American Journal of Orthopsychiatry, 43,* 611–21.

——— . (1977, February). Violence toward children in the United States. Paper presented at the meeting of the American Association for the Advancement of Science, Denver.

——— . (1978). Violence toward children in the United States. *American Journal of Orthopsychiatry, 48,* 580–92.

——— . (1979). Reply to Pelton. *American Journal of Orthopsychiatry, 49,* 372–74.

Gibson et al. v. *Ginsberg et al.,* U.S. District Court for the Southern District of West Virginia, Civil Action No. 78-2375, Consent Decree, September 28, 1981.

Gil, D. G. (1970). *Violence against children.* Cambridge, MA: Harvard University Press.

——— . (1973). Statement of David Gil, Professor of Social Policy, Brandeis University, Waltham, MA. In *Hearings before the Subcommittee on*

Children and Youth of the U.S. Senate on the Child Abuse Prevention Act (pp. 13–48). Washington, DC: U.S. Government Printing Office.

————. (1981). The United States versus child abuse. In L. H. Pelton (Ed.), *The social context of child abuse and neglect* (pp. 291–324). New York: Human Sciences Press.

Giovannoni, J. M., & Becerra, R. M. (1979). *Defining child abuse*. New York: Free Press.

Giovannoni, J., & Billingsley, A. (1970). Child neglect among the poor: A study of parental inadequacy in families of three ethnic groups. *Child Welfare, 49*, 196–204.

Goldschmidt, I. (1986). National and intercountry adoptions in Latin America. *International Social Work, 29*, 257–68.

Gordon, L. (1988). *Heroes of their own lives: The politics and history of family violence*. New York: Viking.

Goriawalla, N. M. (1976). Inter-country adoptions—Policy and practice with reference to India. *Indian Journal of Social Work, 37*, 151–58.

Governor's Budget Message for Fiscal Year Ending June 30, 1967. (1966). Trenton, NJ: February 14.

Governor's Budget Message, Fiscal Year 1977–1978. (1977). Trenton, NJ: February 1.

Gruber, A. R. (1978). *Children in foster care: Destitute, neglected . . . betrayed*. New York: Human Sciences Press.

Gunther, P. (1981). Fire-cause patterns for different socioeconomic neighborhoods in Toledo, Ohio. *Fire Journal, 75*, (May), 3–8.

Hancock, B. L., & Pelton, L. H. (1989). Home visits: History and functions. *Social Casework, 70* (1), 21–27.

Handler, J. F. (1973). *The coercive social worker: British lessons for American social services*. Chicago, IL: Rand McNally.

Harrison, W. D. (1980). Role strain and burnout in child-protective service workers. *Social Service Review, 54*, 31–44.

Hechler, D. (1988). *The battle and the backlash: The child sexual abuse war*. Lexington, MA: Lexington Books. D. C. Heath & Co.

Herskowitz, J., & Smith, E. W. (1985). *Children in voluntary placements: June 30, 1984*. Boston, MA: Massachusetts Department of Social Services, April 10.

Hooe, B. (1973). Memo from Barbara Hooe, Research Assistant, to Fred E. Friend, Commissioner. Nashville, TN: State Department of Public Welfare, January 4.

Horowitz, B., & Wolock, I. (1981). Material deprivation, child maltreatment, and agency interventions among poor families. In L. H. Pelton (Ed.), *The social context of child abuse and neglect* (pp. 137–84). New York: Human Sciences Press.

Hoshino, G. (1971). Money and morality: Income security and personal social services. *Social Work, 16* (2), 16-24.

Immigration and Naturalization Service. *1980 statistical yearbook of the Immigration and Naturalization Service.* Washington, DC: U.S. Department of Justice.

Immigration and Naturalization Service, Statistical Analysis Branch. (1987). Detail run 401. Immigrants admitted by class of admission and country of birth–fiscal year 1986. Washington, D.C.: Author.

————— . (1988). Unnumbered table. Immigrant orphans admitted to the United States by country or region of birth–fiscal year 1987. Washington, D.C.: Author.

Jaffe, E. D. (1982). *Child welfare in Israel.* New York: Praeger.

Jayaratne, S., & Chess, W. A. (1984). Job satisfaction, burnout, and turnover: A national study. *Social Work, 29,* 448-53.

Jenkins, S., & Norman, E. (1972). *Filial deprivation and foster care.* New York: Columbia University Press.

Jeter, H. R. (1922). *The Chicago Juvenile Court.* Doctoral dissertation. Chicago, IL: University of Chicago.

————— . (1962). *Services in public and voluntary child welfare programs.* Washington, DC: U.S. Children's Bureau.

————— . (1963). *Children, problems and services in child welfare programs.* Washington, DC: U.S. Children's Bureau.

Jeter, H. R., & Lajewski, H. C. (1958). *Children served by public child welfare programs–1957, with trend data 1946-1957.* Children's Bureau Statistical Series No. 45. Washington, DC: U.S. Children's Bureau.

Joe, B. (1978). In defense of intercountry adoption. *Social Service Review, 52,* 1-20.

Jones, M. A., Newman, R., & Shyne, A. W. (1976). *A second chance for families: Evaluation of a program to reduce foster care.* New York: Child Welfare League of America.

Jones, M. A. (1985). *A second chance for families: Five years later.* New York: Child Welfare League of America.

Kadushin, A., & Seidl, F. W. (1971). Adoption failure: A social work postmortem. *Social Work, 16,* 32-38.

Kaplun, D., & Reich, R. (1976). The murdered child and his killers. *American Journal of Psychiatry, 133,* 809-13.

Katz, M. B. (1986). *In the shadow of the poorhouse: A history of welfare in America.* New York: Basic Books.

Kaufman, J., & Zigler, E. (1987). Do abused children become abusive parents? *American Journal of Orthopsychiatry, 57,* 186-92.

Kempe, C. H. (1973). Position paper. In *Hearings before the Subcommittee on Children and Youth of the U.S. Senate on the Child Abuse Pre-*

vention Act (pp. 179-224). Washington, DC: U.S. Government Printing Office.

Kempe, C. H., Silverman, F. N., Steele, B. F., Droegemueller, W., & Silver, H. K. (1962). The battered child syndrome. *Journal of the American Medical Association, 181*, 17-24.

Kim, D. S. (1978). From women to women with painful love: A study of maternal motivation in intercountry adoption process. In H. H. Sunoo & D. S. Kim (Eds.), *Korean women in a struggle for humanization* (pp. 117-69). Memphis, TN: Association of Korean Christian Scholars in North America.

Knitzer, J., Allen, M. L., & McGowan, B. (1978). *Children without homes.* Washington, DC: Children's Defense Fund.

Krichefsky, G. D. (1961). Alien orphans. *I & N Reporter* (U.S. Department of Justice, Immigration and Naturalization Service), *9*, 43-51.

Kulkarni, A. (1976). Adoption and foster-care—Domestic and international. *Indian Journal of Social Work, 37*, 165-70.

Lee, M. G. (1980). Characteristics of social change. In S. Park, T. Shin, & K. Z. Zo (Eds.), *Economic development and social change in Korea* (pp. 273-87). Frankfurt, Germany: Campus-Verlag.

Leiby, J. (1978). *A history of social welfare and social work in the United States.* New York: Columbia University Press.

Lerman, P. (1982). *Deinstitutionalization and the welfare state.* New Brunswick, NJ: Rutgers University Press.

Levit, L. D. (1979). *Characteristics of DYFS (Division of Youth and Family Services) children in residential and foster care.* Trenton, NJ: Division of Budget and Program Review, Office of Legislative Services, New Jersey State Legislature, August.

Light, R. J. (1973). Abused and neglected children in America: A study of alternative policies. *Harvard Educational Review, 43*, 556-98.

Low, S. (1957). *Staff in public child welfare programs—1956, with trend data 1946-1956.* Children's Bureau Statistical Series, No. 41. Washington, DC: U.S. Children's Bureau.

———. (1958). *Financing public child welfare services—1956, with selected trend data.* Children's Bureau Statistical Series, No. 46. Washington, DC: U.S. Children's Bureau.

———. (1966). Foster care of children: Major national trends and prospects. *Welfare in Review*, October, 12-21.

Lubove, R. (1965). *The professional altruist.* Cambridge, MA: Harvard University Press.

———. (1968). *The struggle for social security, 1900-1935.* Cambridge, MA: Harvard University Press.

Maas, H. S. (1969). Children in long-term foster care. *Child Welfare, 48*, 321-33.

Maas, H. S., & Engler, R. E., Jr. (1959). *Children in need of parents*. New York: Columbia University Press.

Magura, S. (1979). Trend analysis in foster care. *Social Work Research and Abstracts, 15* (Winter), 29-36.

————. (1981). Are services to prevent foster care effective? *Children and Youth Services Review, 3*, 193-212.

————. (1982). Clients view outcomes of child protective services. *Social Casework, 63*, 522-31.

————. (in press). [Review of *Protecting abused and neglected children.*] *Child Welfare.*

Maluccio, A. N., Fein, E., & Olmstead, K. A. (1986). *Permanency planning for children*. New York: Tavistock Publications.

Mandell, B. R. (1973). *Where are the children?* Lexington, MA: Heath.

Martinez, A. (1977). Statement of Arabella Martinez. In *Hearings before the Subcommittee on Select Education of the House of Representatives on the Proposed Extension of the Child Abuse Prevention and Treatment Act* (pp. 115-98). Washington, DC: U.S. Government Printing Office.

Maximus, Inc. (1983). *Child welfare indicator survey*. McLean, VA: Author.

Mayo, L. W. (1955). Directions in child welfare programs. *Children, 2*, 149-53.

Mayor's Task Force on Child Abuse and Neglect. (1983). *Report on the preliminary study of child fatalities in New York City*. New York: Author. November 21.

————. (1987). *High risk factors associated with child maltreatment fatalities*. New York: Author. January.

Maza, P. L. (1984). Adoption trends: 1944-1975. *Child Welfare Research Notes #9*, August. Administration for Children, Youth, and Families, U.S. Department of Health and Human Services.

McCord, J., McCord, W., & Thurber, E. (1960). The effects of foster-home placement in the prevention of adult anti-social behavior. *Social Service Review, 34*, 415-19.

McMahon, J. (1979). Mom's jail term suspended in fatal fire. *Newark Star-Ledger*, December 18, p. 8.

Meier, E. G. (1962). Former foster children as adult citizens. Ann Arbor, MI: University Microfilms.

Mennel, R. M. (1973). *Thorns and thistles: Juvenile delinquents in the United States, 1825-1940*. Hanover, NH: University Press of New England.

Mierley, M. C., & Baker, S. P. (1983). Fatal house fires in an urban population. *Journal of the American Medical Association, 249*, 1466-68.

Millen, L., and Roll, S. (1985). Solomon's mothers: A special case of pathological bereavement. *American Journal of Orthopsychiatry, 55*, 411-18.

Mnookin, R. H. (1973). Foster care—In whose best interest? *Harvard Educational Review, 43*, 599-638.

Mott, P. E. (1976). *Meeting human needs: The social and political history of Title XX.* Columbus, OH: National Conference on Social Welfare.

Murphy, H.B.M. (1964). Natural family pointers to foster care outcomes. *Mental Hygiene*, July.

Musewicz, J. J. (1981). The failure of foster care: Federal statutory reform and the child's right to permanence. *Southern California Law Review, 54,* 633–765.

National Center on Child Abuse and Neglect. (1977). *How to plan and carry out a successful public awareness program on child abuse and neglect.* Washington, DC: U.S. Department of Health, Education, and Welfare. DHEW Publication No. (OHD) 77-30089.

National Center for Health Statistics. (1988). *Vital statistics of the United States, 1985. Volume II–Mortality.* Part A. Hyattsville, MD: Public Health Service.

National Center for Social Statistics. (1973). *Adoptions in 1971.* Washington, DC: U.S. Department of Health, Education, and Welfare.

————. (1975). *Adoptions in 1973.* Washington, DC: U.S. Department of Health, Education, and Welfare.

————. (1976). *Adoptions in 1974.* Washington, DC: U.S. Department of Health, Education, and Welfare.

National Committee for Adoption. (1985). *Adoption factbook: United States data, issues, regulations, and resources.* Washington, DC: Author.

National Safety Council. (1985). *Accident facts.* Chicago, IL: Author.

Nelson, B. J. (1984). *Making an issue of child abuse.* Chicago, IL: University of Chicago Press.

Nersesian, W. S., Petit, M. R., Shaper, R., Lemieux, D., & Naor, E. (1985). Childhood death and poverty: A study of all childhood deaths in Maine, 1976 to 1980. *Pediatrics, 75,* 41–50.

Neugeboren, B. (1985). *Organization, policy, and practice in the human services.* New York: Longman.

New Jersey Bureau of Children's Services. (1968). Children under supervision chargeable to counties, December, 1968. Trenton, NJ: Author.

New Jersey Division of Youth and Family Services. (1974). Children under supervision chargeable to counties, December, 1974. Trenton, NJ: Author.

————. (1984). *Mission Statement and Service Principles.* August 6. Trenton, NJ: Author.

New Jersey State Child Placement Advisory Council. (1984). *New Jersey Judiciary 1984 report on child placement review.* Trenton, NJ: Administrative Office of the Courts.

Nicholas, R. (1976). Letter from Robert Nicholas, Acting Chief of the Bureau of Residential Services, New Jersey Division of Youth and Family Services, to the administrator of the institution. July 6. With attachments.

Pannor, R., Baran, A., & Sorosky, A. D. (1978). Birth parents who relinquished babies for adoption revisited. *Family Process, 17*, 329–37.

Pelton, L. H. (1974). *The psychology of nonviolence.* Elmsford, NY: Pergamon.

————. (1976). *The conflict dynamics of parent-agency interaction in child abuse and neglect cases.* Trenton, NJ: Bureau of Research, New Jersey Division of Youth and Family Services.

————. (1977a). Child abuse and neglect and protective intervention in Mercer County, New Jersey: A parent interview and case record study. Trenton, NJ: New Jersey Division of Youth and Family Services. Published, in slightly modified form, in L. H. Pelton (Ed.), *The social context of child abuse and neglect* (pp. 90–136). New York: Human Sciences Press, 1981.

————. (1977b). *A survey of the criteria and procedures governing child removal decisions in state child welfare agencies.* Grant proposal submitted by the New Jersey Division of Youth and Family Services to the U.S. Department of Health, Education, and Welfare, July 15.

————. (1978a). Child abuse and neglect: The myth of classlessness. *American Journal of Orthopsychiatry, 48*, 608–17.

————. (1978b). Children in need of decisions: Foster children and the alternatives of continued foster care, return home, and adoption. Trenton, NJ: Bureau of Research, New Jersey Division of Youth and Family Services.

————. (1979). Interpreting family violence data. *American Journal of Orthopsychiatry, 49*, pp. 194, 372.

————. (1981a). Analysis of state aid disbursements. Memo to Director Bernice Manshel. Trenton, NJ: New Jersey Division of Youth and Family Services, June 24.

————. (Ed.). (1981b). *The social context of child abuse and neglect.* New York: Human Sciences Press.

————. (1982a). *Displaced children: Has review made a difference in New Jersey?* Draft. Newark, NJ: Association for Children of New Jersey, January 5.

————. (1982b). Personalistic attributions and client perspectives in child welfare cases: Implications for service delivery. In T. A. Wills (Ed.), *Basic processes in helping relationships* (pp. 81–101). New York: Academic Press.

————. (1983). *Home safety training program for child welfare workers: Resource manual.* New York: Vera Institute of Justice.

————. (1987a). The institution of adoption: Its sources and perpetuation. *Journal of Social Work and Human Sexuality, 6* (1), 87–117. Also published in D. Valentine (Ed.), *Infertility and adoption: A guide for social work practice* (pp. 87–117). New York: Haworth Press, 1988.

————. (1987b). Not for poverty alone: Foster care population trends in the twentieth century. *Journal of Sociology and Social Welfare, 14* (2), 37–62.

Pelton, L. H., & Bricker-Jenkins, M. (1988). Child protection and family preservation. In M. Bricker-Jenkins (Ed.), *Resource handbook for assessment,* Tennessee Department of Human Services Certification for Social Counselors, Nashville, TN.

Pelton, L. H., & Fuccello, E. (1978). *An evaluation of the use of an emergency cash fund in child protective services.* Trenton, NJ: Bureau of Research, New Jersey Division of Youth and Family Services, December.

Pelton, L. H., & Rosenthal, M. G. (1988). Whose neglect? The role of poverty-related factors in child neglect cases and court decisions in the United States. *International Journal of Law and the Family, 2,* 167-82.

Pfohl, S. J. (1977). The "discovery" of child abuse. *Social Problems, 24,* 310-23.

Phillips, M. H., Shyne, A. W., Sherman, E. A., & Haring, B. L. (1971). *Factors associated with placement decisions in child welfare.* New York: Child Welfare League of America.

Piliavin, I., & Gross, A. E. (1977). The effects of separation of services and income maintenance on AFDC recipients. *Social Service Review, 51,* 389-406.

Piven, F. F., & Cloward, R. A. (1971). *Regulating the poor: The functions of public welfare.* New York: Vintage.

Platt, A. M. (1977). *The child savers: The invention of delinquency* (2nd ed.). Chicago, IL: University of Chicago Press.

Pless, I. B., & Arsenault, L. (1987). The role of health education in the prevention of injuries to children. *Journal of Social Issues, 43* (2), 87-103.

Polansky, N. A., DeSaix, C., & Sharlin, S. A. (1972). *Child neglect: Understanding and reaching the parent.* New York: Child Welfare League of America.

Resnick, R. P., & Rodriguez, G. M. (1982). *Intercountry adoptions between the United States and Colombia.* New York: International Social Service.

Richmond, M. (1900). What is charity organization? *The Charities Review, 9,* 499.

Riding, A. (1985). Brazil's time bomb: Poor children by the millions. *The New York Times,* October 23.

Rivara, F. P., & Barber, M. (1985). Demographic analysis of childhood pedestrian injuries. *Pediatrics, 76,* 375-81.

Rivara, F. P., & Mueller, B. A. (1987). The epidemiology and causes of childhood injuries. *Journal of Social Issues, 43* (2), 13-31.

Roberts, M. C., & Brooks, P. H. (1987). Children's injuries: Issues in prevention and public policy. *Journal of Social Issues, 43* (2), 1-12.

Rosenthal, M. G. (1983). *Social policy for delinquent children: Delinquency activities of the U.S. Children's Bureau, 1912-1940.* Doctoral dissertation, Graduate School of Social Work. New Brunswick, NJ: Rutgers, The State University of New Jersey.

Rosenthal, M., & Louis, J. A. (1981). The law's evolving role in child abuse and neglect. In L. H. Pelton (Ed.), *The social context of child abuse and neglect* (pp. 55-89). New York: Human Sciences Press.

Ross, L. (1977). The intuitive psychologist and his shortcomings: Distortions in the attribution process. In L. Berkowitz (Ed.), *Advances in experimental social psychology* (Vol. 10). New York: Academic Press.

Rubin, T. H. (1979). *Juvenile justice: Policy, practice, and law.* Santa Monica, CA: Goodyear.

Rutter, M. (1972). *Maternal deprivation reassessed.* Baltimore, MD: Penguin.

Ryan, W. (1971). *Blaming the victim.* New York: Vintage.

S.K.L. v. *Smith*, 480 S.W. 2d 119.

Schlossman, S. L. (1977). *Love and the American delinquent: The theory and practice of "progressive" juvenile justice, 1825-1920.* Chicago, IL: University of Chicago Press.

Schuchter, A. (1976). *Prescriptive package: Child abuse intervention.* Washington, DC: U.S. Department of Justice, Law Enforcement Assistance Administration, National Institute of Law Enforcement and Criminal Justice, Office of Technology Transfer.

Seekins, D. M. (1982). The society and its environment. In F. M. Bunge (Ed.), *South Korea: A country study* (3rd ed., pp. 49-105). Washington, DC: U.S. Government Printing Office.

Shudde, L. O., & Epstein, L. A. (1955). Orphanhood—A diminishing problem. *Social Security Bulletin, 18,* 17-19.

Shultz, W. J. (1924). *The humane movement in the United States, 1910-1922.* New York: Columbia University Press.

Shyne, A. W., & Schroeder, A. G. (1978). *National study of social services to children and their families.* Washington, DC: U.S. Children's Bureau.

Skinner, A. E., & Castle, R. L. (1969). Battered children: a retrospective survey. *N.S.P.C.C.,* London.

Slack, S. (1976). Memo from Sarah Slack, Program Specialist, Adoptions, to Horace Bass, Commissioner. Nashville, TN: State Department of Human Services, July 1.

Smith, S., Hanson, R., & Noble, S. (1975). Parents of battered children: A controlled study. In A. W. Franklin (Ed.), *Concerning child abuse.* Edinburgh: Churchill Livingstone.

Sohoni, N. K. (1976). Role of adoption and foster care in child rehabilitation. *Indian Journal of Social Work, 37,* 121-34.

Spiegel, C. N., & Lindaman, F. C. (1977). Children can't fly: A program to prevent childhood morbidity and mortality from window falls. *American Journal of Public Health, 67,* 1143-47.

State v. *Goff*, 66 Or. App. 695, 675 P. 2d 1093 (1984a).

State v. *Goff*, 686 P. 2d 1023 (Or. 1984b).

State of New Jersey Pension Survey Commission. (1932). *Report No. 5: State care of dependent children in New Jersey.* April. Trenton, NJ: Author.

State of New Jersey v. *Lucille Lewis*, Superior Court of New Jersey, Docket No. A-4686-76, unpublished opinion and unpublished dissenting opinion, May 16, 1978.

Steele, B. F., & Pollock, C. B. (1968). A psychiatric study of parents who abuse infants and small children. In R. E. Helfer and C. H. Kempe (Eds.), *The battered child.* Chicago, IL: University of Chicago Press.

Stein, T. J. (1985). Projects to prevent out-of-home placement. *Children and Youth Services Review, 7,* 109-21.

Stein, T. J., & Gambrill, E. D. (1985). Permanency planning for children: The past and present. *Children and Youth Services Review, 7,* 83-94.

Steiner, G. (1981). *The futility of family policy.* Washington, DC: Brookings Institution.

Sudia, C. E. (1981). What services do abusive and neglecting families need? In L. H. Pelton (Ed.), *The social context of child abuse and neglect* (pp. 268-90). New York: Human Sciences Press.

Tatara, T. & Pettiford, E. K. (1985). *Characteristics of children in substitute and adoptive care: A statistical summary of the VCIS National Child Welfare Data Base.* Washington, DC: The Voluntary Cooperative Information System (VCIS), American Public Welfare Association, June.

Tatara, T., Shapiro, P., Portner, H., & Pettiford, E. K. (1987). *Characteristics of children in substitute and adoptive care: A statistical summary of the VCIS National Child Welfare Data Base, based on FY 84 data.* Washington, DC: American Public Welfare Association, Voluntary Cooperative Information System (VCIS), June.

Tatara, T., Shapiro, P., Portner, H., & Gnanasigamony, S. (1988). *Characteristics of children in substitute and adoptive care: A statistical summary of the VCIS National Child Welfare Data Base, based on FY 85 data.* Washington, DC: American Public Welfare Association, Voluntary Cooperative Information System (VCIS), July.

Testa, M., & Lawlor, E. (1985). *The state of the child: 1985.* Chicago: The Chapin Hall Center for Children at the University of Chicago.

Thompson, L. A. (Ed.). (1919). *Laws relating to "mothers' pensions."* Bureau Publication No. 63, Legal Series No. 4. Washington, DC: U.S. Children's Bureau.

Thurston, H. W. (1930). *The dependent child: A story of changing aims and methods in the care of dependent children.* New York: Columbia University Press.

Tiffin, S. (1982). *In whose best interest? Child welfare reform in the Progressive Era.* Westport, CT: Greenwood Press.

Tomaszewicz, M. C. (1985). *Children entering foster care: Factors leading to placement.* Trenton, NJ: New Jersey Division of Youth and Family Services, Bureau of Research, Evaluation and Quality Assurance, August.

U.S. Bureau of the Census. (1913). *Benevolent institutions, 1910.* Washington, DC: U.S. Government Printing Office.

———. (1927). *Children under institutional care, 1923.* Washington, DC: U.S. Government Printing Office.

———. (1935). *Children under institutional care and in foster homes, 1933.* Washington, DC: U.S. Government Printing Office.

———. (1975). *Historical statistics of the United States: Colonial times to 1970.* (Part 1). Washington, DC: U.S. Government Printing Office.

———. (1983). *Current population reports,* Series P-60, No. 140, Money income and poverty status of families and persons in the United States: 1982. Washington, DC: U.S. Government Printing Office.

———. (1984). *Statistical abstract of the United States–1985* (105th ed.). Washington, DC: U.S. Government Printing Office.

U.S. Children's Bureau. (1947). *Children's services in the public welfare agency.* Child Welfare Reports, No. 3, May. Washington, DC: Author.

———. (1953). *Personnel in public and child welfare programs, 1952.* Children's Bureau Statistical Series No. 16. Washington, DC: Author.

———. (1961). *Child welfare statistics–1960.* Children's Bureau Statistical Series No. 64. Washington, DC: Author.

———. (1962). *Child welfare statistics–1961.* Children's Bureau Statistical Series No. 66. Washington, DC: Author.

———. (1963). *Child welfare statistics–1962.* Children's Bureau Statistical Series No. 72. Washington, DC: Author.

———. (1964). *Child welfare statistics–1963.* Children's Bureau Statistical Series No. 75. Washington, DC: Author.

———. (1966). *Child welfare statistics–1965.* Children's Bureau Statistical Series No. 84. Washington, DC: Author.

U.S. Department of Health and Human Services. (1981). *National study of the incidence and severity of child abuse and neglect.* Washington, DC: DHHS Publication No. (OHDS) 81-30325.

———. (1988). *Study of national incidence and prevalence of child abuse and neglect.* Washington, DC: Author.

U.S. Office of Civil Rights. (1980). *1980 children and youth referral survey of public welfare and social service agencies.* Washington, DC: Author.

Van der Waals, P. (1960). Former foster children reflect on their childhood. *Children, 7,* 29-33.

Wald, M. S. (1975). State intervention on behalf of "neglected" children: A search for realistic standards. *Stanford Law Review, 27,* 985-1040.

———. (1976). State intervention on behalf of "neglected" children: Standards for removal of children from their homes, monitoring the status of children in foster care, and termination of parental rights. *Stanford Law Review, 28,* 623-706.

Wald, M. S., Carlsmith, J. M., & Leiderman, P. H. (1988). *Protecting abused and neglected children.* Stanford, CA: Stanford University Press.

Weil, R. H. (1984). International adoptions: The quiet migration. *International Migration Review, 43*, 276-93.

Weston, J. (1974). The pathology of child abuse. In R. Helfer & C. H. Kempe (Eds.), *The battered child* (2nd ed.). Chicago, IL: University of Chicago Press.

Wickley, M. (1989). Personal communication with Mark Wickley, Chief of the Bureau of Research, Evaluation and Quality Assurance, New Jersey Division of Youth and Family Services, January 12.

Williams, H. A., Jr. (1973). Letter to Senator Walter F. Mondale. In *Hearings before the Subcommittee on Children and Youth of the U.S. Senate on the Child Abuse Prevention Act* (p. 2). Washington, DC: U.S. Government Printing Office.

Wills, T. A. (1978). Perceptions of clients by professional helpers. *Psychological Bulletin, 85*, 968-1000.

————. (1981). Downward comparison principles in social psychology. *Psychological Bulletin, 90*, 245-71.

Wilson, M., & Baker, S. (1987). Structural approach to injury control. *Journal of Social Issues, 43* (2), 73-86.

Wolock, I., & Horowitz, B. (1979). Child maltreatment and material deprivation among AFDC recipient families. *Social Service Review, 53*, 175-194.

————. (1984). Child maltreatment as a social problem: The neglect of neglect. *American Journal of Orthopsychiatry, 54*, 530-43.

Woodroofe, K. (1968). *From charity to social work.* London: Routledge and Kegan Paul.

Yarrow, L. J. (1961). Maternal deprivation: Toward an empirical and conceptual re-evaluation. *Psychological Bulletin, 58*, 459-90.

Yeatman, H. L. (1970). Memo from Herman L. Yeatman, Commissioner, to regional, county, and area offices. Nashville, TN: State Department of Public Welfare, November 5.

Young, L. (1964). *Wednesday's children.* New York: McGraw-Hill.

Author Index

Subject Index

abandonment, 2, 65-66, 100, 102, 131, 132
abortion, 86
accidents. *See* nonintentional injuries
adoption, 14, 54, 80, 83-96, 159; annual number, 84-86, 88; characteristics of children placed through public agencies, 88-92, 96; disruptions, 92-97; foreign, 87-88, 99-103, 104; by foster parents, 89, 92; institution of, 83-84; and poverty, 97-104; relinquishment for, 98-104; shifting sources of children for, 84-89; subsidies, 80, 90, 92, 97, 137-138
Adoption Assistance and Child Welfare Act (AACWA) of 1980 (P.L. 96-272), 4, 51, 53, 54, 76, 79, 80, 91, 92, 97, 103, 127, 136, 137, 138, 160
advocacy for families, 150, 151, 158, 161-162, 164-166, 167, 175
Aid to Dependent Children (ADC). *See* public assistance

Aid to Families with Dependent Children (AFDC). *See* public assistance

"battered child syndrome." *See* child abuse
best interests of the child, 65, 66, 67
blaming the victim, 29, 108, 141-142, 155, 157, 175
Boston Children's Aid Society, 55
Brace, Charles Loring, 12
burnout, 139

CBS Evening News, 31, 32
case management, 134, 135, 136, 164
case records, 76, 135
Charity Organization Societies, 112, 113, 142
Chicago Juvenile Court, 13, 14, 16, 114
child abuse: and "battered child syndrome," 23, 28, 34; crusade against, 23-45, 47, 79, 82; definition of, 30; "discovery" of, 23, 115; "epidemic" proportions of, 26; in foster care, 58;

ABOUT THE AUTHOR

LEROY H. PELTON received his Ph.D. in psychology in 1966 from Wayne State University in Detroit. He also holds an M.S.W. in social policy and administration from the Rutgers University School of Social Work in New Brunswick, New Jersey; an M.A. in psychology from the New School for Social Research in New York City; and a B.S. in mathematics from Brooklyn College.

After teaching psychology at the State University of New York at Albany, and then at Susquehanna University in Pennsylvania, Dr. Pelton joined the Bureau of Research, Planning, and Program Development of the New Jersey Division of Youth and Family Services, the state child welfare agency. He later served as special assistant to the director of the Division.

In recent years, Dr. Pelton was a consultant to several social welfare agencies and has returned to teaching. He has taught in the schools of social work at Rutgers University and the University of Tennessee, Knoxville. Currently, he is professor and chair of the Children and Family Services Concentration in the School of Social Work at Salem State College in Salem, Massachusetts.

Dr. Pelton is the author of *The Psychology of Nonviolence* and editor of *The Social Context of Child Abuse and Neglect.* He has authored numerous journal articles and other publications in psychology and social work.